CRUISES WITH *KATHLEEN*

CRUISES
WITH
KATHLEEN

Donald Hamilton

David McKay Company, Inc.
NEW YORK

Chapters or portions of chapters in *Cruises with Kathleen* have appeared in different form in the following leading nautical publications: *Boating, Cruising World, Pacific Skipper,* and *Yachting.* The author and David McKay Company, Inc., gratefully acknowledge their courtesies and contributions to this book. The publishers are particularly grateful to the publisher of *Trailer Boats* magazine for that publication's permission to excerpt material from a number of Donald Hamilton's monthly *Trailer Boats* columns.

Frontispiece photograph by Buddy Mays

Library of Congress Cataloging in Publication Data
Hamilton, Donald, 1916-
Cruises with Kathleen.

1. Kathleen (Cutter)   2. Sailing—North America.
3. Sailing—West Indies.   I. Title.
GV822.K34H35   797.1′24   79-23120
ISBN 0-679-50961-5

10 9 8 7 6 5 4 3 2 1
Manufactured in the United States of America

For Kathleen—and *Kathleen*

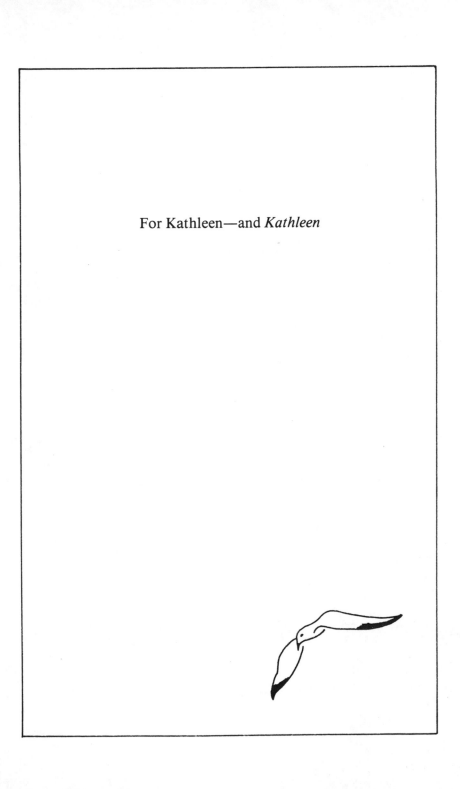

CONTENTS

1

How to Become an Offshore Cruiser

I finally learned the secret. Starting offshore cruising is really very simple. You just point the bow at the empty horizon and keep sailing until you can't see anything but water astern.

It sounds easy enough, but it took me a long time to get around to it. There are hundreds of boatmen, maybe thousands, who never quite manage it although they want to very badly. They keep taking just one more boating course, buying just one more chart or bilge pump or anchor, making just one more "test" cruise along the coast, overhauling just one more piece of gear to make everything quite perfect on board. After all, you can't go offshore until boat and crew are totally prepared. Can you?

Well, my son, Gordon, and I made our first offshore passage in a new 27-foot sailboat—a thousand-mile jaunt from Vancouver to Los Angeles. Gordon's total boating experience consisted of crewing in a couple of races on an inland lake and accompanying me on a week's familiarization-and-shakedown cruise in sheltered Northwestern waters. My own experience was somewhat more extensive, but in recent times it had involved only outboard fishing craft. Aside from the shakedown trip just mentioned, and a few trial runs in Vancouver harbor, I'd done no sailing for twenty years. Gordon didn't know any navigation at all; I'd recently played around a bit at home with a plastic sextant and an artificial horizon. Neither of us had ever taken a sailing vessel out of sight of land.

I'd selected the design of my new boat for rugged seaworthiness, and

I'd loaded her with every affordable piece of gear I could think of. However, except for her brief maiden voyage, she was as untried as her crew. Obviously, we were all far from ready to make a long offshore run down the rugged Pacific coast. I mean, clearly the thing to do was send Gordon to seamanship school and me to navigation school, meanwhile checking out our little ship on progressively more ambitious coastal cruises until . . .

We left Vancouver, B.C., early in June. By the time we reached Neah Bay, Washington, after beating out the Straits of Juan de Fuca, things were looking even less favorable. Of our five halyards, only four were operative. Of our eight winches, only seven could be relied upon. Of our three bilge pumps, we could possibly count on two. Of our half-dozen navigational instruments, only four were still functional. There was plainly only one sensible thing to do: sail back to Vancouver and get everything fixed. I looked at Gordon and he looked at me. We both shrugged—to hell with being sensible—and we headed out to sea. The rugged Washington coastline dwindled to nothing behind us. Sixteen days later we saw California appear on the horizon ahead.

The fact is that while it takes seamanship to win races, or even just to pick up a mooring under sail, very little sailing skill is needed to blow downwind along the Pacific coast, if you stay a hundred miles out where there's nothing solid for you to hit. Furthermore, I discovered it's quite amazing how fast you can master the basics of celestial navigation when there's no other way to find your way home.

As for the boat, the jammed halyard had mysteriously freed itself. The shaky winch had been tightened. The nonpumping pump, which I'd had installed at the last minute, had turned out to have a hidden seacock (closed) in the line that we hadn't been told about. The erratic new chronometer had steadied down nicely, or maybe I'd misread it in the first place. The distance log still didn't work, but we'd got along fine by simply jotting down our hourly runs as indicated by average readings of the knotmeter. Actually, we'd had enough gear on board that none of our casualties had been critical; in every case there had been something else available to do the job. And if we'd waited until all systems were operating perfectly, we would still be at the dock in Canada.

I am not, of course, advocating taking a completely untried vessel to sea with a completely unprepared crew. But when you've done a reasonable amount of homework, accumulated a reasonable amount of equipment, and run a reasonable number of tests and checks, then it's time to go—and keep going. If you wait until everybody on board knows everything about the sea and everything on board is working just right, you'll never leave, because it will never happen.

In planning your first offshore cruise, you'll naturally stack the cards in your favor. For instance, you'll stay out of the Caribbean during the summer hurricane months, and you won't tackle the North Atlantic during the winter storms. And even in a good season, you won't make your first real ocean voyage a nasty beat to windward against strong prevailing winds and currents—even experienced offshore sailors try to avoid such passages. And if you've never done any celestial navigation to amount to anything, you're a damned fool if, the first time out, you pick a destination that's just a small dot way out in the middle of a wet nowhere. I've heard of inexperienced navigators trying to find Bermuda, for instance, and returning to the mainland convinced that the elusive little island is just a figment of somebody's overactive imagination.

Now you've got your boat loaded with enough gear that half of it can fail without embarrassing you seriously. You've even got most of it working at the moment. You've got a nice deepwater cruise all laid out, straight downwind to a long, friendly coastline you can't possibly miss. So what's keeping you at the dock?

Most likely, it's the same old two-faced fear that holds everybody back at first: the fear of the sextant and the fear of storms. Let's take a good hard look at these twin terrors of the open sea.

Sextant first. This instrument intimidates a lot of people, but it's really quite a simple tool, call it a celestial protractor, for measuring an angle accurately. I think where sextants are concerned, the big mistake most budding Slocums and Chichesters make—I did—is to go for the cheapest, figuring to start at the bottom and work up. I got myself a fifteen-dollar instrument first (well, it's a bit more now) and then really splurged on another plastic number over three times as expensive and thought myself a terrible spendthrift. That one got us to California, and we hit the Santa Barbara Channel dead center, but after the cruise was over I marched out and blew several hundred bucks on a *real* sextant. I just wished I'd saved myself a lot of frustration by doing it earlier.

Not that the plastic jobs aren't real enough. Even the least expensive one will take you where you want to go. It may not be quite as accurate as the high-priced instruments; but true fractional-mile accuracy is generally unobtainable from the unstable deck of a small boat at sea. Accuracy is not the problem. Ease of operation is. The old offshore salt who's accustomed to capturing a wildly dancing sun in the waving mirrors while clinging to the gyrating rigging with his toes can get by with a minimum sextant if he has to; the beginner, who has trouble simply staying on board and keeping a grip on his instrument, needs all the assistance he can get. The smooth-working micrometer adjustments of the more expensive jobs; the sharp and easily focused telescopes; and the large, clear mirrors, will all help to get him over the hurdle of those first few sights at sea when the whole operation looks impossible.

Once you've got yourself over that jump, the rest is easy—if you'll let it be easy. The trouble is that most navigation teachers and writers can't seem to resist telling the hapless, helpless student all about the ancient origins of the universe and the immutable principles governing the movements of the heavenly bodies. The poor dope gets the impression he'll never be able to navigate anywhere until he can name the major stars and constellations, identify all the planets and describe their orbits, and give a lucid explanation of the celestial triangle.

Forget it. The only object in the sky that needs concern you at the start is the large and conspicuous sun. And the only theory you need to know . . . well, there isn't any. It's all been worked out for you in easy-to-consult tables; and how it was worked out is, right now, the least of your worries. This is cookbook navigation, of course: take a heaping cup of altitude and half a pint of time, season with a dash of corrections, stir well, and bake quickly in a hot computer—and there actually are little computers available now that'll do the job in less than a minute, if you can afford them. If not, all you have to do is pick a few numbers out of the aforementioned tables that other people have constructed for you with their computers, and do a little adding and subtracting, say five minutes' worth. Here let me recommend to you *Self-taught Navigation,* by Robert Kittredge. A slim volume of 80 pages, it's the one navigation manual I've found that doesn't try to make me a practicing astronomer when all I want to know is where the hell I am.

So the sextant and its accompanying calculations aren't really the terrors they're cracked up to be. What about storms?

A good many experienced cruising people will assure you that's nothing to worry about, either. They'll tell you, many of them, that they've spent umpteen years at sea in small boats, made a dozen ocean crossings, and never encountered a real storm. They're perfectly sincere: the trouble is that after all that sailing, their idea of what constitutes a *real* storm is apt to be considerably different from yours.

Take it from one who's just been there. If you're embarking on a passage of any length, you're probably going to get hit by something *you* call a storm. And you're going to find it a scary and uncomfortable experience.

What seasoned seagoers seem to forget is that even a little gale, one they'd barely reef for, one it wouldn't occur to them to count as truly heavy weather, looks like the end of the world to the beginner on his first offshore cruise. My son and I were hit three times on our way south, and we were petrified all three times. However, we did manage to work out a simple formula for coping with the boat-handling problems involved. Here it is:

1. Take down all sail.
2. Lash the helm hard over.
3. Go to bed.

Please understand, this is not the way to survive a Caribbean hurricane, a China Sea typhoon, or a Cape Horn howler. At least I don't think it is; I haven't had the dubious pleasure of facing any of those meteorological cataclysms. What I'm talking about here is an ordinary summer blow off the Pacific coast. I suspect a summer gale off the Atlantic coast would respond to the same treatment, although I'd worry a bit—or a bit more—if I were anywhere near the Gulf Stream.

There are, of course, many other popular remedies besides (as it's called) lying ahull. The sea anchor has pretty much fallen out of favor these days, but some people still believe in it. The British generally seem to prefer the traditional approach of heaving to under trysail or deeply reefed mainsail, with a small, stout headsail backed to windward. And then there are the gung-ho folks who, if the storm is blowing their way, just run along with it under reduced sail or bare poles. There are arguments in favor of all these solutions. The big advantage of lying ahull is simply that it requires no labor on deck you wouldn't perform anyway—when the wind rises above a certain point you have to get the working sails off her no matter what—and that once you've committed yourself to this system you have no further decisions to make, and no more work to do. All you have to do is go below, close everything up tight, and tough it out.

It does take a certain kind of boat, one that is reasonably tractable, indestructible, and noncapsizable. Our boat, fairly heavy for her 27-foot length, of stout fiberglass-sandwich construction, with 3,000 pounds of lead in a fairly long keel, simply took up a position across the wind and drifted to leeward slowly, except when a big wave would boost her along for a couple of yards as it passed. Whenever her bow would get knocked off to leeward, and she would try to run, the hard-over rudder would round her right up again.

Down below, things were active, to say the least; I wasn't kidding when I recommended going to bed. In a small boat under storm conditions, the only safe place to be is in a reasonably narrow bunk protected by a high bunkboard which won't let you get tossed across the cabin. What about a lookout? You've got to be kidding! Even if I had wanted to put myself or my crew out in that crazy weather, we wouldn't have been able to see much except a lot of crazy water standing on end. If we had spotted something coming at us, we wouldn't have been able to do anything about it. It would have run us down long before we could free the tiller, open the exhaust valve, and start the motor; and trying to dodge anything in those towering waves would have been hopeless anyway. As it happened, we hardly saw a ship the whole way down the coast, even in good weather. I guess the moral is: just don't let a storm catch you in a busy traffic lane.

Not only was it violently active below, it was unbelievably noisy. The constant, high scream of the wind in the rigging never ceased for an instant, and it was punctuated by explosive crashes like the crack of doom. The first few times we got clobbered by breaking waves I just knew we were shipwrecked for sure, and I scrambled out of the sack to plug the gaping holes, but there weren't any. Each time I'd climb back into my bunk, here would come another one: ssssKABOOM! Again I'd make my way aft to count the doghouse windows, quite certain that at least one of them had been smashed, but they'd all be there, streaming but intact. But it took me quite a while to realize that this was exactly what my sturdy little boat had been designed and built for, and all I had to do was leave her alone to do her job.

Okay, it's quite an experience. I'm not trying to scare you, or maybe I am. At least I'm trying to let you know what to expect. You should understand that this is the way it is when it blows out there, and all that's required of you is to hang on, try to get a bit of sleep, eat a little if you can (I could), read a little if you can (I couldn't), and eventually it will stop. Riding out a gale isn't the fun part of offshore cruising, but it's a necessary and inevitable part, and you should be aware of it before you leave the dock. All too many people head out there blithely with all the equipment they can cram aboard, and not a scrap of psychological preparation. When that menacing shriek sounds in the rigging, and the whole ship shudders to the impact of the breaking seas, and water roars across the decks, they can't believe this is just a perfectly normal gale situation, and not a horrid disaster created especially for them. They're instantly convinced that their vessel is doomed, and they get on the horn in a panic and call for help, instead of reminding themselves that hundreds of other small boats have survived, why shouldn't they? If you just hang in there, eventually it *will* stop, and you'll stick your head out the hatch to see the sun shining and the whole world washed clean, including your own little floating world. And you'll say to your crew, "Well, the old girl made it again," and you'll reach casually for the old sextant to find out where you've drifted to and what course you should set . . .

As a new member myself, I bid you welcome to the club.

DONALD HAMILTON
Santa Fe
New Mexico

2

Kathleen

Kathleen is a fairly husky little lady, weighing in at over 9,000 pounds in cruising trim, with a beam of close to nine feet, a draft of four feet, and a length of twenty-seven feet. She is a rather old-fashioned girl in some respects, with rather old-fashioned virtues. If your taste runs to sleeker and sexier nautical playmates, you're on your own. *Kathleen* is a Canadian-built Vancouver 27—smallest boat I could find designed to do the offshore job I wanted done. She seemed to be the best available compromise between the sturdy, slow, heavy sailing vessels, often pointed at both ends as far as they're pointed at all, that most yachtsmen think of when real ocean cruisers are mentioned, on the one hand, and the light fin-keel-and-spade-rudder ocean racing types that go like stink but tend to be rather uncomfortable and temperamental for lengthy voyaging, on the other. (The advocates of both kinds of sailing craft will disagree violently with this analysis. Please, friends, don't tell me how fast your sturdy Westsail goes, or how your hot Half Ton racer is as gentle as a baby's cradle and will sail herself all day without anybody at the helm. To swipe a line from somebody: my mind is made up, don't confuse me with the facts.)

Actually, I pretty well left speed out of my calculations. I'd owned a fast boat, thanks. After skimming over the sea with 230 horsepower at forty knots, was I going to worry about whether my new sailing vessel could make six knots or a sizzling seven?

Fast is fast and slow is slow. Sail is slow. The difference between slow and slightly slower wasn't, I figured, going to keep me awake nights. This is not to say that *Kathleen* won't get out of her own tracks. I doubt that she'll ever hang up a great racing record, at least under her present skipper and under the present rules, but she'll get me where I want to go at a very adequate speed for a sailboat her size. What's really more important than absolute velocity is that she's very responsive and maneuverable and a lot of fun to sail.

In selecting a cruising boat, I worked from the ground up. I mean this quite literally. If you'll promise to keep it to yourself, I'll whisper the shameful secret that my cruising career has involved quite a few unintentional contacts with terra firma, and I have no reason to think there won't be more. I've seen a newfangled sailing craft wipe out its unsupported steering apparatus completely, just bouncing a couple of times on a sandy shoal. I'm not about to let this happen to me if I can help it. When I ground somewhere, I intend to have something very solid down there to protect essential items, like rudders and propellers. I also want my boat not to scare me to death by threatening to topple over every time I have to put her on the ways for a simple paint job, perhaps in some out-of-the-way port with primitive equipment. This all means a fairly long, straight keel with a strong rudder post firmly attached to it. (Whatever sacrifices of performance I may have made, I already have my reward. When we pulled *Kathleen* recently, the gent operating the marine railway watched her emerge and said with honest emotion in his voice: "Oh, my, isn't that a lovely underbody!" You just knew he was comparing her safe and solid stance with the precarious balance of the fin-keel specimen he'd just put back into the water.)

As for the rest of the hull, I figured the designer, a nice guy named Bob Harris, knew more about such things than I did. I didn't consciously pick *Kathleen* for her simple transom stern and easy-to-repair outboard rudder, or for the substantial bulwarks that give her decks a much more secure and shippy feeling than the minuscule toerails currently fashionable. I did, however, take a good look at the cockpit to make sure it was small enough, acting on my theory that anybody who combines seagoing ambitions with a large cockpit ought to consult a head doctor about his suicidal tendencies. I also checked for a high, solid bridge deck between cockpit and cabin; a small, tough, main hatch, and small, strong windows and ports in the doghouse and cabin.

Although the hull has some old-fashioned attributes, the rig is strictly modern—tall and narrow. *Kathleen* regularly wears two sails forward of the mast. I call her a cutter, although some purists may argue with this use of the term. The forestaysail is the heart of this rig. Except when the wind is so light that you want to spread a big overlapping genoa jib or reacher, or so heavy that you have to resort to the storm sails, it's always up. The sizeable working jib ahead of it is roller-furling, and is the first thing to come off when the wind increases. We control it from the cockpit and it rolls up like a windowblind. The next step is to reef the mainsail, easily done with reefing lines that are always rigged. If two reefs won't do it, she'll handle pretty well on most points of sailing under forestaysail alone, with the mainsail furled. If things get even worse, it's time to break out the storm canvas.

Kathleen attracts a lot of attention in strange marinas. Partly, of course, it's her jaunty lines; with her graceful sheer she stands out among the humpbacked racing machines. She looks like a sailboat, not a submarine with a mast.

However, there's also the fact that, for a sturdy cruising craft, she's pretty well loaded with gear. (The standard dockside comment is "Mister, you've sure got a lot of stuff on that little boat!") Well, I'm a middle-aged gent with the usual middle-aged back ailments, not to mention a case of the lazies that seems to be incurable. You're not going to catch me pulling hard if I can get a winch to do the pulling for me. *Kathleen* carries eight winches, nine if you want to count the big Powerwinch for the anchor rode. I use them all and I love having them. She's also got two compasses, one on each side of the main companionway, so the helmsman can watch whichever's more convenient, whether he chooses to sit to windward or to leeward. There's a digital depthfinder, a knotmeter, and a log that registers the number of miles we've run. The instruments haven't made a great navigator of me yet, but I'm still hoping.

So much for the hull and rig. Auxiliary power is supplied by a one-cylinder Yanmar diesel under the bridge deck, rated at ten continuous horsepower. It kicks her along at a maximum of six knots, cruises her at five, and has the shocking fuel consumption of one quart—yes, I said a quart: I told you it was shocking—of Diesel No. 2 per hour. With a twenty-five gallon tank, this figures out to a cruising radius under power of close to five hundred miles.

Moving below . . . but first let me reminisce a bit. Some summers ago, I was cleaning up my powerboat after a day's fishing, when the sailboat occupying the next slip returned after a two-weeks' cruise. She was just about the same length as my Mako 22, although the mast and cabin made her look somewhat larger. Out of this little vessel trooped Mama and Papa, Sonny, Grandma and Grandpa, and a large shaggy dog. You can always tell if a cruise has been a success. If everybody lights out for home after just the barest of cold goodbyes, things probably haven't gone too well. These people, however, could hardly bear to part with each other and the boat. Obviously, they'd had a wonderful time and hated to see it end—five people and a dog on a 22-foot sailboat!

Judging by the number of mattresses stuffed into the average sailboat sold, there are a lot of nice, gregarious folks like those around. Unfortunately, perhaps, I'm not such a person; call me antisocial if you like. One of the things that attracted me to *Kathleen*'s design was the fact that there were only two good bunks on board—but they were "good." They didn't have to be rebuilt every night out of a lot of odd cushions and boards, including the dining table. They weren't crammed far up in the bow out of sight, as if sleeping was something you ought to be ashamed of. They were comfortable, permanent bunks, practically amidships, almost parallel to the centerline of the boat.

The ordinary V-berths forward are usually uninhabitable while actually sailing. When the boat heels, the leeward sleeper (?) has his feet raised higher than his head and tends to slide aft, while the windward one slides forward or falls on top of the other guy. Furthermore, if there's a sea running, the motion in the bow can be ferocious, particularly going to weather. (You'll point out that *Kathleen* has her plumbing up there. Well, I don't know about you, but Montezuma's Revenge excepted, I spend considerably more time in the sack than I do in the head. I guess it all depends on where you feel you must be comfortable, doing what.)

Dinettes don't function too well as sea berths, either; and when one is made up there's generally no place left on a small boat for somebody to sit out of the wind and have a quiet cup of coffee. Of course, most small-boat sailors don't plan on doing much night sailing. When they do cruise after dark, it's an unusual and exciting event, and everybody stays up to participate, or naps in any handy corner. For serious voyaging, however, you've got to be able to get a good night's rest while the boat keeps going. Although I still have no way of knowing how far my seagoing ambitions will eventually take me, *Kathleen*'s arrangement seems to work pretty well.

Aft of the sleeping cabin is the main cabin, with the galley to port including a deep sink; a big icebox; and a husky, two-burner kerosene stove with oven, gimbaled to stay level regardless of the heel of the boat. On the bulkhead is a small cabin heater also burning kerosene. Under the cabin sole is a 45-gallon water tank. Aft of the galley is a permanent navigation nook using the top of the icebox for a seat—a real joy for anyone who has navigated from his lap.

Kathleen's *after cabin, or main saloon if you prefer, has galley and nav station
to port, settee to starboard. Table is seen in stowed position.*

Opposite the galley is a full-length settee. Clips on a small dresser support one end of a removable table that stores neatly out of the way when not in use, and has generous space for two breakfasts or dinners when set up. (Under way, most lunches seem to get eaten in the cockpit.) For writing, which happens to be my business, the same table has a lower setting that holds a typewriter at working height. The backrest of the settee swings up to form an upper berth and, of course, somebody can sleep on the comfortable cushion below, but we're not expecting to entertain a lot of guests. *Kathleen* is laid out and equipped to cruise two people in reasonable luxury—well, "reasonable" for a 27-foot boat— rather than four or five just camping out on board.

Okay. She's a great little boat, so what's wrong with her?

Actually, there's very little wrong with her that doesn't have to be. If you want a small cockpit for safety, you can't have a big cockpit for social functions. If you want a high bridge deck and a small hatch for protection against boarding seas, you can't have a low bridge deck and a big hatch for easy access below. (Brightside note: climbing that ladder is good exercise for a gent who's been warned that his waistline is getting slightly out of control.) No, *Kathleen* is everything I'd hoped she'd be. She handles well under both sail and power. She's stood up to some fairly rugged weather without flinching. She's as comfortable to live on as a vessel her size can be. Well, there's the boat. Now let's see how I arrived at my choice of design in the first place.

I had been asleep, so to speak, for the twenty years before I bought *Kathleen;* I was a sailboat Rip Van Winkle. I had sailed a lot, years ago, but now I was a confirmed powerboat man. The romance of sail I recalled as consisting largely of a lot of hard, wet cork—and to hell with it. I was living in New Mexico, and I was completely happy with my handsome 40-knot Mako 22 and her two thundering Johnson 115s.

Then the fuel shortage came along.

Suddenly sailboats began to look very good to a lot of people, including me. I found myself conveniently forgetting what it was like to wrestle a lot of soggy sails in a screaming squall, and remembering only the pleasure of gliding along silently on a fine summer day without a single worry about whether the stuff in the tanks would get us to the next pump (and would there be any fuel when we got there?). I devoted a lot of time to studying sailboats during that winter of scarcity. I read Chichester and Hiscock, and went back and reread Slocum.

It sneaked up on me. Gradually I came to realize the dreadful fact that I was hooked once more. Like an old, reformed alcoholic taking that first fatal drink, I was falling off the powerwagon. The pernicious craving for canvas was coming back full force; I had to get out there and

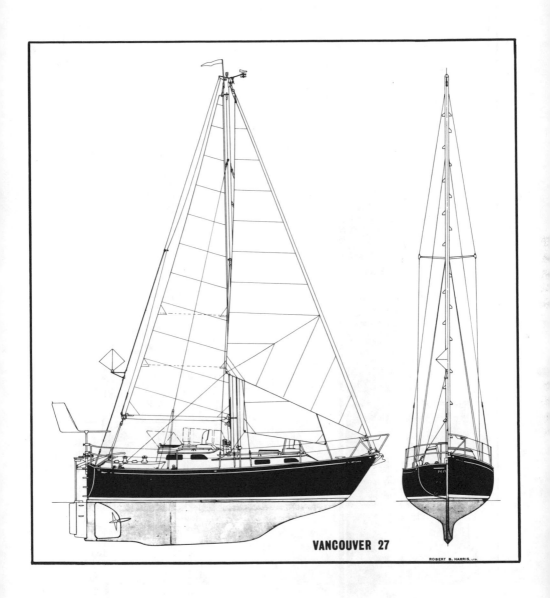

VANCOUVER 27

ROBERT B. HARRIS, LTD.

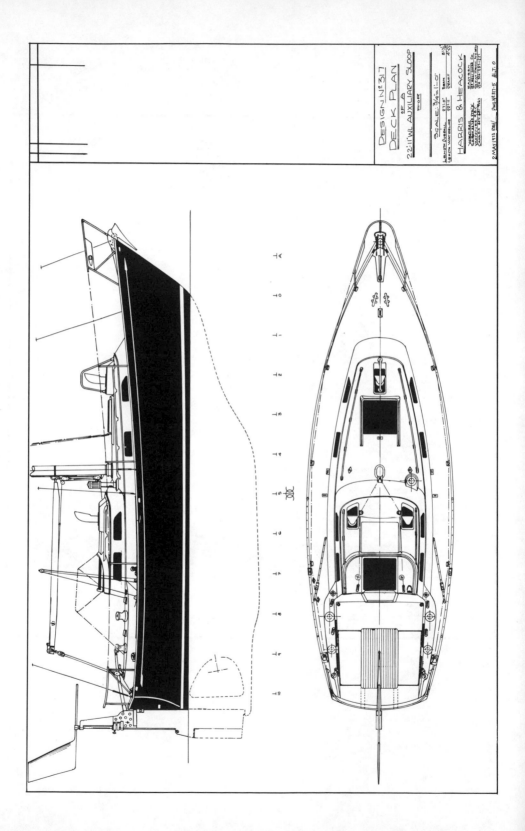

Design No 317
DECK PLAN
OF A
22'11" WL AUXILIARY SLOOP
FOR

Scale: 3/4" = 1'-0"

Length Overall _____ 31'1"   Beam _____ 8'11"
Length Waterline ____ 22'11"   Draft _____ 4'2"

HARRIS & HEACOCK

2 MAY 1943 CRB//   Dwg Nº 317-5 Alt. 0

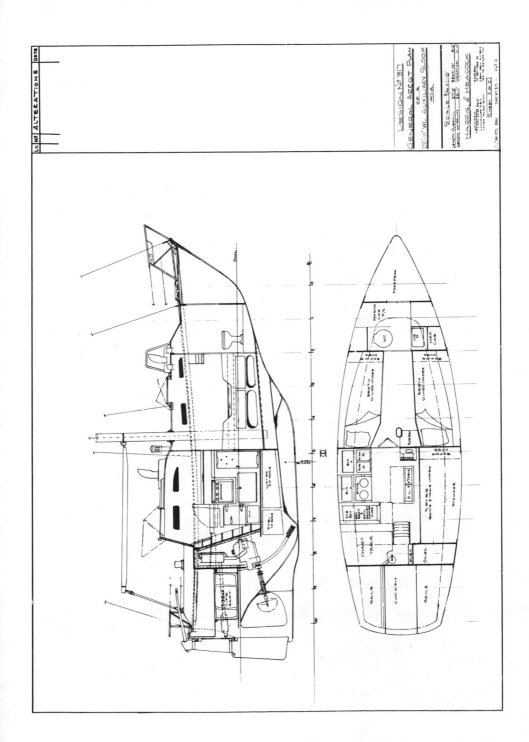

try the windships again, before I got too old to pull on all those strings. But what kind of sailboat, for what kind of sailing?

I decided that daysailing was too simple and circumscribed. On the other hand, racing, particularly ocean racing, had become much too complicated, cutthroat, and expensive for my limited skill and bank account. Obviously, cruising was the logical objective—real offshore cruising, not just the kind of cautious harbor hopping I'd been doing under power.

I studied all the published sailboat plans I could find before I found *Kathleen*. I learned that the standard, stock "cruising" sailboat in the size range I was considering (from somewhere below 30 feet to somewhere above 40) often isn't really a cruising sailboat at all. If you have any doubts, read the ads. If the tub has won a tin cup anywhere, that's the first thing mentioned proudly in the copy. Obviously it's a racing sailboat that can be cruised if you're willing to put up with its high-strung temperament. That's kind of like putting a comfortable Western saddle on Secretariat and taking him for a wilderness pack trip.

The typical stock auxiliary seems to be a masthead sloop sporting a fairly small mainsail and an enormous single jib. To reduce sail, you switch to a smaller jib. With a good racing crew on board, it's one of the simplest and probably one of the fastest and most efficient sailing rigs known to man. However, certain rugged memories inclined me to the belief that all that headsail changing would make considerable demands on a small cruising crew or singlehander, particularly when things started getting wet and violent up forward. Furthermore, reports from my secret operatives indicated that trying to get a boat like this to heave to, when this type of rig is combined with the fin-keel underbody currently fashionable, can sometimes be lots and lots of fun—if you have a sturdy, waterproof sense of humor. (One of the things most shocking to this Rip van Winkle about the current sailing scene was the compulsive secrecy that seemed to have struck the boating industry; how the hell were you supposed to know if you liked a boat if nobody would publish the lines?) Again, my agents reported that a fin-keel boat can sometimes be a treacherous handful driven hard downwind, and doesn't always take kindly to self-steering.

Common sense dictated that my new cruising sailboat should be a stock, fiberglass model—a boat with a good resale value if my ambitious offshore cruising plans didn't work out. But is common sense really a factor when a grown man decides it's time to go knocking around in a small sailboat? If we were truly sensible and practical, would we fritter away our time and money on a useless and unprofitable activity like sailing?

I didn't like the simpleminded two-sail rigs. I didn't trust the fragile, far-out shapes. I didn't like the accommodations in most stock boats, and I wasn't about to shell out the price of a house and lot for a type of boat that gave me no pleasure and inspired me with no confidence.

Having thus ewiminated a large percentage of the stock boats on the market, I looked elsewhere. I found that for serious cruising, I had four choices: (1) motor sailers, (2) character boats, (3) classic ocean cruisers, and (4) modern ocean cruisers.

Motor sailers had come a long way since I'd last been aware of them. There were still some fairly clumsy craft around that were little more than slow motorboats with steadying sails, but there were also some truly pleasing vessels with just a little less sail aloft, and a little more power below, than the average auxiliary. They were very tempting. It was the easy way out. It had been a long time since I'd handled a sailboat, but motorboats and I were now good friends. In a motor sailer, if I encountered problems I couldn't solve under canvas, I could always turn to the nice big diesel under the hatch—but that was just the trouble. If a motorboat was what I wanted, I already had one. Why trade? The whole idea was to go sailing. Anyway, what if fuel got truly scarce once again?

So I filed the intriguing motor sailer brochures away and turned to the character boats, so-called. This was another new development since Rip van Winkle's time: picturesque sailing vessels that were not true replicas of any particular historical craft, but simply seemed to have an old-fashioned flavor. They were generally quite attractive, clipper-bowed ketches. Sometimes they even went in for carved taffrails and other "period" details, and I could live without such quaint frills. However, these boats, obviously designed without a single glance in the direction of the IOR, did have the long keels and well-protected rudders and propellers I was looking for. The report of my intelligence network, unfortunately, wasn't altogether favorable.

The "technical analysis committee" indicated—well, okay, a couple of salty gents who ought to know warned me—that just like the IOR racers, these boats had been known to give trouble downwind in heavy weather, but for different reasons. Where the tricky rudder of a modern boat sometimes stalled out under severe conditions, in the character craft it was the pretty clipper bow that was the culprit. Generally associated with very fine lines forward, this kind of bow, it seemed, sometimes had a tendency to dive, and trip the vessel as she rushed down the face of a wave, particularly if, as was often the case, the stern was quite full and buoyant.

Well, that was rather heavy technical stuff to hand a recent powerboat jockey. However there was another serious count against the character vessels that I found quite easy to understand: they practically all had bowsprits.

A 90-foot schooner I'd sailed years before had a bowsprit, a tremendous, varnished, telephone pole extending 50 feet beyond the stem—well, would you believe 15? Clinging to the end of that slippery suicide stick one lively Chesapeake day, I'd sworn a sacred oath: "Never again!" I'm no better at balancing on precarious spars today than I was twenty years ago. I therefore vowed to keep that oath, even though modern bowsprits seem to have been somewhat sanitized and deodorized by means of platforms and pulpits.

So the character boats followed the motor sailers into the growing reference file. I turned to what I'm calling the classic ocean cruisers—the boats you know can go anywhere because they've been there, navigated by intrepid sailors whose names are familiar to every yachtsman and a lot of landsmen as well. There are in existence several modern replicas of Joshua Slocum's round-the-world *Spray*. At one time Harry Pidgeon's round-the-world *Islander* was quite a popular design—years ago, I almost bought a set of the plans myself. Currently, it seems, the offshore popularity contest is being led by the husky type of double-ender associated with designers Colin Archer and William Atkin, and made famous by hardy seamen such as Vito Dumas and Robin Knox-Johnston.

With either sloop or ketch rig, these rugged craft have made unbelievable voyages and survived incredible storms. Obviously, bowsprit or no bowsprit, such a boat is exactly what's needed by a semilandlubber like me heading out there for the first time: a tough, time-tried, practically unsinkable little ship that will forgive a stupid skipper's stupid mistakes. Obviously.

There's just one catch. Reliable and safe as these boats are, there have been so many of them, and they've been around so long, and have been so thoroughly tested under all conceivable conditions that they are, well, to put it bluntly, kind of dull. I'm not referring to performance, although I gather it's hardly sparkling, and I most certainly don't mean to downgrade their achievements. I just mean that when I arrive at that South Sea Island (a man can dream, can't he?), I really don't want to overhear the natives saying in bored tones: "Oh, God, not another Colin Archer!"

A large number of talented naval architects have been working at a large number of drawing boards since Archer and Atkin did their noble work. Surely, I told myself, at least one of these trained, imaginative men has come up with something newer, fresher, and in some respects

Accompanied by his wife Pat, Kathleen's designer Bob Harris attends the launching at Vancouver's False Creek Marina.

(considering the advances in materials) more satisfactory—a truly modern ocean cruiser.

For a while it seemed as if this category simply didn't exist. To be sure, I found a number of boats billed as rugged, go-anywhere cruising crafts in the modern idiom. However, when I studied them carefully, I discovered disconcertingly un-seagoing details. There were enormous companionways opening directly into enormous cockpits. There were vast expanses of vulnerable glass. There were also double berths, or dinettes converting into double berths—quite practical, no doubt, in a boat owned by a compatible cruising couple planning to anchor every night but, it seemed to Rip van Winkle, hardly the best bedding arrangement for a hard, 600-mile thrash to Bermuda.

The breakthrough, when it came, was an accident. I was cleaning out my file on character boats. What was I doing, I asked myself, with a description of a magnificent, flush-decked, pseudo-clipper ship almost 50 feet long? The novel-writing business has been good to me, but not that good. I was about to crumple up the magazine page when something prompted me to turn it over. There, on the other side, was My Boat.

There wasn't any doubt about it. She just looked up at me from the printed page and said, "Hi, Skipper." She was a smaller craft than I'd really planned on, but she was big enough. Twenty-seven feet long and specifically designed for rugged offshore work, she could be ordered with a modern cutter rig. There was a reasonably long keel, sensibly tucked up a little at the stern to protect the rudder in case of grounding. The rudder was outboard, and a simple type of vane self-steering gear was optional. There was space for a life raft ingeniously provided under the cockpit sole. A small diesel supplied auxiliary power.

Of course, the jaunty little Harris-designed Vancouver 27 I'd just discovered is by no means the only sensible offshore sailing vessel around. I've come across several other attractive designs since—Jerry Cartwright's handsome Nantucket 40, for instance—but they're all bigger boats and more expensive. And they are also less suited to a lazy middle-aged gent making a sailing comeback, who may have to manage singlehanded from time to time.

Obviously I went about this whole project too fast and the wrong way around. Instead of working from books, magazines, memories, and theories, I should have been out there sailing. I should have spent several years chartering here and there, relearning my sailboat seamanship, and getting thoroughly acquainted with the modern sailing scene, maybe even acquiring a secondhand boat temporarily, for experience, before I finally took the drastic step of gambling a very large (for me) sum of money on a

A December launching doesn't always yield good fitting-out weather.

brand-new cruising vessel of my own. That would have been the sensible thing to do; but as I suggested earlier, if we were thoroughly sensible we probably wouldn't be sailors.

My armchair decision was put to the test. Not too much later, the boys in Vancouver informed me that Hull No. 3, My Boat, had just come out of the mold, looking great. You've already read how the design worked out in practice.

3

South to Seattle

I had waited long enough. It was March, a fairly rugged time of year for Northwestern cruising, but I was ready to go sailing. I had my new boat at last, and a little weather—even March weather—wasn't going to keep me at the dock.

The ostensible purpose of this early spring expedition was to legitimize my Canadian-built *Kathleen* by bringing her through U.S. Customs at Blaine, Washington, and then letting the U.S. Coast Guard in Seattle have a look at her for documentation purposes. We also had to shake her down thoroughly to make certain she'd be ready to go offshore when we headed south a few months later. Well, those were the official reasons for the cruise.

Unofficially, I was heading out to find the answers to a couple of unspoken questions. First of all, I wanted to learn if a middle-aged gent who'd spent the past decade in powerboats—actually, my last sailboat cruising experience dated back to the early 1950s—could still handle a wind-powered vessel adequately. To be sure, I had a fairly husky son along to help me, but Gordon's limited sailing experience meant that the problems of seamanship and navigation were largely up to me.

I had no real doubt we'd survive; sailing isn't all that difficult, particularly in the relatively sheltered waters we'd be cruising. The big question was: Would I still enjoy it as I had in the past? Or had I spent more money than I could really afford, and sold a fine, fast, convenient

Entering the U.S. at Blaine, Washington, the crew makes Kathleen *shipshape while waiting for Customs clearance.*

little fishing boat that gave me much pleasure, just to burden myself with a great, complicated sailing machine that would provide me with nothing but expense, worry, work, and hardship. I had a hunch my reaction would be determined largely by the answer to the second question: Had I picked the right boat?

For me, part of the fun of boating is the daring gamble of selecting a vessel very carefully, on paper, for the use I have in mind, and then seeing how well my armchair theories work out in practice. I'd done it a couple of times with my outboard fishing boats with good success; but this was by far the most elaborate project I'd tackled. I'd known what I wanted—a rugged cruising sailboat capable of real offshore work. *Kathleen* had a neat cutter rig to which I'd added roller-furling gear for the jib, and she had a separate sleeping cabin with two very comfortable bunks. She had, in fact, everything I'd thought of—but had I thought of the right things? Or had I made an umpty-thousand-dollar boo-boo that I'd either have to live and suffer with or, red-faced, unload at a loss if I could find somebody to take her off my hands? The answer, named *Kathleen,* now lay in Vancouver at the comfortable False Creek Marina, where their dedicated young resident cabinetmaker had just finished dressing up her rather plain-Jane interior with a beautiful cabin sole of teak, and some other jewels of meticulous carpentry.

From Vancouver, it's over 40 nautical miles down to Blaine, on Semiahmoo Bay. In an effort to time our arrival at Customs during business hours, Gordon and I cast off at 0430. The railroad bridge over False Creek opened in response to three toots on the horn. The husky, one-cylinder Yanmar diesel chugged away cheerfully below while the lights of Vancouver receded astern at a five-knot clip. As the sky lightened with dawn, we found the buoy off Point Grey and swung south. Well, more or less. It turned out that the still-uncompensated state of our compasses made the exact course a matter of conjecture. (Oh well, this was a shakedown cruise, wasn't it? Make a note in the log under work to be done: "comp. compasses.")

"I guess we'll just have to keep the coast to port and hope we don't get fog," I said.

"What about doing some sailing?" asked my eager-beaver crew. "I think we're getting a wind."

It was full daylight now. A nice westerly was beginning to ruffle the water around us. I rounded up into it while Gordon yanked the stops off the mainsail. I manned the starboard winch at the aft end of the cabin trunk and hauled and cranked while he made sure the slides ran freely up the track. I switched over to the port halyard winch and, at his ready-signal, ran up the forestaysail. Finally, he returned to the cockpit and heaved on the jib sheet while I kept a little tension on the roller-furling

Gordon takes the helm on Kathleen's *shakedown cruise to Seattle.*

line. The working jib unrolled smoothly. It was a ritual we'd already practiced a time or two, but it had a special significance now—this wasn't just another test sail in Vancouver Harbor. I stopped the diesel, and our little ship settled down to her cruising stride, at last heading for a real destination over the horizon.

It was a fairly cold, gray, misty day, but we were prepared for it with plenty of insulation under our foul-weather gear. As we hissed along at a good six knots, I was doing optimistic navigational sums in my head that added up to an early arrival in Blaine. Soon we picked up the cluster of navigational marks off the end of the miles-long jetty protecting the entrance of the Fraser River. The tide rips off the river mouth came as an unpleasant surprise, and the wind chose that moment to increase markedly and back into the southeast—dead ahead. A gust put the lee rail down, just as an erratic wave of impressive dimensions came crashing over the weather bow.

"Let's get that jib in," I said, using what I hoped was a calm and captainlike voice.

Gordon had to put the furling line on a handy winch while I tried to keep the flogging sail under control with the sheet. I had a moment of doubt—I'd never been shipmates with one of those seagoing windowblinds before—but the big jib rolled itself up obediently. However, we still had too much canvas up, and could no longer lay our course. Much to the disgust of my son, already turning into something of a sailing purist, I started the motor and helped him douse the rest of the sails.

Slowly, we powered clear of the churned-up area, but things no longer looked very favorable. We now had the strong wind right in our teeth as we hammered down the coast. Although I was running the Yanmar as hard as I cared to push a new motor, we were being brought almost to a halt by every third or fourth big wave. I clocked us between two buoys— two and a half knots over the ground. By this time it was past noon. With some 20 miles still to go, we weren't making it fast enough to reach our destination in daylight, and I had no faith in my ability to locate Blaine in the dark with the compasses haywire.

"Well, let's try the sails again," I said. The wind had eased slightly, letting us set full working sail, but we still averaged no more than two or three knots through the water, not to mention what we now lost over the ground by having to tack down the coast. The wind rose once more so we had to furl the jib. It kept rising and we reefed the mainsail—an operation we'd never practiced except to check out the gear at the dock. It went quite well just the same—I discovered that jiffy reefing, new to me, was a real blessing. *Kathleen* balanced perfectly under forestaysail and single-reefed mainsail, but she was still being stopped in her tracks by those steep, short seas rolling up from the south. I crossed my fingers and started the diesel once more.

It was a scientific miracle. Two and a half knots under sail, two and a half knots under power, add the two together to make five knots? It shouldn't have worked; boats don't behave like that. But it did. Suddenly we were carrying our momentum right through and over the waves, and the knotmeter was swinging between four and six instead of between four and zero. It was rough and wet, of course. She'd come lunging off one wave to split the next like an axe, throwing spray everywhere. I was happy to note that unlike some boats I'd known in the distant past, she was producing no teeth-rattling crashes up forward no matter how hard she was driven. Bob Harris, who'd become a good friend during the lengthy construction process, had apparently done his design job well.

We tacked south and got another miracle—the wind had veered just enough to let us lay Point Roberts, the last land we had to clear before bearing off across Semiahmoo Bay. We fought our way past the point and the buoy beyond, and were able to ease the sheets for a final, exhilarating reach—power off now—to Blaine. We tied up at the harbormaster's dock at four in the afternoon.

The Customs and Immigration formalities, under the guidance of a broker I'd alerted in advance, took surprisingly little time. Afterward, the crew of *Kathleen* celebrated her first landfall with suitable libations from a fairly expensive bottle brought along for the occasion and carefully protected from sea damage—in case you're curious—in the oven of the gimbaled Shipmate stove. It was pleasant and warm in the cabin with the kerosene heater hissing away, and I was aware of a funny little sense of pleasant achievement, and the knowledge that none of my trailerables could have made that run against that wind and sea. I put the disloyal thought away. One day's sail doesn't make a cruise.

After the rugged first day, the second was a breeze—or rather, there was no breeze at all. We simply motored southward in a flat calm, passing through Hale Passage, Bellingham Bay, and Padilla Bay, and stopping finally in the little town of La Conner on the Swinomish Channel. The friendly Texaco serviceman topped up our tank and then let us stay at the end of his dock overnight, no charge. Accustomed to a powerful twin-motor outboard that gulped over 20 gallons per hour if I got a little gay with the throttles, I was startled when my calculations showed that *Kathleen's* hourly fuel consumption under power had been just about one quart!

The following day began as a repeat of its windless predecessor, except for a slight early-morning hassle that almost put us aground after emerging from the south end of Swinomish Channel, when the navigator

The skipper at the tiller during Kathleen's maiden voyage. March weather isn't exactly tropical in the great Northwest.

directed the helmsman toward the wrong navigational marker. The digital depth sounder saved the day. Safely back in the channel once more, we proceeded south under power until a slight breeze came up from astern.

Soon we were gliding down Saratoga Passage with the main vanged down to port and our 320-square-foot genoa, the biggest sail on board, poled out to starboard. (I have very strong feelings on the subject of spinnakers, all negative.) At three and four knots, we ran wing-and-wing all day, basking in hazy sunshine and watching the rocky, pine-covered shores slide past. After a very pleasant 25-mile sail, we docked in the equally pleasant marina in the city of Everett late in the afternoon. Fortunately, there was electricity available to power our portable electric heater, as the kerosene heater had developed a leaky valve. (Note in the log: "repr. htr.")

In the morning, not having found the harbormaster, I tucked some dollar bills under his door in payment for the night's lodging. Four hours of motoring through another calm morning brought us down Possession Sound into Puget Sound and so to Seattle's giant Shilshole Marina, claimed to be the largest in the Northwest. *Kathleen* had reached the southernmost point of her planned trajectory.

In Seattle, we looked up some old friends, ran some errands official and unofficial, checked out the good marina restaurant called the Windjammer, and waited for the Coast Guard to take a look at the boat as required by the complicated documentation process. To keep things legal in the meantime, we re-registered *Kathleen* as a Washington vessel and pasted numbers on her bow to prove it. Water in the bilge caused us a bit of concern until we traced it to the stuffing box. (Log note: "tighten stuff. bx.") At 1500 on our third day in Seattle, I finally learned over the phone that all Coast Guard requirements had been taken care of.

"We're cleared for takeoff," I said, coming down to the dock. "But it's getting kind of late in the day, and it's blowing pretty hard out there. . . ."

My gung-ho crew was having none of that timid nonsense, and pretty soon *Kathleen* was poking her nose back out into Puget Sound. Earlier in the day, there had been a full gale blowing. Now it was easing, but the southerly wind was still gusting to well over 30 knots. I noted that the small-craft advisory over the marina astern was busily flapping itself to rags. Well, if you worry about those funny red flags in that area at that time of year, you'll never get any cruising done.

"Two reefs," I said.

"Aye aye, sir."

Even with only the abbreviated mainsail set, *Kathleen* took a pretty good knockdown before I could bear off, then she straightened up and

Kathleen *spends the night in LaConner, Washington, on the Swinomish Channel.*

Awaiting Coast Guard inspection as part of the documentation process in Seattle's Shilshole Marina.

began to fly. The addition of the forestaysail really gave her wings. As I squared off dead before the wind, Gordon shoved the little headsail out on the collapsible whisker pole at its shortest extension. We roared up Puget Sound wing-and-wing, jibed the staysail over, and shot into Edmonds at the mouth of Possession Sound, out of which we'd come a few days earlier. The attendant at the fuel dock of the small marina directed us to a nearby berth where we relaxed after our short, brisk sail, happy to be cruising once more.

The wind had dropped to more manageable velocities by morning. With the tide behind us, we reached and drifted up Puget Sound and Admiralty Inlet, taking the more direct but less sheltered route back north. As we came abeam of Port Townsend on the western shore, where Admiralty Inlet joins the wide Strait of Juan de Fuca, things got considerably breezier and the rising wind headed us. I didn't like the looks of the sky. It was time to get ashore anyway—I wasn't going to tackle the Strait crossing that late in the day—but there was a nasty-looking tide rip clearly visible between us and the town. A big ferry came charging through the frothing mess, proving that there was plenty of water over there. The trouble was, it was all standing on end.

I realized that we were fast being carried out into the Strait of Juan de Fuca by the current. There was nothing to do but tack into the meatgrinder and hope for the best. We came about smartly and tied a few things down, then we were in it. It was worse than the rip off the Fraser River: big seas tumbling every which way. Furthermore, although the knotmeter indicated reasonable progress through the water, a range on shore showed that we weren't really gaining against the tide. Disregarding the stern disapproval of *Kathleen*'s resident sailing purist, I started the motor. Eventually, after a good shaking up, we reached Port Townsend Boat Haven, a sizable marina with a Coast Guard vessel guarding the entrance like a well-trained watchdog.

Looking for a place to have a belated lunch, we discovered Harbor Seafoods opposite the Coast Guard station. The small establishment in the corner of the big, red building didn't look like much, a simple fish-and-chips place, but it served the most delicious fried clams I can remember. We went back in the evening for a repeat performance, introduced by a bowl of magnificent chowder, and washed down with cold beer. The proprietor advised us to watch ourselves if we were heading towards Friday Harbor in the San Juan Islands across the Strait (we were), as you sometimes hit a pretty mean rip outside the San Juan channel.

That night it blew so hard that I crawled out of my warm bunk at midnight to double the dock lines. The resulting seas were running high where we emerged into the Strait after breakfast, but the southerly wind was light. It dropped to nothing around 0900. We took off the slatting headsails, strapped down the main, and motored north, rolling heavily in the big swells. Presently I saw white water flashing far ahead. Puzzled, I had a reef put in the main for insurance. We could see the San Juan Islands large on the horizon, but without a reliable compass—I still hadn't managed to work out a proper deviation table—it was impossible to tell which of the several low points was the channel we wanted, and which was Haro Strait to the west. Rosario Strait to the east—the wide, main water highway leading up to the Strait of Georgia and Vancouver— was easier to spot; but we had read a lot about the San Juans, and it seemed a pity not to have a look at them while we were there.

Suddenly we were surrounded by cresting seas (those white flashes I'd seen). A strong west wind heeled us well over although we had nothing but the reefed mainsail set. We ran up the staysail and shut down the motor. *Kathleen* picked up speed as the wind gained power. Soon the shrouds were humming and we were hitting six knots even under reduced sail. I glanced to windward. It looked dark and mean up there; more wind was on the way. When we hardened up to where I thought the San Juan Channel ought to be, we started taking heavy spray forward. It would be a wicked slog across those big Strait rollers, and I didn't know just what I was heading for over there. If I missed the narrow entrance, or hit an impossible rip such as the restaurant man had warned about, we'd be in trouble.

"To hell with it," I said. "Let's run for Rosario Strait and Anacortes. We can cut back through the islands tomorrow."

We'd barely eased the sheets when the full weight of the new wind hit us. The knotmeter began to pass seven knots on the swings, trying for eight. Smith Island came abeam to starboard, and the waves got steeper and higher as we cut across the shoals reaching out from it. I waited until things smoothed down a bit, in deeper water again, and turned the tiller over to Gordon so I could check the chart.

Below, the motion wasn't too bad, certainly not as insane as it had been the first day crashing to windward. I spent a little time memorizing the buoys and markers ahead. When I started back up the companionway ladder, I was shocked to see the size of the combers rolling up astern. I'd served my sailing apprenticeship on Chesapeake Bay, which can get rough, but the Chesapeake has few strong tidal currents. These onrushing mountains of water, bucking the ebb pouring out of the straits ahead, had a nasty, vindictive look. Gordon was gripping the tiller hard and doing quite well, but it was really no place for a novice helmsman. Later, he admitted that for the first time he'd been happy to have me take over.

Kathleen was also doing just fine, I decided, as I settled down to steer;

A defective stern tube installation resulted in a serious leak and a dash to Sidney, B.C., where Kathleen *was hauled at Philbrooks Boatyard.*

she was tracking like a locomotive—well, a runaway locomotive. The helm was reasonably light and quite positive. There was never any question of losing control and broaching to. I'd hear a big fellow snarl a warning astern, I'd feel her lift and go into her run, spray would flash up amidships as the roaring bow wave rose high on each side, and the steam gauge would start to climb . . .

Gordon poked me. "Look!" he shouted over the general uproar.

Busy holding course, I had glanced away from the knotmeter. Now I saw that, charging down the face of the big wave, we'd just pegged the instrument at ten knots—not bad for a moderately heavy little cruising boat that wasn't really designed to plane. The needle fell back as the crest hissed past. I heard another growler bearing down on us and glanced aft. It was an intimidating sight. "I think you'd better slip the boards in place and close the hatch," I shouted, hoping I seemed as nonchalant as a skipper should, "before one of those monsters decides to come aboard uninvited."

But it didn't happen. Time after time, hearing that warning growl astern, I'd look over my shoulder apprehensively, hook an elbow around the nearest winch, and wait for the Strait of Juan de Fuca to fall into the cockpit, hoping Gordon had a good grip on something. Time after time, despite her chopped-off transom stern, *Kathleen* would rise buoyantly and the crest would go foaming past. Driving hard under too much sail, we raced for the mouth of Rosario Strait through high, crazy-looking seas like nothing I'd ever seen, but they couldn't seem to get a good crack at us.

Then the entrance was past. The waves subsided as we got out of the direct path of the wind blowing in from Cape Flattery and the open Pacific. An hour later we docked at the Skyline Marina around the corner of Fidalgo Island from Anacortes. That evening, as we relaxed with our predinner drinks below, I heard Gordon give an odd little laugh. He patted the bulkhead beside him.

"She did real well out there, didn't she?" he said. "Now that I've stopped being scared stiff—wasn't that a beautiful ride?"

I realized that he'd spoken for both of us, and for the whole cruise as well as the day's wild sail. In a sense, our test voyage was finished. We still had some pleasant days left before returning to Vancouver, but we'd already accomplished our mission, and answered our questions. Our little ship had done real well out there, right from the start. She was the right boat, she'd given us a beautiful 200-mile ride, and I'd enjoyed every minute of it.

Of course, I reminded myself, this inshore cruising, even in March, was one thing. The open Pacific Ocean, next on the master plan, might be something else again.

4

Springtime in Vancouver

It rains in the Pacific Northwest. I mean it *really* rains. Anyway, it rained on us that spring as we prepared *Kathleen* for The Great Adventure—our 1,000-mile offshore passage from Washington to California. Rain is one of the disadvantages of Northwestern cruising. The others are tides, tows, and logs.

The advantages are hundreds of beautiful islands and inlets, with hundreds of beautiful harbors, set against a scenic background of magnificent mountains. There's also that great game fish, the salmon, for those who are piscatorially inclined.

When I write of Northwestern cruising, I don't have the ocean in mind. I refer instead to the long, relatively sheltered, often branching, inland sea that commences at the southern end of Puget Sound around Olympia, deep in the state of Washington. It runs north past Seattle to the Strait of Juan de Fuca where you can turn west towards the real ocean if you insist. The great waterway continues north through or past the U.S.-owned San Juan Islands. Beyond these, you are in British Columbia, with the Strait of Georgia before you, and the craggy 300-mile length of Vancouver Island off to port, between you and the Pacific.

If you choose to proceed up the eastern shore, you'll come to the picturesque and pleasant city of Vancouver, on the mainland. North of this handsome metropolis, you'll find numerous spectacular inlets that rival the fjords of Norway. Across the Strait of Georgia from Vancouver are the Gulf Islands just above the San Juans, also well worth exploring. To the north, the wide strait tapers off into a maze of intriguing channels that eventually lead to the ocean at the upper end of Vancouver Island.

Kathleen's shakedown area was limited by Seattle in the south and Pender Harbor, forty miles above Vancouver, in the north. The basic reference work for this spectacular region is the expensive *Marine Atlas, Volume 1, Olympia to Malcolm Island*. This volume set us back close to twenty-five bucks, but it was worth every penny. It's a complete book of detailed and comprehensive charts covering the whole region, each chart keyed to lists of marinas, docks, and other boating facilities. In the nature of things, such an elaborate volume can't be brought up to date every year, and the reader is warned not to use the charts for navigation because they may not contain the very latest dope. Frankly, we often ignored this warning and had no trouble. However, we did supplement the book judiciously with current U.S. and Canadian charts, also with the *Pacific Boating Almanac* (Northern Edition) which had the latest word on shore facilities. We also had tide-and-current tables; these were essential.

There's some big water up there. Crossing the Strait of Georgia, for instance, can be a milk run, but people have also drowned trying it. My wife, Kay, and I once made the crossing on a car ferry that was rolling like a rowboat and taking spray clear over the bridge; later that day, many parts of the British Columbia ferry system had to shut down completely because of the high winds and seas in the Strait—and they run some big ferries. It takes a lot to stop them.

But it's the tides that play the most menacing role, and this is particularly true if your craft, like *Kathleen,* is a sailboat that is capable of barely six knots under power. There are some narrow passages between those islands that any small boat should avoid when the current is running hard. We learned that if it's called a "pass" or a "narrows," watch out. (If it's called a "rapids," watch out twice.) Run it only at slack tide, either ebb or flood. Preferably, go in while the current is still slightly against you, so it will turn while you're in the slot and squirt you out the other end, but not too fast. The official tables give you the times when you can shoot the chutes safely, for all the major passes. Hit them wrong, and the boat may be spun around like a toy by eddies and whirlpools, slammed against rocks, and sunk.

But the tides are predictable. Two other hazards of Northwestern cruising aren't: the tows and the logs. These inland waters are full of tugs hauling something somewhere. If you see a little boat moving slowly and a big one behind that seems to have absolutely nothing to do with it, stand off. There's probably a cable between the two, and if you hit it, goodbye. If you come upon a large bunch of logs apparently just floating loosely on the water, and way off on the horizon there's a tiny tug you think is totally unconcerned with all that lumber, you're wrong. That distant tug is towing that raft of logs; and again there's one hell of a cable connecting them that you don't want to approach under any circumstances. We made it a principle to sail well around anything that could possibly be tied to something else, no matter how far away it seemed.

Tugs and barges and log rafts are fairly conspicuous, however. The truly sneaky menace of those northern seas is the floating individual log. The waters are full of these booby traps. They range from scraps of lumber that'll merely cream your prop, to redwood-sized tree trunks that'll accordion your whole boat. The worst are the deadheads, timbers that have got waterlogged at one end so only a few inches of the other end show above the surface. This floating junk makes night cruising inadvisable; and autopilots should be given a nice vacation with pay. You want somebody alert at the helm all the time, ready to respond instantly to the sight of lumber ahead. You can't relax just because you haven't seen any debris for a while. To the best of my knowledge, no place in the region can be considered safe. We later found logs thirty miles out at sea off the Strait of Juan de Fuca.

Finally, there is that rain. There's nothing unpredictable about that— it's going to rain; you can count on it. The natives told me it sometimes stops and gets sunny for whole days at a time during the summer. I'm happy to hear it, but I was there during the winter and spring, and I'll take along complete foul-weather gear (long underwear and several sweaters) if I ever cruise up there again—regardless of the season.

Well, every cruising area has its problems. You can incur sunstroke after grounding in the endless shallows around Florida, or apoplexy trying to run your boat on watery Mexican fuel. If boating isn't a bit of a challenge, what's the point? Every boatman ought to know how to read a tide table; genius is not required. Tows aren't dangerous once you know about them. You can avoid the logs easily enough if you keep your eyes open. As for the rain, all you have to do is dress for it, and it just makes the sun feel that much better when it does come out.

We didn't expect balmy trade winds and swaying palm trees in the Northwest, and we didn't find them. What we did find was rugged sailing in a spectacular setting, and we loved every minute of it, particularly in *Kathleen*. But our thoughts were on sunnier climes— California, a thousand miles to the south.

5

Hang a Left off Flattery

There's nobody out there.

I mean that literally. I'm not merely saying that the Pacific is a great big ocean disturbed by just an occasional ship or plane. I'm saying that there's *nobody* out there. A hundred miles off the west coast of North America there's a vast sea area that's got no people on it at all. Gordon and I sailed for almost two weeks out there without seeing any other craft, seaborne or airborne, except for a single, ghostly light, glimpsed during a midnight watch. Not that we were alone. There were plenty of nonhuman inhabitants of the region to keep us company.

Kathleen was ready for her offshore passage—and so were we; I had read Joshua Slocum's *Sailing Alone Around the World,* hadn't I? Gordon and I had loaded *Kathleen* with 60 gallons of water, 25 gallons of number 2 diesel, 6 gallons of kerosene for the stove and heater, $57 worth of charts, and $163 worth of groceries, not to mention other essentials, such as booze and beer. Our little vessel was fully found; we were prepared for anything and everything—except the emptiness of it all out there, and after we got over the initial surprise, that didn't really bother us.

We said goodbye, regretfully, to the friendly, competent folks at

Vancouver's False Creek Marina who had gone far beyond the call of normal boatyard duty to watch over *Kathleen* and help us prepare her for her first ocean test. Then we were off, across the Strait of Georgia, and through the San Juan Islands, where we cleared U.S. Customs at Friday Harbor. Next we crossed the Strait of Juan de Fuca to Port Angeles and proceeded out the strait to Neah Bay, just inside Cape Flattery.

Our sailing directions to Los Angeles were simple: Sail west from Flattery 100 miles and hang a left. We'd been strongly warned not to try to play the coast. It's a lee shore in the winds that normally prevail at that time of year, and whenever the weather turns bad enough that you need shelter, practically every harbor instantly becomes unavailable due to an entrance bar that breaks viciously in any significant sea. Our experienced friends had warned us to get clear down past California's stormy Cape Mendocino, at the very least, before thinking of closing with the land. We'd decided to do the whole distance well offshore.

So on that first morning at sea we motored out of Neah Bay and set sail off Tatoosh Island. The wind was southerly, where the Pilot Chart had promised it wouldn't be. Well, never mind. At the moment, westing was preferable to southing. We headed out on a close reach with the sturdy one-cylinder Yanmar diesel still thumping away under the bridge deck to help us clear the land. The rugged coastline gradually shrank to nothing astern, and the last fishing boats dropped below the horizon. We had the gray Pacific to ourselves, except for some friendly porpoises of a variety with which I was not familiar. They had a lot of white on them, and they made sharp, startling noises, like boilers blowing off steam, whenever they surfaced.

In the evening, with 50 miles behind us, we shut down the motor. *Kathleen* continued to jog westward under forestaysail and doublereefed main. The wind wasn't all that strong, but for our first night at sea I was taking it very easy. Gordon went below, leaving me alone on deck. We had decided on the Swedish watch system—a mixture of four-, five-, and six-hour stints so arranged that each man gets two fives and a four one day, and a six and a four the next. I was beginning to regret the lack of self-steering, but we'd been unable to locate a suitable system in Vancouver. Anyway, we'd wanted to learn just how our vessel handled before turning her over to a wind vane.

A sudden *Pzzzut!* jerked me out of my thoughts. The porpoises were back, now leaving luminous trails as they gamboled around the boat. This far north the night, although cloudy, was far from totally black; there seemed to be a bright moon behind the clouds. It was chilly, however, and I was encased in my full Northwestern cruising regalia, consisting of cotton long johns, topped by insulated long johns, topped

The author cons his ship west along the Strait of Juan de Fuca toward her first ocean test in the Pacific.

by a khaki shirt and pants. Over that I wore two wool sweaters and my foul-weather suit. I looked forward to the time I'd be able to dispense with some of that insulation. South of Mendocino, I reflected, things ought to start warming up.

The wind shift caught me by surprise. Suddenly, it seemed, we were being headed no matter which way I steered. Then the new breeze steadied in the northwest. By the time Gordon came on deck for his watch, we were rolling through the semidarkness on a beam reach, still angling westward but also making progress toward Los Angeles at last. We were really on our way.

With daylight, and a more or less clear sky, I suffered an acute attack of celestial navigation. I'd done quite a bit of practicing with a plastic, fifteen-dollar Davis sextant and an artificial horizon in the back yard of my home in Santa Fe. That's fairly steady real estate, however. Even though I was now employing a more expensive (but still plastic) Ebbco instrument, with a micrometer that made it somewhat easier to use, I found that all my work on solid ground hadn't prepared me for the problem of capturing an elusive sun in a pair of tiny mirrors while clinging to the unsteady deck of a 27-foot boat in the middle of the heaving Pacific Ocean. Eventually, I managed to put together a fix that made some kind of sense, although it was about 20 miles from my dead reckoning position. Well, maybe my dead reckoning was that far off. At least I hadn't put us in downtown Seattle, or on top of Mt. Rainier.

We made good progress that day, accompanied by a great soaring bird (albatross?) that skimmed the waves so closely we kept watching to see if he got his wing tips wet, but he never did. The following afternoon the wind headed us once more, forcing us to tack west. It picked up strength during the night. By the time I came on deck at 0800, *Kathleen* was storming along under staysail and singlereefed main. Gordon helped me take a second reef before going below. The wind continued to increase; big seas began to show their teeth all around us. At last I stuck my head down the hatch and yelled for the watch below. Gordon came on deck promptly.

"I figured you'd be calling me when I found myself sleeping on the side of the boat," he said with a grin. "I guess we'd better do something about that mainsail, right?"

The Dacron cracked like machine-gun fire as we brought it down. *Kathleen* was still charging along at six knots with just the 80-square-foot working staysail set. A sudden gust put her rail down, and water sluiced through the lee cockpit winches.

"What about trying the storm staysail?" Gordon yelled. The wind was rising steadily, and so were the white-capped waves around us.

The skipper was timid on his offshore jaunt to California, witness the reef in the main, almost a permanent fixture.

"To hell with it," I shouted. "Let's just get that sail off and see how she lies ahull."

We got the staysail down and secured and the helm lashed just in time. A screaming squall hove *Kathleen* down to her rail cap under the bare pole along—but I noticed that she escaped the full effect of it by yielding a little to leeward with each wave that passed. Any time she fell off and started moving forward, the hard-over rudder would bring her back. In spite of the racket and confusion, things seemed to be under some kind of control.

We went below, closed the hatch, and got into our bunks to keep from being thrown across the boat. A shattering crash caused us to sit up and look around apprehensively, but nothing seemed to be broken and there were no torrents of inrushing water to be seen. The funny thing was, I'd been there before. In dozens of cruising books, I'd read about this— about what it's like to heave to in a storm and listen to the shriek of the wind and the occasional end-of-the-world crash as a breaking wave smashes against the hull. It gave me a very odd and unreal feeling to be experiencing it myself; but the thought was consoling, too. Others had survived. It seemed likely—well, possible—that we would, too.

It was a long day. In the early afternoon, the wild scream of the wind died to a steady howling somewhat lower in pitch. Perversely, *Kathleen*'s motion became more violent as the pressures on her mast and rigging eased. We pulled on our foul-weather gear and climbed on deck to set the 30-square-foot storm staysail, not only to steady her but to give her a little drift offshore. I wasn't feeling very confident about my navigation. If this blow should last for days, and if my position was out by a significant amount, we could drift into trouble if we allowed ourselves to be blown too far to the northeast.

I was preparing to follow Gordon below when something caught my eye off to starboard. A miniature seal, looking no bigger than a dachshund, was resting calmly, belly-up, in the stormy sea. As I watched, a second seal, no larger, joined him, and they started to play happy games around the hove-to boat, with complete disregard for the gale. I called Gordon, and we watched their playful antics for several minutes. The sight made us feel better about the hostile roar of the wind, the menace of the big waves bearing down on us, and the half-seasick feelings we were both experiencing. At least we had a couple of little friends out there.

In the late afternoon the wind, still strong, veered into the west, leaving *Kathleen* fore-reaching in a northerly direction, back where she'd come from. We made our way on deck once more and brought her around so she was at least pointing the way we wanted to go. At midnight, I woke from an uneasy sleep, realizing that something was missing: the tremendous noise. Everything was quiet. Leaving Gordon asleep, I pulled on my foul-weather gear and safety harness and went on deck to find *Kathleen* drifting among great, disorganized swells that hissed angrily as they broke of their own weight. There was, however, only a moderate breeze from the northwest.

The following day we were feeling pretty cocky about our stout, stormproof little vessel. It came as a shock to discover that she wasn't quite perfect. Up to this point she'd been in all respects the ideal cruising boat. Maybe she wouldn't go upwind with an IOR racer, but she'd do quite well for a husky cruiser, thanks. On a reach she was terrific, not only fast but miraculously light and steady on the helm. She was the only boat I'd ever sailed in where, driving fairly hard with the wind on the quarter, I could simply leave the tiller and move off to pour myself a cup of coffee, and find her still holding course within a point or so when I returned. And we had just learned that she could ride out heavy weather like a duck.

Now, as the breeze veered north, and our albatross returned, and the navigator announced that we were far enough offshore and could head due south at last, we discovered that our four-and-a-half-ton sweetheart did have a hidden flaw. Although we'd checked her out in all points of sailing in sheltered waters and found nothing wrong, in the big seas of the open Pacific, when turned straight downwind, she rolled. It was a rather spectacular roll. It took us quite a while to learn how to cope with it, mainly by unlearning everything we knew about steering a boat downwind.

My deeply implanted instinct, at least, says that in large waves, when a boat running before a stiff breeze slings her mast over to starboard, that means she's getting ready to broach to port, and you'd better heave hard on the tiller to prevent it. With *Kathleen,* given her tremendous direc-tional stability, this was exactly the wrong response. We learned that no matter which way her mast was swinging, she had absolutely no intention of broaching to. Muscular steering tactics were not only unnecessary, they strongly aggravated her rolling tendencies. The answer was simply to give her her head and, if necessary, wait until you could steer with a roll instead of against it, gently nudging her back on course—and at the same time damping, instead of increasing, the oscillation.

Of course, the problem could be avoided altogether simply by taking the wind slightly on the quarter and tacking southward on courses that just kept the headsails full. By the time we had all this worked out, we were nearing the latitude of Cape Mendocino, which in West Coast nautical circles has a reputation much worse than that of Cape Horn.

After all, people have, occasionally, rounded the tip of South America in reasonably good weather. It has never, I'd been assured, happened to anybody trying to get past Mendocino.

It didn't happen to us. On the day my shaky navigation said we had the infamous point of land abeam about 110 miles to port, we saw a gray roll of cloud bearing down on us. By midnight we were hove to again. This time we used the 30-square-foot storm trysail. It worked very well, holding *Kathleen* quite steady some six points off the wind; but by the following afternoon the little sail was starting to overpower the boat, and we brought it down. The gale continued to blow and seemed to get worse. *Kathleen* was taking a real beating. Finally Gordon had the bright idea of also lowering the roller-furling jib and lashing it along the rail. Relieved of the windage of the long roll of sail forward, *Kathleen* rode much better, and the waves that did catch us struck near the bow, away from the more vulnerable dog house and cockpit aft.

This was a sunshine gale, with the wind screeching under a clear blue sky that in turn seemed to emphasize the spectacular violence of the angry sea. It was an impressive sight, and I couldn't help sticking my head out the hatch occasionally to watch it, as well as to check on the tiller lines (okay), and the amount of water accumulating in the cockpit (none). The second or third time I popped my head up for a look, I saw a familiar splash to port: there were our friendly little storm seals again, or perhaps another couple had been assigned to watch over us in this area.

Seals or no seals, it was getting to be kind of an ordeal. To put it another way, being hove to in a long gale is the most boring way of being terrified I know. Finally, I got impatient with it and dug out some charts and books, with considerable difficulty.

"What are you looking for?" Gordon asked from the depths of his sleeping bag.

"San Francisco," I said. "This is getting ridiculous, and I've got a backache from lying in that lousy bunk."

It turned out that you can't get to San Francisco. The books are quite clear on this point. If you don't simply run straight onto the rocks in the everlasting fogs, the savage tidal currents will put you there anyway. I said to hell with it; it couldn't be that bad. I plotted a course from our estimated position.

The gale lasted 52 hours. Again I woke up in the middle of the night to find us rolling in a near calm. After I'd got some sail up and settled down to steer, Gordon stuck his head out and glanced at the compass, and at me.

"What happened to San Francisco?" he asked.

"Go back to bed," I said. "I'll take her until 0400."

That day we encountered two large whales proceeding north in a businesslike manner. The following night I met the chickens. We were running along at four and five knots, using the three-way masthead running light—red, green, and white—now authorized for sailboats in international waters. Located high above the cockpit, it's a great improvement over lower lights that always seem to have been carefully placed to render the helmsman totally blind. There was no moon, and when I checked the horizon through a full 360 degrees, as my duty required, I could hardly distinguish between the sea and the sky. Suddenly, I became aware of hearing unmistakable barnyard sounds.

Let me explain that since an operation some years back I've got an ear that isn't quite all it should be. I frowned, seeing myself reporting back to the clinic: "Doctor, you won't believe this, but I keep hearing chickens in the middle of the ocean." Then I looked up and saw that there were actually birds above me, many smallish white birds with long, forked tails. They fluttered around *Kathleen*'s masthead light like bats, and chattered and clucked furiously. I watched them for a while, fascinated, until I realized that I was neglecting my nautical duties. I looked around routinely—and there was a green running light glaring at me from the port quarter. In the moment of discovery it looked so close that I panicked and, after switching on the masthead strobe to make sure we were seen, called Gordon on deck in case quick evasive action should be required.

"Keep an eye on that green light," I said. "I think the bearing's changing aft safely, but check me."

"What green light?" he asked after a moment, studying it through the big 7 × 50 Bushnells. "That's a white light, and it's definitely going away from us."

He was quite right. It must have been a brief optical illusion. When I looked again, through the binoculars this time, the light was white, and receding. But Gordon wasn't too upset about being aroused unnecessarily. He stayed on deck for a while, watching the gleam of light dwindle in the northwest.

"Do you realize that's the only ship we've seen in nearly ten days?" he asked at last. "And there haven't been any planes either . . ."

The third gale hit us a couple of days later (complete with toy seals). After listening to the same old screaming wind for 24 hours, I told myself that enough was enough. We were now past San Francisco, a fact established not only by the sextant, but by RDF bearings on the powerful and reassuring 150-mile radio beacon on the Farallon Islands. I struggled out of my bunk and read up on Monterey, the next logical shelter along the coast.

You can't get to Monterey, either, because of the constant and impenetrable fog; but by this time I was catching on. The fact is, you'd never enter any harbor if you took seriously all the gruesome obstacles listed in the *Coast Pilot* and similar works. Braced against the gyrating chart table, I laid out a course to Monterey. Some hours later, the wind started to moderate. I cooked myself a good breakfast of bacon, eggs, and coffee to celebrate, although it took a bit of doing (God bless gimbaled stoves). Then I went topside and set the staysail. After a while, Gordon woke up and helped me hoist the reefed main. He glanced at the compass as I steadied on course again.

"What happened to Monterey?" he asked slyly.

"Get yourself something to eat so you can take over here," I said. "I want to take some sights as soon as the sun gets up a bit."

Abruptly, as if we'd crossed an invisible line on the ocean, the weather turned fine and stayed that way. The seas went down; the air became quite balmy; we shed our heavy clothing. The winds remained favorable. Our solitude was broken at last by two navy ships behaving in a mysterious fashion. Later, a wedge-shaped military plane circled over us before going on about its business. An airliner passed high overhead, flying west. We began to see occasional freighters as we closed with the coast. Finally, a bunch of porpoises, the plain brown kind that don't scare you to death by hissing at you, came to meet us, accompanied by a full-sized seal, or sea lion, that really looked rather gross compared with our neat little friends of the storms. Sixteen days after losing sight of Cape Flattery astern, we saw land ahead.

It was Point Arguello, guarding the entrance to the Santa Barbara Channel that would take us inside the coastal islands to Los Angeles and Marina del Rey. The navigator drew a secret breath of relief. It was a lovely sight, appearing right where it should have been, off the port bow.

Various people have various standards for successful cruising. I once read a story by a gent who misjudged his weather, goofed his navigation, got himself into a mild pickle, lost his nerve, and called the Coast Guard to haul him in—yet he considered his cruise a huge success and could hardly wait to do it again. On the other hand, on his last long voyage Sir Francis Chichester sailed alone across the Atlantic and back at the age of 70, saved his boat by a magnificent feat of seamanship and endurance when it was damaged by a storm in the Bay of Biscay, but considered that his venture had been kind of a flop because he hadn't achieved his goal of sailing 4,000 miles in 20 days.

In some ways, let's admit, this cruise was kind of a flop. For one thing, it was slow. It's only a little over 1,000 miles from Cape Flattery to Point Arguello the way we sailed, but we took a little over 16 days to do it, averaging a mere 65 miles a day. Granted that we were held up by bad weather; if speed is a criterion, the trip was a bust.

Well, I'm not all that sold on sailing fast. My Mako could make 40 knots without breathing hard. I didn't switch to sail in order to burn up the ocean. However, we had hoped to learn what it was like to reel off the sea miles happily, day after day. On this trip we never got in the groove, so to speak. Either we wound up hove to, waiting for the wind to stop yelling at us, or we got distracted by problems of boat handling.

And what about the boat and her downwind handling?

The answer is that I didn't really know what I was doing out there. In fairness to *Kathleen* and her designer, I must report that a sister ship followed us down the coast as far as San Francisco a month later, and she didn't misbehave at all. Her owners, Humphrey and Claire Jones, experienced sailors, drove *Saraband II* hard, averaging 100 miles a day for their 600-mile passage. They were wing-and-wing most of the way, and except when they carried too little canvas, they didn't roll, indicating that our problems were caused by an over-cautious skipper. (My crew said, "I told you so.") So we didn't make much speed sailing south, and we didn't enjoy the pleasant and relaxed cruising experience we'd hoped for. That's quite an indictment—but let's hear the argument for the defense.

On the plus side: although hampered by inexperience, lousy weather, and some boat quirks we didn't quite understand, we nevertheless made it across 1,000 miles of ocean and had learned a tremendous amount in the process. I don't.claim we became great seamen and navigators in the 16 days we spend offshore, but we certainly got a lot better than we were when we started. We knew a lot more than we did about a lonely, wonderful world the harbor-hopping coastal cruiser never sees.

We made it, and we made it without serious emergencies or breakages. We had no rigging failures except for a running backstay that came dropping down beside me one calm afternoon. Earlier, the main halyard had fouled on that particular mast fitting, and apparently the yanking and jerking involved in freeing it had wiped out a split ring holding a pin in place up there. (Yes, I know—it should have been taped; it is now.) Since *Kathleen*'s running backstays exist mainly to keep the skipper happy—they're my substitute for a security blanket—this was hardly a major crisis. No significant leaks developed anywhere, even in the worst blow; 20 strokes of the pump cleared the bilge after 50-odd hours hove to. There was no structural damage, and nothing went adrift above or below except one dollar-ninety-five flashlight I had neglected to secure properly (which still works OK if you squeeze the bottom a certain way).

The cutter rig functioned beautifully. We couldn't help wondering at the folks who go cruising with rigs that require constant juggling of sail bags and handling on and off of headsails. With roller furling for the jib and a downhaul on the forestaysail, the halyard of which leads aft, we seldom had to visit the foredeck. Everything up there could be set or doused from the cockpit. The only sail bags handled were those for the little heavy-weather sails when those were needed.

Not only did we make it, we made it comfortably, storms excepted. The supplies held out well—although I admitted later I had eaten enough canned stew for a while. The sleeping cabin just forward of the mast, with its well-arranged bunks and bunkboards, could hardly have been more satisfactory. The compact galley aft, with its deep sink and gimbaled Shipmate stove, turned out a hot meal whenever anybody felt like cooking, weather notwithstanding. The navigation space, although small for full-sized charts, worked very well with the plotting sheets used offshore.

As for the crew, our vague seasickness symptoms lasted only through the first gale; after that we seemed to be immune. We found that, contrary to some reports, a two-man crew was quite adequate for a passage of this length, even without the help of selfsteering. We never approached exhaustion, nor did either of us, I think, feel any psychological effects attributable to the utter emptiness of the ocean on which we sailed. In fact, that very emptiness was a relief—we'd been expecting to have to dodge big freighters and tankers the whole way down the coast.

We did get fed up with the violent weather. At least I did, and I think a couple of times I half persuaded the junior partner in the enterprise that cop-out time had come. But each time we (I) started entertaining such cowardly notions, the gale would stop blowing, and it would seem idiotic to quit short of our destination with the crew healthy and the boat intact and a fresh, fair breeze helping us south.

Now, with the harbor in sight, I decided that the next time I would do a little more downwind experimenting to learn if I really did have a problem boat on my hands, and, if so, how serious the problem really was. And the next time, if it didn't blow *too* hard, maybe I'd get up nerve enough to try running with some of these gales instead of just lying in my bunk swearing at them. But that would be next time; Ventura, California was off the port bow. We motored in through the Ventura Breakwater after a wild night ride along the Santa Barbara Channel.

Inside, I put the helm over to round up at the gas dock. As we swung sharply, I saw Gordon turn to look at me in surprise. I realized that I was making the landing, if you want to call it that, 15 feet out. I spoke a few short words appropriate to the occasion, and took *Kathleen* around

Her thousand-mile passage completed, Kathleen *enters Marina del Rey.*

Kathleen *under full working canvas, showing her paces before the camera outside Marina del Rey.*

again. This time I managed to get a little closer—say eight feet. Gordon made a mighty heave and got the line to the attendant on the dock, who reeled us in—an undignified ending to a long voyage. I realized that after all that time offshore with nothing solid in sight I'd become land-shy, psychologically unable to take my boat in close to that hard and threatening dock.

That is one of the few times I can remember that I haven't thoroughly enjoyed docking a boat. Generally, I consider close-quarters maneuvering to be one of the more interesting and stimulating parts of a boating day. It is one of the few real challenges to our boat-handling skill. Bringing a boat neatly alongside, or putting her accurately into a slip, is what really separates the men from the boys, the women from the girls, the real sailors from the landlubbers.

Of course, there are boats and boats. Listing the types in order of decreasing maneuverability, they are:

1. Twin outboard or inboard-outboard
2. Twin inboard
3. Single outboard or inboard-outboard
4. Single inboard
5. Sail with outboard auxiliary
6. Sail

For sheer close-quarters handiness, a twin-outboard (or I/O) installation can't be beat. At the other end of the scale, backing an auxiliary sailboat, especially against a breeze, is exciting, to say the least. She may back the way her prop turns (probably counterclockwise, to port), but you're never really sure, which adds spice to things.

Knowing your vessel is everything; each one is a law unto herself. You have to know under what circumstances the prop will be the major influence, and at what speed the rudder will start to take effect, both ahead and astern. Yet some pretty fancy maneuvering can be done with a boat like this by a skipper who has really learned his ship's idiosyncrasies. Sailboats are designed to be controllable at practically no speed; their rudders are enormous by powerboat standards. Sailboats also tend to be deep and well ballasted, with a good deal of inertia and a good grip on the water. In spite of their rigging they're generally not greatly affected by the wind while maneuvering under power in sheltered waters. In *Kathleen,* for instance, I soon found that I could, and should, take it very easy around the docks. Nothing had to be done fast. Approaches could be made at a ridiculously slow crawl; she'd steer when she hardly seemed to be moving at all. If I made a mistake creeping up to the dock I had all the time in the world to correct it. Once I got her to the right place, she'd lie there docilely waiting for me to put the lines ashore instead of blowing off across the harbor with the first gust that hits, like previous powerboats.

I was cautious when we docked in Ventura—*too* cautious, my crew said—and I was downright startled a short time later when a friend suggested sailing *Kathleen* into her slip in California's crowded Marina del Rey. I crossed my fingers and gave him the go-ahead and he made a beautiful landing.

Actually, I grew up docking and picking up moorings under sail for the simple reason that most of the boats I sailed back then, even the larger ones, had no motors. It's time all sailboat owners (myself included) learn (relearn in my case) how to bring their little windships home, all the way home, by means of the free and inexhaustible motive power for which they were designed. Sailing offshore down the Pacific Coast had made me feel like a very salty character indeed, but I have to admit that maneuvering around the docks is still the true test of plain old-fashioned boat-handling skill.

6

East to Texas

There are a number of different routes by which a seaworthy cruising boat such as *Kathleen* can be moved from Pacific to Atlantic waters; specifically from Los Angeles, California, to Marathon in the Florida Keys. The classic one involves the Panama Canal and about 4,000 miles of sailing.

Sorry, folks. I can't tell you a thing about that. I did it the easy way. I simply telephoned an outfit called Boat Transit, Inc., in Newport Beach and told them I had a 27-footer I wanted hauled from Los Angeles to Houston, Texas.

If you want to read how others have transited the Big Ditch, you might sample Eric and Susan Hiscock in *Voyaging Under Sail,* William Robinson (*Svaap*) in *10,000 Leagues Over the Sea,* Gordon and Nina Stuermer in *Starbound,* or, more recently, Maurice and Katie Cloughley (*Nanook*) in *A World to the West.* Granted, their passages were from the Atlantic to the Pacific, but the problems and principles of handling a small vessel in those immense locks is pretty much the same, whether your passage is west-east or east-west. Follow their advice; they've done it—this intrepid navigator chickened out.

I made my long-distance telephone call.

My destination: Marathon in the Florida Keys. My first problem:

A giant Travelift at Aggie's Chris-Craft Boatyard in Marina del Rey deposits Kathleen *on a truck for her land voyage to Houston, Texas.*

moving *Kathleen* from Marina del Rey on the Pacific Coast to the Gulf of Mexico, actually to the Clear Lake Boat Center off Galveston Bay near Houston, Texas, where I could enter the Gulf Intracoastal Waterway for the long haul to the Keys.

I was tempted to buy a king-sized trailer and do the hauling myself, but a little research indicated that this was not a practical solution, financially speaking. A good, husky trailer capable of handling *Kathleen*'s 9,000 pounds would cost me at least twice as much as the trucking charges for the distance involved. Since I expected to keep *Kathleen* in Atlantic waters, it didn't seem advisable to purchase a highly specialized trailer that I might never need again. For a one-shot deal, trucking was cheaper. It also involved less effort.

Not that it was altogether easy. The whole move had to be synchronized like a military operation. I had to find out when a truck would be available from Boat Transit. Then I had to determine if Aggie's Chris Craft boatyard at Marina del Rey could take out *Kathleen*'s mast and pick her out of the water and place her on the flatbed trailer at that time. Finally, having organized the California phase of the maneuver, I had to call Texas to make certain the planned delivery would occur when the Clear Lake Boat Center had a lift and operator available for unloading.

After running up a considerable phone bill at home, I caught a plane to Los Angeles, picked up a rental car at the airport, and checked in at the Marina del Rey Hotel. I drove around to the far side of the harbor, where my little ship was docked in a slip. Accustomed to the comfortable and friendly atmosphere of the small Canadian marina where *Kathleen* had been launched and fitted out, I found gigantic Marina del Rey a rather cold and impersonal place; and *Kathleen* seemed to feel the same way. She was apparently in perfect condition except for some discoloration of the rigging—I guess they still haven't invented a stainless steel that's totally resistant to Los Angeles smog—but she looked small and plain and sturdy and lonely among all the large, sleek shiny racers and cocktail cruisers. I had the feeling she was watching me expectantly and waiting eagerly to learn where we were going to voyage next. For a moment I was tempted to call the truck deal off. After all, hell, they'd dug that perfectly good ditch down there in Panama just so boats could be sailed from the Atlantic to the Pacific and vice versa . . .

But I simply didn't have the time for a 4,000-mile cruise that fall (maybe I didn't have the courage, either), so I got into work clothes and boat shoes and started on the job of stowing things solidly for *Kathleen*'s long highway ride. The mainsail came off the boom, and the boom itself was detached from the mast and struck below. Various minor items of running rigging, like flag halliards, that could easily be rerigged later, were removed and carefully coiled and put away. The anchors, already below, were wedged and lashed into place so they wouldn't start smashing around. By afternoon, my part of the work was done. I started the diesel and chugged across the wide marina to the boatyard and tied up to the floating dock next to two big Travelift installations.

The following day I watched the unrigging process, rather regretfully. After all, we'd finally got *Kathleen* into pretty good shape, and I hated to think of all the work that would have to be repeated to put her back into full commission again.

By evening the mast was lying on a couple of sawhorses on shore with all stays, shrouds, halyards, and electrical wires securely taped into place and covered with protective plastic where they might be vulnerable. I saw that the aluminum mast surface was noticeably marked where the halyards had been whipped against it by galeforce winds offshore. When I asked if anything should be done about this, I was told that I could have the spar painted at considerable cost; but that actually these were honorable scars that probably didn't do any harm and (wink) they did show that *Kathleen* was a boat that didn't spend all her time in harbor.

In the morning, the truck was late. When it finally arrived, I ran *Kathleen* under the lift, went ashore, and watched the slings pick her up and deposit her on the long flatbed semi-trailer. The bottom-paint job didn't look too good. The Vancouver builder had apparently failed to get all the wax off the gelcoat before applying the anti-fouling; it was peeling badly. (Maybe that's why the Vancouver 27 is now being produced by a different boatyard.) It took a while to get the hull firmly chocked and braced in place and the mast lashed down. Then I gave the driver his certified check and watched the truck roll away.

The following week, back in Santa Fe, I was notified that *Kathleen* had arrived safely in Texas; but it was several months before I had time to head down there, well after Christmas, in fact. It was a relief to find her floating jauntily, undamaged except for the name on the port side that had been scraped off against a dock or piling. The yard accepted responsibility for, and promptly repaired, this minor blemish. I'd asked them to repaint the bottom after a thorough sanding and it seemed they had done a good job.

It was a small marina, mostly devoted to powerboats stored afloat in covered slips. Mastless, *Kathleen* had spent the past few months in one of these protected spaces; but she'd just been moved to an open dock in anticipation of my arrival. I was eager to get the mast stepped; but the first day of hard work accomplished only such routine chores as getting the sails and working anchor out of the cabin so there'd be room to move

Entering the Gulf ICW at Port Bolivar, Texas.

Kathleen spent the first rough night of her Texas cruise made fast to this drydock *near Siever's Cove, but later sought a less exposed location.*

Tows in the Texas ICW look terrifying but the skippers are considerate and the problems are minor—as long as you're under way.

around down there, and remembering where I'd hidden items like spreaders, masthead lights, and other essential odds and ends. The second day was spent working on the mast, removing tape and plastic, checking fittings, reinstalling lights and spreaders, sorting out miles of wire and dacron rope, and helping the yard's mechanic trace the electrical connections. Here we discovered the one serious casualty of the trip from California; the masthead strobe had ceased functioning. The only replacement available locally didn't fit my bracket; so rather than have this rebuilt I decided to do without a strobe temporarily, hoping to repair the old unit or find one like it. (A mistake: nobody wants to fix the old one and the model is no longer manufactured.)

The following morning I ran the boat under the crane and the mast was picked up and lowered onto the step on the cabin top. Somehow, most of the standing rigging I'd sorted out once had got fouled again during the subsequent work, and we had quite a time getting the headstays to run forward and the backstays to run aft the way the designer intended. Finally, we had enough wires tacked down all around to keep the stick in place. I motored back to the slip and spent most of the afternoon playing with turnbuckles, first squaring the mast up athwartships until the main halyard touched evenly on both sides of the boat, and then lining it up fore-and-aft more or less by eye. Meanwhile, the yard's expert was hooking up the electrical wiring below. From time to time I had to stop what I was doing and tell him if the right light turned on aloft when he pulled a certain switch. I installed the main boom in its proper place, bent on the mainsail, and furled it neatly. When I left her that night, *Kathleen* looked like a sailboat again.

Now the real work could begin. Kay, who had been seeing the sights of Houston, came aboard with a sharp pencil. Together we took inventory from bow to stern, organizing the haphazard accumulations of gear that had been stuffed away into any convenient drawer or locker during the year since *Kathleen* had been launched in Canada. Each stowage space was allotted a page in the engineering log and its contents were neatly listed. That took care of the old stuff. Next day we had the tedious job of lugging aboard, logging in, and stowing the truckload of new equipment we'd brought from New Mexico (the nautical mail-order business loves me, and I love it). Then, at last, we headed for the local supermarket with an arm-long list of the provisions needed for our winter cruise along the Gulf Intercoastal Waterway.

7

Winter Along the Gulf

Kathleen had taken her 1,400-mile truck ride and she was a sailboat again. She tugged gently at the docking lines as though she was eager to go. I was eager, too. The calendar said it was winter in Texas, but who worries about winter along the Gulf? Cruising the protected waters of the Intracoastal Waterway would be a pleasant milk run, I figured—even in winter. After all, *Kathleen* had been well tested in waters much tougher than those of any muddy ditch. She'd cruised the rugged sounds and inlets of the Northwest, and she had made a thousand-mile passage down the Pacific Coast.

The weather was clear when we motored out into Galveston Bay, and the wind was light, so light that we didn't attempt to sail, although mainsail and forestaysail were bent on with sheets properly led so that if the motor should fail—which had never happened before—we'd have something to fall back on. Two anchors were in readiness, the big 35-pound CQR (*Kathleen*'s combination storm and working anchor) resting in its bow fitting, and a new 12H Danforth secured in a bracket on the stern rail. Both had their rodes attached, on deck, and ready to go. An old 13S Danforth from a previous boat was stowed below for a spare. Diesel and water tanks were full; adequate provisions were on board. We

Seeking shelter from the stormy Gulf Intracoastal Waterway, Kathleen *found refuge alongside the* Silver King II, *Captain Blood commanding.*

were, I felt, ready for just about anything the ICW could throw at us, but I wasn't really expecting many difficulties on this simple inland voyage.

It was obviously going to be a new kind of cruise for *Kathleen*. As the shore faded from sight astern, the digital depth sounder still read no more than eight or ten feet, a change from the open Pacific where the charted depth had generally been measured in thousands of fathoms.

Then we turned into the buoyed and dredged ship channel, with soundings in the thirties, and dodged freighters and tows until, well after noon, we picked up the buoy off Port Bolivar and headed into the Intracoastal, which here runs right up the long, low, narrow Bolivar Peninsula. The small-craft chart showed two possible places to tie up for the night. The first, when we reached it, seemed to consist mainly of an exposed and broken-down old dock, so we proceeded to the second at Siever's Cove. (If the community itself has a different name from the nearby bay, we never learned it.)

It turned out to be a small fishing harbor on the south side of the Waterway at one of the few points where, for a change, the channel is open to Galveston Bay to the north. I threw the 12-horsepower Yanmar out of gear and let *Kathleen* coast slowly into the entrance. Instinct caused me to favor the right side by the rocky breakwater. Instinct was wrong. Abruptly, I felt us start to lose way. I slammed the little diesel into reverse and hit the throttle. There was a moment of suspense before a range on shore told me we were pulling free. Okay, try the left side. We got only a little farther there before the same thing happened. I backed off the mud again and paused to take stock of the situation. It was the first time in the year since she'd been launched that *Kathleen* had touched bottom—truck beds don't count—but I had a sudden premonition that on this trip it wouldn't be the last. Well, that was why I'd got a boat with a moderate draft, a fairly long keel, a protected propeller, and a well-supported rudder, wasn't it?

Kay nudged me. I looked up and saw a sporty runabout approaching at a good clip. When I waved, the young skipper, alone in the boat, cut his power and swung towards us.

"Can I get four feet of draft in there?" I yelled.

"Shouldn't have any trouble. The shrimpers draw almost that much. Just stay right in the middle."

I felt a little foolish. "Where can I tie up?" I shouted.

"Come on, I'll show you."

In the exact middle of the entrance, *Kathleen* slid through with a foot to spare. Inside, the harbor branched, one arm running straight inland, the other leading off to starboard. At the corner so formed was a small dry dock protected by heavy clusters of creosoted pilings wired together with rusty cables. The youth in the runabout headed over there. He sounded with his boat hook and held it up, pointing to show that there was plenty of water for us. We ran in, thanked him, and secured to the dry dock with a line out to a dolphin astern, just around the corner from a heavy commercial fishing boat named *Little Sheppard*.

It was snug and pleasant in the cabin with the little Taylor kerosene heater burning cheerfully. Kay served up sizzling hamburgers for dinner. In the middle of the night, however, I awoke, aware that our cozy situation had changed somehow. There was a familiar storm note in the rigging—the last time I'd heard it, *Kathleen* had been hove to a hundred miles off the Farallon Islands. The boat was testing her lines and fenders uneasily. We'd turned out the heater before retiring, and the cabin was very cold. On deck I found it even colder; when I stuck my head out the main hatch I got an icy blast of wind in the face. A Texas norther was blowing right off Galveston Bay and through the harbor entrance, hitting us astern where we lay just inside. I shone my flashlight around. All secure. I went back below and tried to sleep, but after a couple of hours I popped upright in my bunk, hearing a new, grinding sound above the scream of the wind.

On deck, I saw that *Little Sheppard* had broken her stern line and swung around to come to rest against the windward side of the cluster of pilings to which our stern line was secured. There was obviously nothing I could do, alone, with a boat that heavy even if I could get aboard, which wouldn't be easy, since any resemblance between Tarzan and me is strictly coincidental. I just prayed, selfishly, that she'd stay put and not break loose completely and come drifting around the dolphin to take a crack at us.

It wasn't a restful night, but in the morning we were still there and so was *Little Sheppard*. Some hours after daylight a couple of men went aboard and hauled her back to where she had been; a little later another commercial boat came along to tow her deeper into the harbor. That left *Kathleen* alone at what I'd begun to think of as the coffin corner just inside the entrance.

The wind was still shrieking, and the temperature was well below freezing. I wondered if the natives knew something I didn't. Finally, I braved the Tarzan jump to the dry dock framework, and the monkey scramble to shore. As is usual in such cases, the small local store was well stocked with contradictory advice. A brace of experts said I was perfectly safe where I was (well, if the wind didn't get up much higher); another pair said they'd get the hell out of there, if they were me, and tie up with the shrimpers in the inner harbor. I decided to go with the second opinion. It took some doing in that wind, but *Kathleen*'s second night at Siever's Cove was a great deal more sheltered and restful than the first.

In the morning, the norther had blown itself out. It had also blown a good deal of water with it, and *Kathleen*'s keel was resting in the mud. Two friendly dockside characters helped me push the bow out while Kay gave her the gun. Slowly *Kathleen* slid off into deeper water, and soon we were chugging eastward along the Intracoastal. In spite of the day's lack of wind, a pleasant change from yesterday's gale, it was bitterly cold. The radio was talking about the coldest winter in recent Texas history, and the rest of the country wasn't exactly overheated either, judging by the news reports of storms and blizzards. Gradually, in the bright sunshine, the arctic temperatures gave way to more bearable conditions, and it turned out to be a pleasant, if still fairly brisk, day. That left us free to consider another hazard—the Waterway traffic.

We'd been treated to numerous horror stories about the terrible tows in this part of the Intracoastal, and I was therefore alert, not to say apprehensive, when I saw the first monster of the day coming at us. Perversely, I was almost disappointed when it gave us plenty of room and slid past with surprisingly little effect on *Kathleen*'s steering. As string after string of enormous barges was met without incident, and a couple even passed us harmlessly heading east—at five knots *Kathleen* was just about the slowest vessel in the ditch—I relaxed, deciding that the warnings had been greatly exaggerated.

It was a low, flat, swampy landscape through which we motored sedately, just endless vistas of mud and reeds with occasional reminders of the oil industry. However, Kay spotted large numbers of spectacular, long-legged birds on which to train her binoculars; and as soon as I thawed out slightly, I found enjoyment in simply holding a tiller after the long months on shore. We had planned to stop early and spend the night in a small, man-made cove we'd been told about near a certain swing bridge, but when we got there we found that the pilings to which we'd expected to tie up had been removed by the construction crews working on a new, high replacement bridge nearby. I started to investigate the small inlet anyway, with the idea of anchoring, but at that moment the bridge tender obligingly started his span swinging open for us without being signaled. It seemed rude not to take advantage of his kindness, and it was really pretty early in the day to stop, anyway. The chart showed a good many other inlets ahead.

An hour or so later, a promising one appeared—a slough running back into the marsh. I approached it at dead slow, which was just as well; *Kathleen*'s keel started dragging before her bow had even entered the opening. We backed off and continued on our way. Farther on was a straight, narrow side canal obviously dug by man, boasting a couple of rickety rowboat docks. We poked our nose inside, barely inside, and were stopped again. Once more we backed away and proceeded eastward.

Finally we found what seemed to be the answer in a relatively wide section of the Waterway. The north side was almost a bay, at the head of which was another slough or creek. We couldn't quite get into that, but I felt that the bay itself would put us far enough out of the main channel to be safe. After careful probing with the indispensable depth sounder, I anchored bow and stern in six feet of water, parallel to the main channel and just off the mouth of the quiet creek. Satisfied with my arrangements, I relaxed in the cockpit to watch a big, deeply laden tow approach.

Suddenly, strange things started happening. As the lead barge came up, *Kathleen* started to move sideways, out toward the center of the channel. Bow and stern anchor rodes came taut. There was a violent swirling of current around the boat. Trying to determine where all the water was coming from, I looked up the stagnant side creek and saw that it was running like a mountain stream. The passing tow was simply sucking it dry, leaving nothing but bare mud. Moments later, as the tug itself passed, the water came rushing back, carrying our boat with it to bring her up hard against her anchors again, unpleasantly close to shore.

Kay stuck her head out the main hatch. "What in the world is going on?"

I said, "Let's get out of here before another one comes along!"

Kathleen has nine winches on board, most of them considerably oversized for the length and weight of the boat. I've heard docksiders joking about the gadget-happy guy who'd got his little cruising craft all winched up like an America's Cup contender; but at the moment, prying the reluctant Danforth out of the mud astern, I wouldn't have traded the big primary cockpit winch I was using for its considerable weight in pure uranium. I doubt that I could have muscled out the well-buried 35-pounder forward without the help of the husky electric Powerwinch on the foredeck, at least not in time to escape the effects of the next oncoming tow. We headed east again, considering our problem.

At last I said, "I think I've got it. We shouldn't have anchored across the mouth of that tributary—that put the boat broadside to the water surging in and out. But if we moor the other way, so the suction works fore and aft, we ought to be all right."

It took us a while to find the right spot. In one place we couldn't back in far enough to set the stern anchor, in another we got ourselves secured, we thought, only to find ourselves too close to the main channel when things settled down. Back to the winches again. Finally, we saw a reasonable side channel leading off the south side of the Waterway that seemed to fill the bill. We backed in as far as the mud would permit and dropped the Danforth, then ran well out and let go the CQR. Finally I took up on the stern rode enough to leave *Kathleen* riding about halfway between the two hooks, a good distance out of the traffic lane.

We drew simultaneous breaths of relief, and Kay went below to see about dinner. I made up all stray lines neatly for the night and watched a tow approaching from the west. I heard the tug's giant power plant slow for us. It seemed very nice of the skipper but, I thought, unnecessary. Then hell broke loose.

As the lead barge crept up to us, *Kathleen* surged forward violently with the rush of water out of the slough, to be brought up short by the Danforth astern. As the whole long tow came abreast, there was a crazy, rotary, washing-machine motion. We swung hard, sideways, against the big plow out ahead. The cockeyed strain was too much for it. It broke out and dragged, allowing us to pivot wildly about the stern anchor. I felt the motion stop short as the boat was literally washed up on the mud at the side of the inlet entrance. The tow passed on, leaving us solidly aground.

I found myself wondering what would have happened if that considerate tugboat captain hadn't slowed his monstrous rig . . . Well, never mind that. At the moment, the problem was to get off before another string of barges came along and made things worse. With Kay tailing, I cranked in the stern line once more. We'd been washed back close enough to the Danforth, fortunately, that it broke out when the rode came taut, almost up and down. That left us free to go ahead out of there—if we could.

Crossing my fingers, I went forward to the Powerwinch; but the bow anchor, having pulled out once, showed no inclination to bite again when I tested it briefly. I returned aft and, now that all lines were safely clear of the prop, tried the motor. It was obvious at once that there wasn't a hope of getting off that way; the faithful little Yanmar couldn't budge her alone. Leaving it idling to feed juice to the battery, I went forward and reeled in some more half-inch nylon. Suddenly, I met resistance. The heavy plow had found something to grab out there.

There was another tow on the horizon now, but I forced myself to disregard it. This had to be done right if we weren't to lose our chance—if we really had one—of getting off unaided, and *Kathleen* had been spun around so far that the line tended straight out to port, rendering the bow roller ineffective. I reminded myself that I'd considered this possibility when I had outfitted the boat the year before, and I had Kay duck below for a certain heavy shackle and massive snatch block while I took the rode off the roller and brought it in through the port hawsehole. The block, secured in the bow, was now necessary to give a fair lead to the windlass drum.

With everything ready, and Kay standing by in the cockpit to give us full power when I yelled, I switched on the winch and took a tentative strain. The anchor held. With four turns on the rotating drum, I leaned back hard, letting the electric windlass really go to work. The line tightened and began to stretch unnervingly. It came in more and more slowly. The strain was obviously terrific; I half expected the snatch block to explode in my face, or the Powerwinch to heave itself right out of the deck. Suddenly, something gave way somewhere else. *Kathleen* shuddered. She'd come upright as her keel settled into the mud, but now she heeled over sharply. Her bow began to swing.

"Hit it!" I shouted.

The whole boat trembled as Kay engaged the gears and shoved the throttle to full. *Kathleen* gave another jerky swing in response to the straining winch. Then the roaring diesel was shoving her forward, skidding her off the mud. A moment later she was upright and floating free. Phew!

I got in the CQR. Kay steered slowly eastward again, letting the tow I'd spotted go past, while I straightened out the mess on deck. Looking aft I could see the sun getting low in the west, lined up with the long Waterway like a red target seen over a shining rifle barrel. Things were, I realized, getting slightly critical. The two rules I'd been given for negotiating the ICW were: Don't anchor in the Waterway, and don't move at night. Now it looked as if I had to make a choice between them, but actually there was no choice. Even if I could stand the cold—the temperature was already dropping sharply as the sun went down—I simply didn't have the instruments or the skill to negotiate these narrow waters in the dark. We had to stop somewhere.

I said, "I think our mistake is messing with these damned inlets. Since we can't get up into them with our draft, we've got to stay away from them and all that water rushing in and out. Maybe, if we can just find a wide enough spot and anchor close to the bank, out of the main channel . . ."

That was what we finally did. We found a place where the dredged channel ran close to the south bank. On the north side was a kind of wide shelf with much shallower depth-sounder readings, too shallow, we hoped, to attract commercial traffic. We moored there bow and stern with a couple of feet of water beneath the keel, and waited for a tow to pass. Presently, one came along. The first barge went by, and the second, and the tug itself. Beyond a little rocking, *Kathleen* didn't move.

"Well, I think a steak is indicated," Kay said after releasing her pent-up breath. "Call me if you need me."

I worked about the deck a little longer in the fading light, watching the effect of the passing barges on our boat; hardly any. I hung out an anchor light and supplemented it with the man-overboard strobe, so arranged that it would keep flashing. I went below and had a stiff drink and a good meal, but that was another night I didn't get much sleep, listening to the freight-train roar of the tows going past, often accompanied by the glare of their searchlights.

Every hour or so I'd stick my head out to check the glowing red numbers of the depth sounder, making sure we were still in the shallows and hadn't drifted out into the deeper channel. Everything looked fine until daylight, when I discovered that the outside world had reversed itself strangely. At some time during the night, unnoticed, *Kathleen* had been swung completely around in spite of the anchors fore and aft. How it had happened I had no idea, and I still haven't. I think maybe I'd rather not know.

Anyway, we'd survived. We gave humble thanks to the skillful tugboat handlers who'd managed to avoid those idiot yachtsmen and their ridiculous little boat. (I don't suppose I need to say that I strongly advise not following our example.) I started the motor, winched up the anchors—I was getting very good at that—and got us the hell out of there while our luck still held. It was another icy-bright morning, and all the geese in the world were honking overhead—flock after flock of beautiful white snow geese with black-tipped wings, crisscrossing the sky with long lines and V-formations, but we weren't permitted to enjoy the ornithological display very long.

Without warning, with the sun still shining and the sky still clear, the light northerly breeze of the morning freshened to another piercing-cold gale. It came from ahead and it brought our five-knot speed under power down to four, and finally to three, knots. With Kay spelling me long enough for me to grab breakfast, and then stoking me with hot coffee at frequent intervals, I kept us plugging grimly eastward, reminding myself that this was my comfortable milk run.

The high wind seemed to have blown all traffic off the Waterway. We had the endless, lonely ditch to ourselves, and the reedy marshes and the frigid gale and the short, steep, choppy little waves. I found that I could make better time under the north bank where there was a slight lee, but it was still several hours before I sighted the high bridge at Port Arthur ahead, and close to noon before we were actually coming up on it.

With binoculars, I could see the seas running white in the bigship channel beyond the bridge. The channel led south to Sabine Pass and the Gulf of Mexico. The Waterway crossed it, I knew, and continued eastward, but I hoped I wouldn't have to, at least not until the weather improved. A small outboard with two well-wrapped men on board was coming down the Waterway towards us. I flagged it down.

"Marina?" I yelled.

"Just ahead on your right," one of the men shouted back.

I'd seen the numbered indentation on the chart, but I hadn't been able to spot the entrance with the binoculars. Now I saw it and cruised slowly past to scout it out. It was a tiny, dredged harbor. At one side of the entrance was a dock at which lay a big white craft, at least 60 feet long, that looked like a party fishing boat. Farther in were some ramshackle slips and boatsheds. A husky shrimper rested in one of the slips, a vacant space on either side of her.

We circled around and drifted in with the wind astern, heading for the nearest vacant slip. Past the party boat, half-way across the little harbor, I felt the by now all-too-familiar sensation of keel meeting mud. Automatically, I threw the Yanmar into reverse, wondering what to do next. We had to find shelter somewhere.

"Over here!" A man had come out on deck aboard the big white boat. "Over here. Tie up alongside."

At the moment, slowly freezing to death in the open cockpit, I thought those were the sweetest words in the English language. It took some maneuvering, and line heaving, and fender juggling, before we were secure, finally, in what was called Le Blanc's Marina. Then I grinned up at the husky gent on the big boat's deck.

"Captain, you're a lifesaver," I said. "Come aboard and have a drink. Maybe you don't need it, but I do. Brr, it's really blowing out there!"

"The prediction was wind northeast 20 to 30 knots," he said. "I'd put it at well over 40, myself. Thanks, I don't mind if I do." He joined us in the cockpit. When Kay and I introduced ourselves, he laughed and said, "You won't believe this, but I'm Captain Blood. They call me Cap."

He gave me his card: Captain A.E. Blood of the *Silver King II,* specializing in scuba diving trips out in the Gulf of Mexico. Down below, over a drink, he explained the run-down and silted-in condition of the little marina; it had been neglected because a planned widening of the Waterway was expected to put it out of existence soon, and the man who'd run it was now associated with a fine new city marina on nearby Sabine Lake. Something stirred in my mind. I glanced at Kay and saw the same thought mirrored in her face.

I said slowly, "This city marina, can we get into it with a four-foot draft? And is it really pretty good? Safe enough that we could leave our boat there for a couple of months—until the weather warms up?"

We had champagne with Captain Blood because it was Kay's birthday. From time to time *Kathleen* would rock a bit and shift position uneasily as tows chugged past in the Waterway outside the little harbor. Suddenly Cap looked up sharply, set his glass aside, and headed for the main hatch.

"Come on! That one isn't slowing down!"

Later we got on deck just in time to see the water start to rush out of the marina as the heavily laden oil barges approached too fast. Cap scrambled forward, and I braced myself against the cockpit coaming aft, both of us pushing hard against the side of the *Silver King II* to keep the boats apart as the docklines came taut and the violent current forced *Kathleen* against the larger vessel. Our efforts made no appreciable difference. I saw that the big air fenders I had out were being squeezed almost flat between the boats—I half expected them to pop like balloons. The whole marina had suddenly been emptied of water except for the dredged-out entrance where we lay. There was nothing but black mud to be seen; all the boats in there were high and dry. I saw that one of *Kathleen*'s lifeline stanchions, normally well clear, had made contact with the *Silver King*'s high, overhanging side and was being pushed inwards. As the roaring tug passed there was a brief respite; but a moment later all the water came flooding back with a rush.

I wasn't an expert on the Gulf ICW, but I had learned one thing: the 350-mile stretch of Waterway between Houston and New Orleans is a commercial waterway, and it makes hardly any concessions to pleasure craft. This does not mean that arrogant tugboat pilots are going to run you off into the tules deliberately; as a matter of fact I was surprised at how often a powerful tug pushing two or three enormous barges would slow down considerably for *Kathleen*'s benefit. The multi-ton hotrodder who gave us trouble alongside *Silver King II* was very much an exception. But it does mean that the luxurious and conveniently spaced marina facilities that are taken for granted along the Atlantic ICW do not exist to any extent along its Gulf counterpart, at least not west of the Mississippi. You'll damn well tie up or anchor where you can, and feel lucky to find a safe spot out of the traffic pattern, never mind showers, electricity, and running water.

I also learned that while the numerous tows aren't very troublesome as long as you're under way in the main channel with a reasonable amount of water under you, they do weird and dangerous things to the shallow side canals and sloughs. When a nine-foot-deep barge comes plowing down a twelve-foot-deep channel, something's got to give. All that displaced water has to go somewhere, and it does. Strangely, the first effect is suction. You'd think a tow would push water ahead of it like a piston; but what it actually does is pull water out of every tributary that it approaches. (Don't ask me why or how; consult your friendly neighborhood hydraulics expert.) This can leave a small harbor or creek practically dry for a moment; and it creates some strange and scary currents along the banks.

Let's face it—the ICW isn't meant for really big sailboats; some bridges have a 48-foot clearance. *Kathleen*'s masthead is 40 feet above the water. Also, the scarcity of facilities, and the rather rudimentary nature of those that exist, means that you want to be well equipped to secure and defend your boat wherever any opportunity for stopping does present itself, however primitive. This involves:

1. Long, strong docklines and plenty of them.
2. Large and numerous fenders, plus fender boards.
3. Hefty ground tackle and lots of it.

Of course, a well-found boat should carry these anyway. I had been told that I would need a couple of fifty-foot lines in the locks to the east. As for the thickness, I'd made a habit of using half-inch nylon even with smaller boats, not because the strength was really needed, but because the heavier line is a great deal easier to throw, it doesn't cut your hands like smaller stuff when you have to pull hard, and it gives you some reserve against unexpected chafe. (*Kathleen* chewed almost all the way through one of her half-inch lines that first blustery night of this leg of the cruise.) Four sound docklines are a must, and a spare or two won't hurt a bit.

I had started out with two big inflatable fenders. I added two big, solid fenders to the inventory very soon. In a crisis situation, the fat, soft inflatables now take the first shock; after which, when the pressure is really on, the skinnier hard fenders keep them from yielding too far.

Lying against a piling or two—which often happens when you tie up with the fishing boats—fender boards are needed, since it's impossible to keep the ordinary fender in position between a boat and a post. Here there are two ways to go. You can hang your regular fenders in place and then suspend a three- or four-foot length of 2 × 4 or 2 × 6 outboard of them; the board bears against the piling, and the fenders keep the board from damaging the hull. This works as long as there's not too much wave action; however, such boards have been known to jump out of place when big wakes come along. For *Kathleen* I bought some commercial fenders specially molded to accept 2 × 4s. The supporting lines go through a board and a pair of these fenders, holding them together as a unit.

In many areas, anchoring is a lost art; the cruising yachtsman sails from marina to marina, and if there shouldn't be a slip available, the local authorities compensate him for the terrible hardship by supplying a nice mooring for his use. Well, if you're in the ICW, you'd better be prepared to anchor on occasion; in fact you'd better be prepared to anchor twice. One anchor up forward and another back aft is a bare minimum. If you do have to drop the bow hook, you very often won't have room to swing around it; you'll need a stern anchor out to hold you in one place. Besides, it's very reassuring to have an adequate ground-hook handy to the cockpit when you're being swept towards a bridge by a stiff current and you don't know if the span is going to open in time.

An almost-essential piece of ICW gear is a good reliable depthfinder. Of course, people made do with leadlines for centuries; and a long boathook clearly marked with your boat's draft will work, also. We didn't use our inflatable dinghy because it was too damned cold to be splashing around in a rubber boat.

I had learned that the ICW isn't a tropical climate the year around. Even in fall and spring a cabin heater can come in handy; we found ours essential in the winter.

Even to a deepwater sailor, there is something fascinating about canal cruising; and the endless lonely marshes of Texas have a great deal to offer. But winter is winter, even in Texas—and frankly, we were cold.

8

Snug in Port Arthur

Sabine Lake lies half in Texas and half in Louisiana, just off the Gulf of Mexico. It is pronounced Sah-bean, not Say-byne. It is roughly sixteen miles long, six miles wide, and five feet deep. They have some fairly thin water in Texas.

Cap had put us in touch with the management of the larger and deeper city marina on Sabine Lake, and a helpful gent named Bob LeBlanc had arranged for us to have a berth in which we could leave *Kathleen* until the weather became more suitable for cruising. LeBlanc had also got a local boatman, Don Boring, a retired engineer, to pilot us through the shallow lake, since I admitted to not being much of a skinny-water sailor. We waved goodbye to Cap and motored away from *Silver King II*. A short time later, Don was sitting up forward rather disconsolately, obviously feeling pretty bad because, only a mile or so inside the lake, he'd put us on an oyster-shell bar not marked on the chart. In fact, when I took a couple of compass bearings and established our position, the resulting X landed precisely on a six-foot sounding that should have had us floating nicely. Along the Gulf Coast in winter the water level tends to drop considerably when the northers come through and blow everything out to sea. To attain even the charted low-tide depths you have to wait until southerly winds prevail and blow everything back.

Unfortunately, eager to get *Kathleen* safely tucked away so we could

95

head for home, we hadn't waited. Fortunately, on the other hand, we had planned to go into the lake on a rising tide. We had miscalculated a bit and come too early, at the last of the ebb, but it was now slacking fast and getting ready to turn. The tides aren't much in that part of the world. After sailing in the Northwest, where a rise and fall of six feet is considered rather skimpy, I found the idea of a six-inch tide a bit ridiculous; but right then inches were what we needed. I leaned out over the stern to look at the rudder again. Had the water come up a bit? I was tempted to try the motor once more, but I glanced at my watch first. After a number of fruitless attempts to get off I'd promised Kay to give the tide a full half hour before having her again join Don Boring and me in hanging out to port on the main boom to heel the boat. She was calmly reading a book below, and there were still ten minutes to go. Well, at least it was a pleasant, warm, sunny day for a change.

Ten minutes later, the water was definitely up a bit; and the ripples of outgoing current around us had died away completely. I started the Yanmar, put it into reverse, gave it full throttle, and scrambled over to throw my weight on the boom with the rest of the ship's complement.

There were a few seconds of suspense; then Don Boring cried: "She's moving! She's coming off!"

Moments later we were heading out of there happily. *Kathleen* scraped and hesitated a couple of times but continued to move. At last the flashing red figures of the digital EMS depthsounder went abruptly to reassuring numbers like 10 and 15. The bridge at the southwest entrance of the lake swung open for us, and we chugged through the slot and back up the big-ship channel to the ICW. Soon we were making *Kathleen* fast once more to the *Silver King II*. Cap Blood didn't seem very surprised to see us back.

"I was afraid you might have trouble," he said. "Water's still low around here, too; and I doubt the tide will make enough difference to matter. You'll just have to wait until the wind goes around into the south."

The following day, with the water still low, Kay took a plane home to Santa Fe. There wasn't any sense in both of us hanging around waiting for the elusive south wind. I hired a car and drove back to pick up my station wagon, which I'd left at Clear Lake Boat Center. With a vehicle at my disposal, I settled in comfortably on board *Kathleen,* doing a little work at the typewriter, cleaning up a number of overdue boat chores and, in the evenings, swapping sailing yarns with Cap Blood, who knew a lot more and better ones than I did.

The following Sunday I woke up and as usual stuck my head out of the hatch first thing to look at the pennant at the port spreader. It was streaming from a new direction: southeast. I looked around quickly, checking various rocks and other tide markers; the water was definitely higher than it had been. The only catch was, there was a heavy fog. I could hardly see across the marina. I certainly wasn't going to try to fumble my way across Sabine Lake in that stuff. I sighed and went back below to make breakfast.

The fog persisted all day, with showers of drizzling rain. The following morning was equally dense; but the wind was still south and the water was still rising. In the afternoon, Don Boring turned up with a strange-looking gadget.

He grinned. "You know, I used to be an engineer. I'd like to check something if you don't mind."

The thing was a giant wooden L-square equipped with a level. He lowered it over *Kathleen*'s side, felt around until the lower arm slid under the keel, squared things up with the level and, at the waterline, read some numbers off a scale.

"Four feet, three inches," he said, straightening up. "That's your real draft. I thought maybe the designer or builder might have pulled a fast one and given you a boat with a five- or six-foot keel without telling you. I've seen some people awfully surprised when they learned their actual draft. But four-three is okay, we can make it." He looked at the shoreline. "It's getting up there, isn't it? What about giving it a try tomorrow morning? Let's meet over at the marina. I've got a tide gauge there."

In the morning, the sky was perfectly clear. The water was still up, although not quite as high as it had been; however, the tide was rising. I ate breakfast hastily and got into my car and drove over to pick up Don, who took me first to the slip where his neat 20-foot sloop was lying. On one of the pilings was a carefully numbered scale. It read three feet, eight inches.

"There's kind of a bar just at the marina entrance," he said. "I measured the shallowest point one day and came right in and nailed up that gauge; it shows what's out there, not in here."

"Pretty handy," I said. "We're seven inches shy, apparently, but the tide's supposed to come up all morning. That bar, it isn't rocks or coral, is it?"

"No, just silt. They try to keep it dredged but it washes in."

I said, "Hell, let's give it a try. All we need is a few more inches, and we can kedge her over the hump if we have to."

"We won't have to. I've got a friend standing by with a 50-horse outboard. He'll be watching for us around noon. If we stick, he'll come out and tow us in."

Obviously, after the earlier fiasco, Don was taking the project very seriously; and I felt that I was in good hands. Nevertheless, I was aware of a certain amount of suspense as, half an hour later, *Kathleen* headed out into the Waterway and made the turn down the ship channel. Presently, we slipped through the swing bridge at the entrance to the lake. It was hard to believe that the whole wide expanse of water ahead was just barely deep enough to drown in.

Soon we spotted the cluster of decaying pilings near the spot we had gone aground the week before. I slowed *Kathleen* well down as we approached and watched the depth-sounder carefully. With the transducer installed two feet below the surface, a reading of 3 means I'm safe. A reading of 2 (actually four feet) means I'll probably be aground shortly— at least the bottom is getting too close for comfort. I started calling out the numbers to Boring who, steering from the port cockpit seat, had the sun in his eyes.

"Seven, six, six, five, six, five, four, four, three, three, three, two . . ." I reached out and pulled the gearshift lever into neutral, letting the boat just coast along, losing speed. I took up the count again. "Two, three, three, two, two, three, four, five . . . Phew, I think we've got it made!" I shivered abruptly. "You know, it's getting damned cold out here."

Tense, concentrating on the instrument, I hadn't been aware of a weather change. Now, putting the motor in gear once more, I looked around and saw that, although the sky was still clear, the water was ruffled around us. A sudden, icy wind had come up. Although it wasn't strong, its effect was increased by the fact that we were motoring almost straight into it; it was blowing out of the north once more. Water levels would soon be starting to drop again, I realized. I had a feeling of a trap closing, and a vision of being stuck out in the middle of this enormous, shallow lake while the water ran out once more as if somebody had pulled the plug.

It was a long, cold ride. The depth-sounder, after giving us some reassuring readings up around 5 and 6, went back to 3 and stayed there, meaning that we were plowing along endlessly with a mere foot of water under the keel. I hoped nobody had sunk a boat or dropped a load of bricks up ahead. At last I could pick up the marina with the naked eye; and the three pairs of pilings that marked the channel that led in to the entrance.

I said, "You folks must spend a lot of your time aground, sailing here."

Boring shook his head. "There's considerably more water in the summer; and in spring you'll have it very easy; that's when the tides are highest. But even during the regular sailing season we don't have much trouble; and there are several boats in the marina deeper than yours . . . Well, I think we can head straight in now. Why don't you take her? If we have to do some quick maneuvering, you know the controls better than I do. Just head right down the middle between the pilings.''

Steering as directed, I watched the marina entrance approach—but right between the two outermost channel markers, the keel started dragging slightly, slowing us down. I reached for the gearshift lever to back out of there, but realized there was nowhere to back to. I certainly wasn't going to retrace our route across those endless shallow miles of lake with a north wind and a falling tide. I grabbed the red-knobbed throttle lever instead and shoved it hard over. With the diesel roaring, *Kathleen* kept moving through the soft silt, but more and more slowly. Just past the middle pair of channel markers she came to a reluctant halt. Boring jumped to his feet.

"Let's get on the bow," he said. "Maybe with both of us way up there, the keel will lift a bit."

It was something that would never have occurred to me; but I suppose if you regularly sail in shoal water you learn all the tricks. Amazingly, it worked. I lashed the tiller amidships, left the motor at full working throttle, and scrambled forward. As my weight joined Don's at the headstay, *Kathleen* started to move once more, slowly, sluggishly, but making perceptible progress towards the opening in the seawall ahead. At last, however, right between the innermost markers, only some fifty yards from the entrance, she stopped for good. I went aft and shut down the Yanmar and looked around.

"I don't see your friend," I said. "Maybe I'd better get an anchor ready for kedging. If we have to, we can inflate the Avon dinghy to run it out . . ."

"There's Weldon now!"

A white boat was coming out of the marina with a husky gent at the helm. He circled under the bow to take the line Boring threw him, and made it fast to a tow-eye at the outboard's stern. I ran aft and started up the diesel again. Boring, in the bow, gave the signal. As the line came taut, I put the little Yanmar to work, hard. For a moment, nothing happened. Then, surprisingly, *Kathleen* took a sudden list to port as if, smart girl, she realized that it's easier to heel a boat sideways than to lift her bodily over an obstacle. With fifty horsepower pulling ahead, and twelve horsepower pushing astern, she started to move.

Five minutes later I was making her fast in a comfortable, sheltered slip in Port Arthur's well-kept Pleasure Island Marina, and giving thanks to my conscientious pilot and his helpful friend, Weldon Denbow,

I spent the rest of that day, and most of the next morning, securing things properly on board and loading the station wagon. As I drove out of there, homeward bound, I paused to look at Don Boring's tide gauge. The wind was still in the north, and the reading was down to three feet. We'd made it at the last possible moment. Sabine Lake was impassable again for *Kathleen*.

Okay, so we quit. To continue trying to negotiate the Gulf Intracoastal during what would probably go down in history as the Great Freeze of 1977 just didn't seem very bright. Twenty-degree temperatures and 40-knot winds don't make for enjoyable cruising, particularly in a vessel with an unprotected steering station.

I felt defeated, of course, all the more so because I had to admit that this brief cruise had hardly qualified as a jewel of meticulous planning and immaculate seamanship. Still, some things had been accomplished. *Kathleen* was back in commission, rigged and ready to go east as soon as conditions improved. We'd learned some hard lessons that aren't to be found in the books. And while her crew hadn't shown up too well either as Arctic explorers or canal cruising experts, *Kathleen* had met every test successfully. I was particularly pleased to know that even in moments of stress her ground tackle could be handled easily by a sedentary-type gent with a delicate back; but she'd been more than adequate in all other departments as well. When ignorance and inexperience had got us into trouble, she'd got us out—with, of course, some help from considerate tugboat skippers and Lady Luck.

So our little ship was snug in Port Arthur, having covered less than a hundred miles of the thousand we'd planned. And if I ever again have to decide between the tough Panama Canal route and the easy route through Texas, I'm not at all sure I'll make the same choice.

After all, it's supposed to be warm down in Panama.

9

Kathleen *Was Seaworthy—But Was I?*

It was a time for taking stock—of *Kathleen* and her skipper.

I like speed; *speed is fun*. And I submit that the 55-miles-per-hour highway speed limit is uneconomical—at least it is in my husky station wagon, which averages 12.4 miles per gallon at 70 and 12.3 miles per gallon at a pokey 55. The same was true of my last boat, outboard-powered *Kay IV,* which averaged better gas mileage at 43 m.p.h. than she did at 8.5!

All right, you say: If you think speed is all that wonderful, why are you knocking about in *Kathleen*?

It's really very simple, friend: when the fuel crisis hit and the cruising bug bit me, I opted for seaworthiness over speed, remembering that there are two good routes to survival afloat. One involves boat-speed enough to get off the water fast when things start looking hostile out there. The other involves boat-seaworthiness enough to stay out and take it.

The one big trouble with sailboats, as far as safety is concerned, is that they're slow. Cruising sailboats of under thirty feet generally won't make more than six or seven reliable knots, no matter how much auxiliary power you have below. This means that, unless you're forever cautious and stay very close to shelter, there will sooner or later come a time when you're simply not going to make it in ahead of an onrushing storm. If you try, you may get yourself caught in tricky waters close to shore, no place to be in an underpowered auxiliary in heavy weather. Your safest bet will probably be to forget about shelter and head offshore to ride it out—if you have a boat that is truly seaworthy.

There seems to be a great deal of misunderstanding and misrepresentation about seaworthiness. All kinds of small craft are advertised as seaworthy these days, vessels that no sensible sailor would dare expose to a real blow. The trouble is, the boating world is full of people who have never experienced a real blow. Right here I hasten to confess that, although I've spent a lot of time around the water, I've never been through an ultimate storm off shore.

I have, in coastal waters, survived several squalls clocked by shore weather stations at over seventy knots—well up in the hurricane range. They didn't last very long (which is why I'm still here), but each one did a lot of damage and drowned a number of people. In each case I made it through without serious trouble because I had under me a truly seaworthy sailing vessel designed for offshore work. I'm grateful for those rugged experiences. They cured me of the foolish notion that I was a hell of a sailor who could survive any old weather in practically any old craft.

For the benefit of folks who think a 20-knot breeze with a few whitecaps is a dangerous gale at sea, let me try to describe what it's like to be hit by a real wind, one up in the 60–80 knot bracket. Take, for instance, the first Chesapeake Bay black squall I encountered.

We were racing. I was attached to the Naval Academy at the time, in a sort of lefthanded way. Actually, I was stationed at the Naval Engineering Experiment Station across the river. This entitled me, after passing a stiff qualifying course, to skipper the Academy's handsome 44-foot yawls. In that race, I had a good crew of midshipmen on board; and we weren't doing too badly in the fleet as we came back across the Bay after turning a buoy near the far shore, but the wind was fading fast, the water had a greasy, glassy look, and there was a funny haze all around the horizon. Then I saw the squall coming, a dark wall of cloud in the north, growing bigger, blacker, and more menacing by the minute.

I went into my Captain Bligh act; and the air crackled with nautical lingo. The crew scurried around getting the storm sails ready while we held onto the racing canvas as long as possible—until I spotted a vicious-looking line of wind rushing at us from the north. At the command, four midshipmen clawed the big mainsail down and lashed it to the boom, while five manhandled the enormous genoa jib to the deck, unhanked it, and dumped it below.

"Secure that blink-blank forward hatch, now!" That was Captain Bligh, who'd never been through a bad squall before and was trying to hide the fact that he was scared stiff.

"Hatch secure, sir!"

"What's the problem with that everlasting storm trysail?"

"Trysail set, sir!"

"Check the ports; what about the one in the head? Is that skylight closed? Get those boards into the main hatchway and close the hatch, tight! Okay, all hands aft. Grab hold of something solid, gentlemen, here we go . . ."

It hit us, and we went. An icy fist of wind slammed us flat in spite of the fact that we had only two tiny, tough scraps of storm canvas up. For an endless time, it seemed, the twelve-ton yawl just lay there, mast almost horizontal, water sloshing into the cockpit; then she started to move. With steerage way, I could bear off a bit before the blast, and she rolled more or less upright once more, before another blast beat her down.

It was suddenly almost dark. Out of the darkness came more rain and hail than I'd ever seen, accompanied by thunder and lightning like a Wagner opera; but all the fireworks and precipitation seemed almost irrelevant. The scary, incredible thing was the wind. It was a screaming, supernatural force no human being could face. It didn't make waves, not the kind you're used to, the kind that go up and down. It simply picked up the whole top surface of Chesapeake Bay and hurled it across our staggering, reeling vessel.

Clinging to the big wheel, trying to steer after a fashion, I couldn't really see the boat at all. There was just the cabin trunk, awash like a half-tide rock, and the mast and rigging, and the heads and shoulders of the crew; the rest was a driving mass of rain, hail, spray, and solid water moving to leeward at seventy knots. I was aware of a midshipman doing something near my feet. He was trying to clear the scuppers so the flooded cockpit would drain; but he came up shaking his head. The scuppers were already clear. We were simply taking the stuff aboard much faster than it could run out.

As I said, that was a seaworthy, oceangoing boat. So she got knocked down, so she got a cockpit full of water, so what? Seaworthy boats are supposed to put up with nonsense like that. She did; and she brought us through, wet but unharmed. (As for the race, a flat calm followed the squall, and nobody finished.)

Nowadays, strolling along the docks, I see boat after cruising sailboat that probably wouldn't have survived that blow. The simple fact is that on a small boat you have to make a choice. You can have comfort and convenience, or you can have seaworthiness, but you can't have both. Many buyers choose the former. That's their privilege, but I wonder if they realize that the sacrifices they've made for comfort may drown them some day if they're not very, very careful.

To be truly seaworthy a sailboat must be: (a) totally selfrighting, and (b) totally watertight.

As far as stability is concerned, don't kid yourself. Your boat may seem steady as a house, gliding along with the wind on a pleasant afternoon; but if you do any amount of sailing any distance from shelter, there will eventually come a howling, shrieking day when she'll go over, all the way over. You'll find yourself perched on an almost perpendicular deck watching the waves playing in the rigging. If she won't come back up—goodbye.

But lack of stability is not my big complaint against many of the small, modern, cruising sailboats I see. The most serious deficiency they exhibit, to my eyes, is that they simply aren't watertight where it counts—everywhere it counts.

The average owner will protest indignantly: "Why, I never have to pump my boat; the bilge is bone dry!"

Well, sure. His boat is waterproof on the bottom, but what about the top?

In a real storm, there'll be water all around the bucket, not just underneath it. When the hull disappears from sight, buried by a breaking wave, or simply smothered by wind-driven spray the general consistency of the stream from a fire-hose, will it come up again? What about the cockpit? Here's the great weakness of the average small sailing cruiser; the cockpit is relatively huge, and leads straight into the cabin. What's between the two? Why, a six-inch sill, perhaps, and a flimsy little door— and sometimes, by God, that door is even louvered for ventilation!

The one thing you can count on, in a real blow, is a cockpit full of water. And without a bridgedeck and a waterproof hatch, that water will go below, into the main cabin.

Who wants to bet his life on a thin little hinged plywood door and dime-store latch? It's true that a high, solid bridge deck between the cockpit and the cabin is an unholy nuisance. Every time you want to go below, instead of simply stepping through a wide, inviting main hatch, you have to hoist yourself up onto the bridge deck, ease yourself through the hatch, and then lower yourself down a steep ladder. It's inconvenient as hell—but any water in the cockpit stays in the cockpit until the scuppers can deal with it.

Even if a boat is waterproof top and bottom, there's still the sheer size of the cockpit to be considered. A big cockpit is very pleasant. It makes a comfortable gathering place for a bunch of friendly people. It's a fine place to sleep on a hot summer night. There are all kinds of nice things to be said for big cockpits—until the wind starts to howl, the heavens open up, and that comfortable big cockpit starts to fill with water.

Kathleen's cockpit, aft of a solid bridge deck, is a small footwell between deck-level seats. The well is about four feet long by two feet wide by eighteen inches deep—that's roughly twelve cubic feet. With water at sixty-odd pounds per cubic foot, this cockpit will hold something over seven hundred pounds, a sizeable burden, but probably not disastrous on a 9,000-pound boat. I've seen boats of half the displacement that may someday be asked to carry two or three times that weight. I don't think they'll make it.

There are boats and boats. Some are designed for use in sheltered waters, preferably harbors; others are designed to go to sea. If you like the comfort of a great big cockpit opening directly below through a great big hatch, I hope you don't have too much sea-rover in your blood. If, on the other hand, you're a roamer at heart, you want a real cruising boat that'll stay out and take just about anything that comes along, hurricanes excepted. Comfort and convenience are great; but there's nothing quite as uncomfortable and inconvenient as a sunken boat.

Small cruising sailboats of suitable design have survived spectacular storms at sea. Judging from a large amount of reading and a small amount of experience, I'll say that the basic secrets of survival in a storm once you have the proper boat are research and preparation. In other words, first you must know what to do; and then you must do it, or get ready to do it, in plenty of time.

Recently I read a story about a young couple in a modest new cruising auxiliary who were caught by bad weather in the Gulf Stream. They were having a rugged time of it, but apparently making it all right, when suddenly a big wave slopped into the cockpit and ran below, flooding the vessel—the main hatch was open! They lost their new boat. Fortunately, they were picked up in their liferaft.

The lesson is obvious. Nothing should be open on your boat when a storm is bearing down on you. Seal up your vessel as if she's a submarine preparing to dive. There should be no traffic through the hatch for the duration. A vessel riding out a three-day blow cannot, of course, maintain this rule; but we're talking now of coastal storms of fairly short duration but, often, extreme intensity. Anybody can stay put for an hour. The moment someone opens the main hatch is the moment a particularly fierce gust of wind will knock you on your beam-ends and the whole ocean will take advantage of that gaping hole—and so goodbye.

Everything that can be got off the deck should be stuck below; and whatever is left should be lashed down securely. You want to be able to keep your crew and yourself safely in the cockpit. You don't want to risk your life, or anybody else's, out on that slippery, plunging, streaming deck or cabin top wrestling with a sail that's suddenly started blowing out of its stops. The same goes for the interior of the cabin. In a real blow, your boat will assume attitudes you wouldn't believe; and the forces generated to sling things around are impressive. You don't want to have to clean a lot of mayonnaise off the overhead, do you? Get that jar into a safe locker and make sure the door stays shut, if you have to use a hammer and nails.

There are a number of well-tested methods of dealing with heavy weather offshore; and most of them apply, with modifications, to riding out a hard squall in coastal waters. There's one thing you can sometimes do inshore that the deep-sea mariner can't: you can anchor.

This assumes, of course, that you possess a hefty storm hook one or two sizes larger than that recommended as a working anchor for your boat, and a couple of hundred feet of husky nylon rope to match, but— and here's the catch—you've got to have something very solid on your boat to secure it to. A lot of the deck-mounted mooring cleats won't take the strain. Will yours?

Anchoring won't work, of course, where the water is too deep, and it's not advisable, except as a last resort, off a wide-open seacoast exposed to the full blast of the storm. However, I know of several people who have used this technique successfully among the Florida Keys where any other method would have involved a serious risk of being blown onto the shallow flats nearby. It has, of course, the tremendous advantage that once the hook is set and everything is secure there's no reason to remain topside. You can go below and ride out the disturbance in relative comfort.

Where anchors aren't usable, for one reason or another, weather emergencies can be dealt with in several ways, some that have the approval of generations of hardy small-boat voyagers, and others that seem to have been invented by armchair navigators and never really tried out, at least not on the kinds of boats for which they're now being recommended. Let's list them and see how practical they are:

1.   Heaving to under power.
2.   Riding to a sea anchor.
3.   Heaving to under sail.

4.   Lying ahull under bare pole(s).
5.   Running before it.

The first choice is not one that normally occurs to the offshore sailor. He generally hasn't got the desire or the fuel to nurse his vessel through a lengthy gale under power, but the coastal sailor often tries it.

A good many years ago, in a borrowed 36-foot sloop, my wife and I were heading home across Chesapeake Bay after an overnight cruise. A black squall came up. I'd been through a couple of these howlers, but always while racing. *Karin* had a reliable 25-horsepower auxiliary. I thought this was great: for once I could take it easy, stow the sails, and just motor through the storm. We got everything tied down and putt-putted along confidently. When the wind hit, I gave her a bit more throttle and shoved the tiller down and headed up into it . . .

Well, that is to say, I tried to head up into it. She wouldn't come around. Even with the old four-cylinder Gray pounding away at full throttle, *Karin* would not turn into that screaming wind. She lay there helpless, knocked flat by the hurricane pressures on her bare mast and rigging. Finally, in desperation, I hauled the tiller the other way and ran off before it. Fortunately, the Chesapeake is a large body of water, and we had room enough to keep running until the storm blew itself out.

Karin was a seagoing sailing craft with a good inboard installation; yet she simply would not maneuver under power alone in that shrieking squall. After that experience and a couple of others, I've lost all faith in the internal combustion engine as a means of dealing with really bad weather in a sailboat. Unless your boat is a powerful motor-sailer, forget it.

The second impulse that comes to the inexperienced sailor caught in a bad blow is to throw a sea anchor over the bow. He's read a lot about these miraculous devices. One day he finds one and can't resist it: a beautiful, big, salty-looking cone of canvas with a husky ring at the open end, to which is attached a businesslike bridle. It makes him feel safe just to know it's on board.

Well, I carried the same sea anchor in a couple of powerboats, but I never even got around to trying it. I've had no experience with sea anchors on sailboats, so I'll call in an expert, Eric Hiscock, who with his wife, Susan, has sailed three times around the world in small boats. In one of his many excellent books, *Cruising Under Sail,* Hiscock writes: "The widely held belief that if streamed from the bow a sea-anchor will hold a yacht's head to the wind, has been disproved so often that one wonders how it survives. No matter how large the sea-anchor may be, the yacht will lie beam-on or nearly so . . . ''

Most experienced ocean voyagers seem to agree with Hiscock.

So much for a couple of popular ideas that probably won't work when the sky turns black and you see that white line of churned-up water racing towards you and know you're going to be hit and hit hard. Now let's look at some classic methods that do work offshore, and may be applicable in coastal waters as well.

Heaving to under sail is the standard way of coping with a gale at sea, as old as the art of sailing. The chief advantage of heaving to is that it sets up the vessel to tend herself, and you can seek shelter below. In order to heave to under sail, you've got to reduce the area of your sails drastically without removing them altogether. You need a storm trysail to replace the mainsail completely, or the ability to reef the main down to pocket-handkerchief size; and you should have a small storm jib.

With any sail up, you can expect some hairy moments when the squall strikes; that first gust is generally something pretty special. You'll have to coax her through it, spilling the wind from the sails as required. After that, you can expect to continue to take a beating as long as the fireworks last. Nevertheless, if you're caught in hostile waters, you have no choice. You have to sail her, just to keep her off the rocks, or out of the way of the freighters and tankers.

The final two offshore storm techniques require adequate room to leeward (so does using a sea anchor if it works). This is often available to the deep-water voyager, but less often to the coastwise cruiser.

The first time I heard of somebody lying ahull, as it's called, it sounded ridiculous and unseamanlike to me. What, just pull down all the sails, lash the helm hard over, and go below and let her drift, broadside to wind and sea? I'd have said it was a sure-fire recipe for suicide; yet innumerable yachtsmen have survived innumerable gales in just this way. A large number of salty adventurers have ridden out severe gales in the cabin, warm and dry, letting their little ships take care of themselves. My son and I used the technique on our first offshore passage with complete success—at least we're still here to talk about it.

The final bad-weather remedy is the one my wife and I wound up using on the rugged day on Chesapeake Bay: running before it. Again, this requires plenty of searoom; but if your destination should happen to be downwind, and there's nothing solid in the way, why not make a little progress in the right direction? Most deepwater sailors seem to agree that running before it—with or without a small storm jib, depending on the boat and the circumstances—is the best answer to a really violent gale.

A lot of folks seem to be trying to sell the notion that stormy weather is a terrible curse on boating. This is kind of like saying that steep rocks are a terrible curse on mountaineering. Wind, strong or weak, is what sailing's all about, isn't it?

A squall now and then is inevitable. Sooner or later a cruising sailer may even have to cope with the killer storm of the season; that sneaky meteorological Sunday punch that lays racing fleets flat without warning and litters the beaches with craft that didn't make it. The question is: will he be prepared for it when it comes?

My advice is, get the hell out there when it blows. Sure you'll get wet. Sure you'll tie in your reefs cockeyed, set the storm jib upside down, and find that the leads for the jib sheets are all wrong. In fact, everything may be all wrong; it's bound to be the first time. You'll be sweating and swearing, but suddenly you'll find everything sorted out after a fashion and you'll be sailing and maybe even getting a kick out of being out there on such a beautiful day. If you keep at it, you'll eventually know exactly what to do when it's got to be done, not for fun and practice, but for real. You'll be ready for the big one if it comes.

10

Locking Through New Orleans

It was late spring and we were heading east again. It's about 254 miles along the Gulf Intracoastal from Port Arthur to New Orleans, our first major objective. There's only one problem: The city of New Orleans is not really available. At least not to private pleasure boats. You can't hardly make it (as they say down there) and it's safer not to try. I learned that the hard way, and it took considerable time and money to repair the damage.

If you're coming from the east you've got a slight chance. But when I was there, that nice wide waterway called the Rigolets that leads directly into beautiful Lake Pontchartrain was closed to *Kathleen*. They had built some bridges across it, and one of them had stripped a gear or burned a bearing or something so it wouldn't open, and nobody seemed to be in a hurry to fix it. It's possible to sneak through the industrial center of the city by the Intracoastal and its tributary canals if all those bridges are working and somebody's willing to open them for you, but it's a fairly lengthy operation.

What about approaching from the west? Well, I tell you, folks, I came that way and my advice is short and simple: forget it. On the west bank of the Mississippi two locks protect the ICW canal system from the river and vice versa: Harvey Lock upstream and Algiers Lock downstream. Naturally, coming from the west, you'll choose Harvey in order to have the current with you for the four- or five-mile run down to the entrance to the city canals at the Industrial Lock. At the time of year we crossed the river—June—it wasn't running hard enough to make much difference, but often, I'm told, it can amount to several knots.

These two locks can be considered negotiable if you don't mind being bawled out by ill-tempered lock keepers. (To be honest, I don't know about the guy at Algiers, but the gent at Harvey was certainly no jewel of gentle forbearance.) But the big obstacle to entering New Orleans, an almost insuperable barrier, is the Industrial Lock on the east bank. Here you've got no choice. You either go through that or you don't go; and it's a lot easier getting a sinner past St. Peter into Heaven than a sailboat past the Keeper of the Industrial Lock into New Orleans.

If you have a rather shabby-looking power craft, maybe you can fool him by smearing some dirt around, wearing greasy dungarees, and carrying a bunch of castoff fishing nets on your cabin and transom. Maybe the guy will think you're a commercial fisherman and let you through. If your vessel is bigger, you might try disguising it as a tug to sneak past the eagle-eyed guardian of the New Orleans gates. But if you have an obvious, uncamouflageable pleasure sailboat, I'm sorry for you. They aren't about to let any of those into their sacred city. In the New Orleans Industrial Lock, pleasure boats simply don't count, and the guy will do everything in his power—and he's got lots of power—to let you know it.

What's that—I sound prejudiced? Well, you try nursing an ailing engine, which you don't dare let stop because the starter isn't working, for a long afternoon under a blazing Louisiana sun, waiting helplessly for permission to enter a lock while everybody else is allowed to go through, and see how objective you feel.

I suppose the real trouble was that we'd had it too easy up to that point. With locks, I mean. Our first experience had involved the Calcasieu Lock a couple of hundred miles to the west. We'd approached it with trepidation, fenders draped over *Kathleen*'s sides, docklines ready on every available cleat. At the lock we found a couple of tows nosed against the bank, waiting—they just push the whole long string of barges right up against the shore and keep the tug's props turning slowly to hold it there. We pulled alongside the nearest tug and asked the captain please to call the lockmaster for us since we had no radio. He obliged and came back out to say that if we'd get into position near the lock entrance, we could go right through as soon as the tow currently in the lock emerged.

Since there wasn't much difference in water level, they'd just open both gates for us if we made it snappy.

It was almost a let-down. We had hoped to gain some experience in these low and easy locks before hitting the Mississippi; but it was certainly nice of everybody concerned. As soon as the emerging tow was clear, I blasted into the long chamber under a full head of steam—well, twelve horsepower and six knots. The friendly lockmaster called for our boat's name as we roared by and we yelled back, "*Kathleen.*" As we neared the far end, the lock gates swung open and out we shot into the ICW, having lost only a few minutes in the process. Beautiful.

There was some question about the Vermilion Lock farther on. We'd heard that it was being repaired and a lengthy canal detour might be required. As it turned out, the conflicting water levels were apparently just right so the lock gates weren't even closed. Our only problem was keeping our little diesel running—we were having trouble with dirty fuel filters due to skipper negligence—as we maneuvered in the holding pattern waiting for westbound traffic to clear the lock. Then we squirted right through as before. Great.

So, as we prepared *Kathleen* for the big Mississippi locks, we weren't as apprehensive as we should have been. Louisiana was a nice—if rather hot—place full of nice people; everybody had been kind to the couple in the funny little sailboat that had come all the way from Seattle, Washington. It was therefore rather a shock, at the Harvey Lock, to meet the attitude that if your boat doesn't work for a living, and if you don't have a radio, you don't belong near Harvey Lock, or maybe anywhere else.

I don't really know what my crime was at Harvey. I made no signal, but neither did the commercial vessel ahead of me. Undoubtedly that captain talked to the lockmaster by radio, but the Coast Pilot states clearly that this in no way affects the requirement for the use of sound signals. Since he didn't use his horn for the three blasts required by law, I figured silence was a local custom and there was no sense in annoying anybody with a lot of noise. It wasn't as if we were invisible. The craft ahead wasn't that big, and *Kathleen*'s mast projects forty-odd feet into the air. Nevertheless, as soon as the leading vessel was past, with the signal light still beckoning green, the drawbridge at the west end of the lock started to come down right in front of us. I slammed the diesel into reverse and hit the throttle hard. The drawbridge stopped closing.

"HEY, GET THAT SAILBOAT IN HERE!" bellowed a bullhorn on the lock wall. As I engaged forward gear once more, and crept cautiously under the menacing span, a man stepped out of the control room and shouted angrily, "If you don't know the rules, you shouldn't be here!"

I still don't know what rule I'd broken. In fairness, the rest of the lock personnel were very obliging, patiently instructing us how and where to secure and when to cast off. After all the yelling, it really wasn't much of a deal. Although the lock walls towered high above us, the lift at this season was only about a foot. Then the east gates opened and we were given the all-clear and powered out into the wide Mississippi. Having crossed it on bridges farther north where it spreads much more extensively, we were actually a little disappointed at how wide it wasn't here, contained by its levees. Still, it was a thrill to be sailing—well, motoring—on the great river at last, with New Orleans now within reach.

Well, we thought New Orleans was within reach. Just one more lock to go and we had it made. We putt-putted for an hour down the rather dilapidated waterfront, past the Vieux Carre, and turned into the entrance of the Industrial Lock. A big tow and some fishing craft and other commercial vessels were waiting to lock through. I approached the tow and asked the tug's skipper please to call the lockmaster for us. He came out shortly and reported that there wasn't room for us this time but maybe we could be worked in next time, stand by.

As I've indicated earlier, *Kathleen*'s motor was ailing and I couldn't even give it a rest because the starter circuits had been damaged and I had to crank it by hand, a rather muscular operation, which I wasn't quite sure I could manage again. However, if we had to wait, we had to wait. I powered slowly across the channel looking for a less-crowded area in which to maneuver while killing time. As we approached a smaller tow coming in slowly, the tug's pilot stepped out onto his open bridge and gestured to where a bunch of fishing boats were now crowding into the lock behind the big tow we'd first hailed.

"Go on in," he shouted. "If you hurry, you can get through."

Figuring he had the latest radio word from on high, I jazzed the ailing diesel unmercifully and headed for the gate. It looked pretty jammed in there, but I had my clearance, didn't I? Then a man stepped out of the control office and a bullhorn blared angrily: "HEY, GET THAT SAILBOAT OUT OF HERE!"

Well, I won't bore you with the rest of that day. Time after time we'd get definitive orders, we thought, and head for the opening; time after time the bullhorn would drive us off. Tow after tow went through, accompanied by unattached tugs and shoals of fishing boats large and small. Trying to find out exactly when we might expect to get admitted, we tangled with a helpful fisherman while he asked questions over the radio that weren't answered. Fending off, Kay hit her head on a projecting fitting, and while I was determining that she wasn't seriously hurt, *Kathleen* damaged a spreader on an overhanging boom. All in all, it wasn't an afternoon I'd care to repeat. We arrived at the lock at two in the afternoon. It was well after six when we were finally admitted, and past eight by the time we were tied up in the marina on Lake Pontchartrain. In a way, I preferred those gales off the Pacific Coast. As far as I'm concerned, New Orleans is a pleasant place to visit—but not in a sailboat.

11

South to the Keys

Coming down the Apalachicola River after another long, hot day under power, I passed a significant milestone just before reaching the town of the same name. I was now in Florida, 350 statute miles east of the Harvey Lock at New Orleans. I'd started this cruise in Texas, 350 miles west of that unfortunate place. I'd covered 700 miles of Gulf Intracoastal Waterway and that, I told myself, was enough. In fact, it was too much. I was disenchanted with the whole project. Either this yachting bit wasn't all it was cracked up to be, or I was getting too old for it. Well, I'd take *Kathleen* all the way to the Florida Keys because I was stubborn and that was the goal I'd set myself. Then, dammit, I'd clean her up and put her up for sale and switch to golf or knitting.

I had spent that icy winter at home making ambitious cruising plans for the spring and accumulating piles of fascinating gadgets to put aboard, including an autopilot and a brand new nonplastic sextant. However, back aboard, heading east once more, we soon found that the coldest winter in recent Gulf Coast history had turned into the hottest summer. Kay jumped ship in New Orleans. She said that a constant 95° in the shade without much shade was a bit too much for cruising enjoyment. I'd always wanted to try sailing *Kathleen* singlehanded,

The Gulf ICW east of New Orleans is often a pretty, sheltered canal, but all the powering eventually made the skipper very depressed.

hadn't I? Well, if I didn't mind, now woulde a good time for it. She would rejoin me when things got cooler, or if I found I really couldn't manage alone.

So I sent her back to the cool mountains of New Mexico and spent a couple of sweltering weeks taking care of overdue boat chores while waiting to get *Kathleen's* damaged spreader repaired. While the mast was down, and other yard work was being done, I had a VHF/FM unit installed. Of course that was money down the drain, I reflected, now that I was through with cruising forever.

In Apalachicola, I made a bad landing, misjudging the tidal current at the dock of the Rainbow Motel and picking up another creosote smudge on the topsides, but I was resigned to those by now. When you're handling a boat by yourself you simply can't juggle docklines and fenders simultaneously, so you get her secured first and protected afterwards. Aside from that, sailing without a crew had posed no problems. Really, I told myself, I should be quite happy at the ease with which I found myself managing my little ship alone. But my depressed mood, intensified by the clumsy landing, persisted even after I'd stretched my legs with a hike through town and had a pleasant chat with the crew of a handsome Pearson 35 called *Harmony* that had just docked when I returned.

In the morning, still morose, I negotiated the highway swing bridge under power and followed the channel buoys out into Apalachicola Bay; by lunchtime I was in Carrabelle, the jumping-off spot for the openwater run that came next.

When planning the cruise, I'd spotted three potential danger areas. The first had been the Mississippi River locks, which had fully lived up to my grim expectations. The last would be the fairly long passage down around Cape Sable—the southwestern corner of the Florida mainland—and across shallow Florida Bay to my final destination at Marathon, halfway out the Keys. But the most serious difficulties encountered by yachtsmen following this route around the Gulf, according to my research, practically always developed in the middle of the cruise, between Carrabelle and Tarpon Springs, although more frequently during the stormier seasons of the year.

This is the Big Bend where Florida stops going east and west and starts going south and north. There's no sheltered ICW to help you around the corner; the Waterway ends off Carrabelle and doesn't begin again until you reach Anclote Key off Tarpon Springs. There's a series of widely spaced navigational markers to help you follow the coast around, that's all. However, I had decided that if I was capable of finding California with my sextant after a 1,000-mile offshore passage from British

Columbia, I could damn well make a lousy little 150-mile jump alone straight across from one part of Florida to another.

After docking at the Isle of St. James Marina, I spent the afternoon doing my laundry and stocking up with ice and groceries. Carrabelle is conveniently arranged for the cruiser's needs, and I found that the marina had a very pleasant restaurant. In the evening, *Harmony* appeared and I had a drink on board. Like me, they were bound for the Keys, and we discussed navigational strategy and agreed to bypass all intermediate harbors, none very easy of access, and rendezvous in Clearwater Beach, 12 miles south of Tarpon Springs. We would maintain radio contact on the way across if possible.

As the smaller, slower boat (perhaps with the more nervous skipper), *Kathleen* departed first. I ate breakfast in the dark and headed out as soon as there was light enough to show me the channel markers. The dawn was quite lovely over the low Florida coast, but I'm afraid I didn't appreciate it as much as I might have; I was more concerned with trying to anticipate what might go wrong on my first singlehanded offshore passage. There wasn't enough wind to bother with, and it came from dead ahead anyway, so I crossed St. George Sound under power and ran through East Pass between the sandy shelter islands, and out into the Gulf of Mexico. I took my departure from the offshore buoy.

Soon there was no land in sight. I was alone out there except for a couple of distant fishing boats; and the southwesterly breeze was beginning to act as if it meant business. After giving it a little more time to show its intentions—apparently honorable—I set the mainsail, while Tilly (my new Tiller Master autopilot) held the bow into the wind. Moments later the forestaysail and roller-furling jib were set and drawing, the diesel was silent, and we were off under sail on a close starboard reach, course 135, speed 4. The sky was clear, the sun was bright, the horizon was sharp, and it was time to activate the navigation department—I wanted to put in some sextant practice in case a fix should be needed the following day to help me make my landfall at Clearwater Beach.

Although I had firmly decided to give up all this nautical nonsense, I was curious to see, while I still had the chance, how a really good sextant worked. I found that it worked very well, much better than I did. Celestial navigation is apparently not one of the things, like shooting or bicycle riding, that you don't forget. It took me most of the morning to manage an error-free calculation; but around noon I got a series of sights that gave me a very good fix. The only trouble was, it put us way ahead and to the west of my dead reckoning position.

"Kathleen, Kathleen, Kathleen, this is *Harmony."*

Although I'd already used the new radio several times for calling, this was the first time I'd received a call. It took me a moment or two to pull myself together and make the proper response and switch to the desired working channel. The *Harmony* sailors had slept fairly late and were apparently several hours behind me. I remembered my navigational problem and asked if they'd noticed any sign of a fairly strong southerly current, maybe a bit southwesterly. They hadn't. We agreed to check with each other again towards evening, and I returned to my charts and figures. Well, did I believe my dead reckoning or my pretty new sextant? I decided that the fix looked just too good to ignore; I remembered being told that the Gulf was subject to strong and erratic currents on occasion. I started a new DR from the circled dot on the chart, changing course accordingly.

It was past time for lunch, so I consumed a sandwich and a can of beer. The wind held steady, and *Kathleen* romped along towards the southeast at a good clip. So far so good, but there was a long, dark night ahead. I wasn't lonely, but I was, let's say, slightly apprehensive. I promised myself I'd take it very, very easy and run no risk at all of, alone on board, being caught with too much canvas up in the middle of the night. Later, after an evening check with *Harmony,* still not in sight astern, I broke out a can of stew that had accompanied *Kathleen* all the way from Vancouver and followed it with a can of Canadian peaches for dessert. Gradually, the sun approached the western horizon. It was time to snug things down for the night.

I cleared the furling line of the jib, and started to ease off its taut sheet; then I cleated it again. To hell with it. The big headsail was pulling like a horse and we were going great. It wasn't as if I'd have to visit the foredeck in the dark if the wind increased; that was why I'd installed roller furling, wasn't it? A precautionary reef in the main? I vetoed that thought, too. It was just too pleasant to have my little ship sailing well in open water after negotiating all those endless muddy ditches under power, day after blistering hot day. I'd reduce sail when I had to, not before, dammit.

I watched night settle over the totally empty sea. No lights showed anywhere except for *Kathleen's* masthead running light 40 feet overhead. Gradually I settled down into a routine of a good look around and instrument check every half hour. The wind held, and we drove on through the night, close-reaching at four and five knots with the rail almost, but not quite awash—it takes a lot of wind to heel her those last few degrees. I found the main cabin settee more convenient in these circumstances than my usual berth in the forward cabin; but although I rested, I don't think I ever really slept. At least I never missed that half-hourly trip to the deck.

After midnight, I spotted something that looked like a distant Christmas tree. It turned out to be a northbound tow well off to starboard, the only traffic seen all night. Around 0300 the wind died abruptly. I took in the headsails and, reluctantly, turned on the Yanmar and resigned myself to spending more time on deck since, under power, I no longer had the right of way over just about anything I was likely to meet. Well, it had been a beautiful seventeen-hour sail that I would always remember.

At dawn, with the sea perfectly calm, the main came down and the cockpit awning went up. I motored along steadily in the increasing light and watched the sun make a spectacular appearance to port. *Harmony* called at 0700; she'd apparently gone by in the night because she expected to be in Clearwater Beach in a few hours. I wasn't so optimistic. My DR wasn't agreeing too well with my depthfinder readings, and I was beginning to have some doubts about my position. I got to work with the sextant once more, but the sun lines that resulted weren't angled right to tell me much except that I was somewhere off the west coast of Florida. I'd have to wait until local noon, well past one o'clock on my watch, since that was set to daylight saving time.

At 1230, watch time, I picked up what seemed to be the tip of a tall smokestack or tower to port, tiny on the horizon. Hopefully, I called it the big powerplant near Tarpon Springs I'd been told to look for, although we were passing too far away for me to be certain. I debated heading over that way to check, but the detour seemed like a waste of time. After all, I was sure to get a noon fix shortly.

When I did, it put me 30 miles south of my charted position, well past Tarpon Springs and Clearwater Beach, closing in on Tampa Bay.

This was strictly impossible. It meant that we must have averaged at least six knots ever since leaving East Pass yesterday morning. While *Kathleen* had been going well under sail last night, she hadn't been going that well; and her cruising speed under power is only five knots. Furthermore, the depthfinder kept insisting that I wasn't where I thought I was at all. Something was very wrong. For a while, I kept plugging along on the same southeasterly course; I couldn't think of anything else to do. The water depth was approaching three fathoms now, decreasing gradually; some kind of a coastline ought to appear soon. None did. The bottom was visible below me, but there was no other land in sight. Eerie. It was like being lost on a glassy, shallow, dream sea that didn't really exist.

At last I said to hell with it: I'd left a definite landmark somewhere astern and even though it was now an hour and a half behind me the only thing to do was backtrack and make sure of its identity. I swung *Kathleen* north. It was a long run back. I must admit that the suspense was fairly great and I was beginning to wonder if maybe I'd imagined that tiny smokestack on the horizon when suddenly it appeared, dead ahead. Well, at least my piloting wasn't totally haywire. But it took another hour before I was close enough to make a positive identification, long after I could see that what my wishful thinking had turned into a distant stack or tower, wasn't that at all.

It was a perfectly good navigational marker. In fact it was #10 in the series of lights that had been installed to help cruising boats follow the coast around from Carrabelle. Instead of being miles south of Clearwater Beach as my sextant had insisted, I was miles—to be exact—16 miles north of Tarpon Springs.

It was a terrible shock to my navigational pride, but at least I knew where I was. I turned *Kathleen*'s bow back south, left the helm in Tilly's care, and ducked below to recheck my calculations and determine where the spectacular error had originated. It wasn't hard to spot, once I applied a few brains to the problem instead of accepting uncritically the products of my shiny new sextant. The numbers were right there: my latitude 28° N, sun's declination 22° N. At noon I had been trying to measure a tiny six-degree angular difference dead overhead or, to put it more accurately, an angle of 84° up from the horizon. Now I remember writers like Eric Hiscock and Don Street complaining about the problem of getting accurate meridian sights in the tropics when the sun was on the same side of the equator as the ship. Well, we weren't quite in the tropics here, and an experienced navigator could undoubtedly have coped with the situation, but it had apparently been too tough for a clumsy beginner with a brand new sextant. Why my giant noon errors had all been consistently south, I didn't really know (and still don't), but that wonderful-looking fix yesterday, obviously a complete fluke, had led me to change course to port, I recalled, explaining how I'd wound up so far up the coast.

Looking on the bright side, it was a good thing I'd learned this lesson in these safe waters instead of, for instance, the coral-studded seas surrounding the Bahamas. I rechecked the chart, glanced at my watch, got the marine operator on the radio, and called Kay and told her not to expect a call from Clearwater Beach tonight. (Making a telephone call from shipboard still made me feel as if I was cruising in a state of marvelous luxury or dreadful decadence, I wasn't quite sure which.) Before I could call *Harmony,* her crew called me. They were in, they'd been in for hours, where was I? I told them I'd got slightly confused and wouldn't make it this evening, which was good for a laugh on me. As I signed off, and glanced around, sitting comfortably in the main companionway while Tilly steered, I spotted something off the port bow: a real smokestack that soon turned out to be part of a real, enormous powerplant. Presently Anclote Key appeared. I headed for the anchorage behind it. Just as the sun dropped out of sight in the west, *Kathleen*'s big CQR went down in eight feet of water.

In the morning, strangely, I woke up feeling great. I couldn't understand it. After all, I'd just made a tremendous navigational booboo that could have had tragic consequences. I'd failed to reach the port for which I'd been heading. I should have been totally disgusted and ashamed of myself, but instead I felt fine, just fine. Singlehanded cruising—hell, any cruising—was a wonderful experience, and I couldn't comprehend how I'd ever thought otherwise. I decided that it was relief; the crossing now behind me must have worried me more than I'd realized. Even so, it seemed as if I was overreacting, but why fight it? For the first time in many days everything looked bright and rosy.

I made myself a big breakfast and, afterwards, sat in the cockpit with my second cup of coffee enjoying the morning. No hurry. I was going only as far as Clearwater Beach today; I had all the time in the world. If I'd wanted to rush around I'd have stuck to powerboats. I washed up and finished writing up the log that I'd been too tired to tackle the night before; then I started the diesel and went forward and let the Powerwinch break out the hook and bring it aboard. There was no wind, but even that didn't affect my mood; I powered happily away to pick up the ICW markers that would lead me inside the Anclote Keys to Clearwater Beach—and I couldn't do it.

I could feel my pleasant euphoria evaporating as I looked down that long line of idiot markers that would lead me south to another bunch of idiot bridges that might or might not open promptly when I hooted the idiot horn. Suddenly I realized what my recent depression had been: I'd contracted a bad case of ICW claustrophobia. I'd got sensitized, allergic; I couldn't take any more crummy little closed-in canals and channels, locks and bridges, certainly not this morning after a fine, free 150-mile offshore passage, even it it had wound up in the wrong place. I shoved the tiller hard over and sent *Kathleen* out towards the open Gulf.

A week later I reached the Keys. I wasn't offshore all that time, of course—as a matter of fact I did stop for fuel and supplies in Clearwater Beach, but I made the approach from seaward, not from the ICW. But I had some great sails, including one black night with lightning flashing all around the horizon and *Kathleen* crashing through the darkness under

A fine reaching breeze carried Kathleen *most of the way across the corner of the Gulf of Mexico from Carrabelle to Anclote Key.*

After many navigational vicissitudes, Kathleen's skipper finally managed to find Clearwater Beach, Florida.

staysail and double-reefed main—and Cape Sable appearing on schedule as the dawn broke violently under a stormy sky. . .

I had left Naples at daylight the morning before and spent an hour under power negotiating the winding and branching waterway leading to the Gulf of Mexico. It was a clear July morning, but the weather report promised afternoon thundershowers—I think they tape that one in the spring and run it all summer. The shores were an odd mixture: stretches of tangled mangroves alternating with manicured lawns surrounding handsome residences, each with its own little dock. As I headed out the final channel into the Gulf, the usual morning breeze came up, blowing off the land. Once clear of the last channel markers, I set sail and turned off the diesel.

The course down the coast was a bit east of south. My first target, ten miles away, was a buoy off Marco Island. I didn't really need to touch base there, but it would give me an idea of how I was doing, navigationally speaking. Then, in another twenty miles, I should pick up the buoy marking the south tip of the long shoal off Cape Romano, after which I'd have, roughly, a fifty-mile run to Cape Sable, which would mostly be made in the dark. I'd have to be careful not to sail too fast here, if the winds were favorable; when closing with the coast in the morning I didn't want to overshoot my landfall before there was light enough to see it.

Cape Sable, the lower left-hand corner of the Florida mainland, consists of three promontories: Northwest Cape, Middle Cape, and East Cape. I was hoping to gauge my progress so that, on a more or less southeasterly course, I'd pick up Middle Cape at dawn; then I'd make sure of my position by finding a navigational marker off East Cape—one of the very few around—and turn due south for the twenty-mile run to Marathon. Well, that was my battle plan. There was nobody on board to criticize it, since I was sailing still alone.

There's no truly deep water in that part of the world. At Naples, for instance, the five-fathom line runs almost twenty-five miles offshore. Florida west coast boatmen are hardened to seeing bottom under the keel even when there's no land visible on the horizon. I'd determined from the chart that on this run to Marathon I'd never have much more than twenty feet beneath me until I reached Cape Sable—and then I'd be lucky if I had eight to ten feet for the last long jump across the open end of Florida Bay.

To a deepwater sailor, this kind of thinwater navigation can be nerve-wracking, but there are compensations. For one thing, along most of that coast there are few surprises offshore. If you're sailing along happily in eight feet of water, you're not likely, if you pay attention to the chart, to find yourself suddenly aground in four feet. For another thing, since the depth changes are almost always so gradual and predictable, your depthfinder serves as a pretty good navigating instrument, giving you a reasonably accurate notion of your distance off the coast. And most important, there is absolutely no danger of being run down by a supertanker in 15 to 20 feet of water.

Ten miles south of Naples I spotted the buoy off Marco Island. When it came abeam I noted the fact that we didn't seem to be going quite as fast as the knotmeter indicated and that we'd slipped a bit to the westward—I'd have to make a bit more allowance for current and leeway.

The offshore breeze had now freshened and swung ahead; even closehauled we could no longer make the course for the next target south. A tack would be required eventually. A couple of small, flat rays (manta?) jumped close aboard, with their ridiculously long whiplike tails flailing—I wondered if they ever got knots in them and, if so, how they got them untied. By midmorning there was enough wind that I pulled down a reef in the mainsail, remembering that back in my younger sailing days a reef had been considered a fairly big deal, but jiffy-reefing has changed all that.

Gradually, the high, blocky shapes of the resorts and condominiums on fashionable Marco Island sank below the horizon. We were opposite the mangrove maze known as the Thousand Islands, too low to be seen from so far out. I must admit that I'm always happier when the last vestige of land vanishes. I'm confident that *Kathleen* can handle anything the open sea can throw at her short of typhoons and hurricanes; it's that hard stuff around the edges that worries me. But with the breeze continuing to veer southwards and freshening—10–15 knots had been predicted—it looked as if I was in for a long, rough ride hard on the wind.

By noon I'd taken in the jib and pulled down the second and last reef in the main. Things were getting wet and lively on board; but an hour later the wind dropped somewhat and I turned out one reef. I'd hardly got back to the cockpit before I realized that I had the Cape Romano buoy off the port bow. At least there was something out there, even though we should still have been well short of, and probably quite a bit to the west of, the buoy. A few minutes later, I could see that it wasn't a buoy at all but a large white ketch coming up from the south under power. I changed course to pass close to her, meaning to hail her, but as we got nearer the big boat turned sharply away, obviously afraid that the bearded pirate in the small cutter intended to hijack their boat.

The depthfinder was giving readings in the thirties now, indicating that we were much too far offshore to find our elusive buoy. I tacked eastwards. The wind eased a bit, and I unrolled the big jib again, watching the depth readings as we crashed along at a great pace. Gradually they diminished, and suddenly there was a real buoy well off to port, dramatically illuminated by a shaft of sunlight piercing the thunderclouds that were now gathering. Remembering the navigational aid I'd mistaken for a smokestack a few days earlier, I made absolutely sure of its identity. It was No. 16 buoy, all right. I tacked south: next target Cape Sable, with a dawn ETA.

By evening, there were black squalls cruising all around the horizon, and we were back down to forestaysail and single-reefed main. However, the wind had backed a little so we could almost lay our course. At twilight, I tucked in the second reef once more. It wasn't really needed at the moment, but we were making pretty good time. There was no real hurry, and I didn't want to have to clamber around the decks in the dark, reducing sail, if the wind should pick up again. *Kathleen* was driving along nicely at three or four knots, her decks almost dry in spite of the short, white-capped seas coming at her out of the growing darkness ahead. There was a steady low note in the rigging to tell me that the weather forecaster had flubbed it; she doesn't start to sing to me like that until it's blowing well over the predicted 15 knots.

Leaving Tilly on watch, I went below to study the chart. Alternative strategy if things got too rough to make headway to windward: bear off and run for Key West, and make a long detour around the end of the Keys. But that would take another day at least. I settled down to the routine I'd established on earlier night passages: lookout and instrument check every half hour, with a detailed log entry—course, speed, depth— every hour. At midnight, I saw a single white light on the port quarter, the only light seen all night—except, of course, for the lightning. That kept flashing all around but, fortunately, never near us. It was a black and threatening night, but nothing seemed to come of all the meteorological menace. At four in the morning I got hungry and cooked myself a big breakfast, breaking out the pot holders for the first time on this sheltered cruise. At five, with the wind dying, I turned out one reef in the mainsail. Half an hour later I heard sudden heavy rain on deck and popped out the hatch to see an inky black squall cloud of impressive dimensions bearing down on us. With two reefs in, I would have gambled on being able to sail through it; with only one, I scrambled to bring the mainsail down, getting thoroughly soaked in the process—and then, of course, no wind came, only more heavy rain.

Disgusted with my poor weather-guessing, I left *Kathleen* loafing along under forestaysail alone and went to wring myself out and make myself a cup of coffee. Then I took stock of the situation. The depthfinder readings indicated that, hammering to windward under reduced sail, we'd been set well offshore. The pencil track on the chart indicated that, inshore or out, we should be pretty well opposite Middle Cape; all we had to do was tack east and find it. As it turned out, there was no question of tacking. Back on deck I found that the rain squall had killed the wind completely, at least for the moment. It was getting light in the east. I started up the Yanmar and set a course at right angles to the one we'd held all night. An hour passed. The water got progressively shallower. The readings went from 24 feet to 20 to 18 to 14, and still no land in sight. Maybe, in spite of strong headwinds, I'd run past Cape Sable altogether; maybe I was now standing into the treacherous shallows of Florida Bay. The suspense was considerable. I forced myself to go below and make more coffee, to be doing something while Tilly steered.

When I emerged from the hatch, cup in hand, I saw the prettiest picture a navigator can hope for: dead ahead was a definite point of land shimmering in the suddenly brilliant sunrise under a low bank of cloud. Pretty soon a second cape rose out of the sea to port, and then a third one appeared on the horizon to starboard, looking like a separate island at first but gradually becoming joined to the expanding mainland. I'd hit Middle Cape right on the nose. The rest of the passage was an anticlimax. At three in the afternoon *Kathleen* was secured in Marathon's Faro Blanco Marina.

Harmony was in Marathon when I arrived. We celebrated our reunion at the excellent restaurant of the Faro Blanco Marina on the Gulf side of Key Vaca. Later, I moved *Kathleen* around to the somewhat less elaborate, but somewhat better protected, Boot Key Marina on the Atlantic side, and put her to bed for the summer.

12

Some Thoughts on Singlehanding

I was looking forward to sailing *Kathleen* in the fall, all thoughts of selling her forgotten. There had been some letdown at the end of my long cruise around the rim of the Gulf, but it's pleasant to know you've accomplished what you'd set out to do. I was particularly satisfied with my singlehanded overnight passages. I am, of course, an instant expert on singlehanding, ready to pass along the fruits of my long experience. Well, let's call them first impressions for the sake of accuracy.

My first first impression is that it isn't really very hard. Any well-executed small-boat passage is certainly an admirable feat, but after singlehanding *Kathleen* about 700 miles, including some overnight jumps of up to 150 miles, I can't really see why a cruise should earn you a lot more credit because you performed it alone. The mechanics of it aren't all that difficult.

A good cruising sailboat of modest size is always pretty much a one-man boat. With a small crew, if everyone's to get enough sleep on long offshore runs, a lone man on watch must be able to handle anything but a major crisis by himself. For this reason, singlehanded ocean racing has often been of greater benefit to the average cruising man than the kind of high-powered competition that involves squads of well-trained crewmen in matching T-shirts thundering across the decks on command.

All right, what are the mechanics involved? First of all, you almost have to have a self-steering device of some kind. Joshua Slocum managed without, but his boat turned out to be miraculously steady under sail, although I suspect that the old captain's nautical genius had something to do with *Spray's* famed self-steering qualities. Anyway, we don't have boats like that these days, and we don't have seamen like that, either. Us decadent modern sailors in our skittish modern sailboats, we need some kind of self-steering.

Some time ago I did extensive research on the subject of wind-vane devices. After all that studying—perhaps because of it—I didn't get one. I got an electric autopilot (Tiller Master) instead. I got it mainly because, unlike the vane-type units, it functions reliably under power; and cruising along the sounds and bays and bayous of the Gulf ICW in calm summer weather, I expected to (and did) spend a lot of time with the motor running. It is also, as a rule, an easier and simpler installation, and often somewhat less expensive. Disadvantages: It is prone to the quirks of all electric gadgets on shipboard (Tilly displayed an unladylike appetite for fuses that took some time to correct), and it does, of course, require an adequate source of electricity, although current consumption is very moderate.

As far as sailboat rigs for singlehanding are concerned, I'm highly prejudiced. I can see no reason for anything but a cutter rig, except in very large boats, very small ones, or if you're in a tearing hurry. In particular, the modern idea of forever dragging sailbags around the ship to set larger or smaller headsails to suit the wind seems pretty nonsensical to me. On *Kathleen,* when cruising, the sail lockers generally remain closed for the duration; the three sails permanently bent on are the only sails employed, unless storm canvas is required.

Under way I almost never venture forward of the mast except for reasons totally unconnected with sail area. When it's time to reduce sail, I can handle the big, light, roller-furling jib from the cockpit; the boat sails on very nicely under mainsail and forestaysail. When the sturdy little staysail has to come down—actually it's usually the last sail taken off in a rising wind; often I use it for heaving to—I cast off the halyard (led to the cockpit) and pull on the quarter-inch braided line that brings it down the stay and keeps it there. It's small enough, and well enough inboard, that it can usually be left unsecured until I can bag it at my leisure. These two headsails together have almost the area of the big genoa I never use offshore—and while a roller-furling jib is supposed to be inefficient on the wind, *Kathleen* tacks readily within ninety degrees, which is good enough for me.

The main halyard also leads to the cockpit. It's useful there for setting the sail, and for changing its shape under way, but I've never yet been shipmates with a Bermuda-type mainsail that would run freely down the track of its own accord, and *Kathleen's* is no exception. A visit to the cabin top and a little pulling and hauling is always required to get the sail all the way down. I suppose a downhaul could be used here, too, but I have visions of it fouling aloft, and I'd rather sacrifice an occasional fingernail to the green gods below. Again because of the rat's nest of tangle-prone lines that would be required, I can't pull down a reef from the cockpit. The jiffy-reeling lines installed involve the clew cringles only. The main halyard is marked, and when it's time to reef I slack it off to the indicated point. Then I move up to the mast and pull the tack cringle, by hand, down to one of two large hooks installed at the boom gooseneck. From the same spot I pull down the clew cringle by means of the reefing line that cleats at the inboard end of the boom, and also take up the slack in the second clewline, if this is the first reef down. Back in the cockpit, I set the halyard up taut again, sheet in the flapping mainsail, and I'm back in business.

Except in a true shipwreck situation, for a singlehander to mess with a life-jacket is, as far as I'm concerned, a waste of good kapok. Wearing a flotation device around the deck only makes sense if there's a chance that somebody will wake up if you go overboard and turn the boat around to pick you up. When you're sailing alone offshore, using any kind of self-steering apparatus, you know damned well that if you part company with the ship, she's not coming back, so you might as well sink like a rock and get it over with. It's not considered nice to say such things, but that's this sailor's opinion. Since you're a goner if you fall overboard, it behooves you not to fall overboard. Therefore, whenever I head offshore I run a hefty dockline along each side deck from the cockpit to the bow, firmly secured at each end but slack enough that it's easy for me to pick up and snap on the hook of my safety harness. I don't wear the harness constantly, but I do buckle it on, and hook it onto one of the jacklines— which allows me to go forward dragging my rope tail behind me— whenever I have to leave the cockpit in breezy weather. In a real blow, of course, even with a crew on board, everybody snaps on religiously any time they're on deck, even in the cockpit.

I had singlehanding in mind when *Kathleen* was built. My big worries didn't concern *Kathleen,* they concerned me: was I really up to handling the boat alone, and even if I was, might I not find it a bit of a drag sailing around all by myself?

Well, I won't keep you in suspense: I had no serious trouble, and it was great.

Why was it great? Why do people go singlehanding, anyway? I won't dodge the issue by pointing out that congenial crews don't grow on every dock, and very often the only way to get your boat out sailing is to take her out alone. It's a factor, to be sure, but there's more to it than that. Various people have tried to answer the question, for themselves and others, and some have come up with answers that seem fairly weird to me. I don't think I'm trying to prove anything when I'm out there alone. After Slocum, Chichester, and all their followers, everybody knows that a single determined seaman can take a good-sized sailboat anywhere in the world there's water enough to float it. What's left to prove? I think the real answer to the question is: total freedom and lack of responsibility.

It may sound antisocial, probably it is, but when I'm singlehanding I'm responsible for nobody's comfort, happiness, and safety but my own. When my wife is along I often carry less sail than I'd like because she doesn't really enjoy it when *Kathleen* heels. When my son is along I often carry more sail than I'd like because he wants to see the rail go down and the spray fly. When guests are along, I try to sail the boat to suit them. I'm happy to do it, of course, but there are times when I like to sail to suit myself.

Alone, I can change destination whenever I please; I can even turn back if I'm so inclined without having to justify my decision to anybody. If I'm in the mood to go storming along like a mad Viking, there's nobody on board who'll get scared or seasick; on the other hand, if I feel like heaving to prematurely instead of slugging it out with the elements, I can do that without frustrating or disappointing somebody on board who'd rather have kept going regardless of the weather. And then, of course, there's the final argument in favor of singlehanding: that lovely lack of responsibility for other people's lives. When I'm alone, no matter what horrible nautical errors I may make, I can't drown anybody but myself.

But the singlehander is never really alone—he or she follows in the wake of too many hardy solo sailors to be *totally* alone. Each has contributed to the art, whether as a result of rugged individualism or a desire to win races. The gear and techniques developed for the Observer Singlehanded Trans-Atlantic Race, for instance, particularly in the area of self-steering, have been of tremendous value to the ordinary ocean sailor.

I feel they hurt the OSTAR when they limited the size of the competing boats to 56 feet or under. Those tremendous, imaginative, one-man sailing machines—70' and up, way up—made the event much more than a race: it was an exciting spectacle even just to read about. It was also an important seagoing testing program. As far as I'm concerned, the last gleam of the original, bright, experimental spirit of the race has been abolished. Well, almost. The first 4000 La Route du Rhum singlehanded race from France to Guadeloupe in the West Indies placed no restriction on size. Perhaps there's hope after all!

The concept of the OSTAR was a brave one: a practically unrestricted race across the Atlantic for lone sailors using any damn boats and equipment the skippers figured would get them across the pond. As few rules as possible. Colonel Blondie Hasler, more than any other man the moving force behind the idea—although Francis Chichester (not yet, then, Sir Francis) played a significant role—felt at the time that the question of boat size would be taken care of automatically by having only one man on board with no power plant to help him. Hasler's ideas on safety and rescue were equally simple and straightforward. At least he's said to have stated, when asked what if one of the boats should sink, that he hoped the chap in charge would have the decency to drown like a gentleman and not cause anybody any trouble. A deadpan, British joke, perhaps, but indicative of the prevailing mood at the time.

In the first OSTAR in 1960 the largest vessel entered, Chichester's 39′ *Gipsy Moth III,* had been considered to be right at, or perhaps a little above, the upper limit of what one strong, experienced seaman could handle alone. Some concern was expressed that the poor old gent would get into trouble trying to handle such a fearfully large yacht all by himself. Of course the poor old gent had no trouble at all in romping home first. In the 1964 race, however, he was edged out of first place by Tabarly in a newly built 44-footer, whereupon Chichester promptly proceeded to get a new 53′ sailing machine, in which he sailed out of our story and around the world to fame and knighthood.

Meanwhile, back at the OSTAR, the 1968 event was won by Geoffrey Williams in a 57-footer. In 1972, out of 55 starters, Alain Colas reached Newport first in a king-sized, 70′ ocean racing trimaran originally built by Tabarly. But hard on his heels was Jean-Yves Terlain in—brace yourselves, now—a unique, three-masted schooner 128 feet long. And the 1976 event (125 starters) that more recently passed into history was won by a reasonably conventional 73′ ketch skippered by our old friend Tabarly, the only two-time victor on record. But right behind him was the 1972 winner, Colas, in a magnificent four-master almost as long as a football field, 236 feet to be exact. (Colas' official placement is lower due to a rules technicality. Colas and his boat disappeared during La Route du Rhum, but he wasn't sailing the 236-foot *Club Mediterranee.*)

Many of the boats developed for the OSTAR have been fascinating designs. To me, Terlain's 128′ *Vendredi 13* (since renamed) and Colas' enormous *Club Med* are the most exciting sailing craft that have appeared in an era otherwise devoted largely to cookie-cutter vessels built to the IOR rule, that are of real interest only to those few who understand this complex handicapping system.

In addition to adding tremendous suspense to the race—Would the giants win? Could Terlain and Colas actually control the brutes?—these spectacular, great OSTAR boats have put us, I feel, on the threshold of a new era of sail. When the world energy situation deteriorates to the point where commercial shipping interests find it profitable to once more look to the wind for motive power, and start searching for effective designs capable of being handled by very small and economical crews, they'll find that the ingenious solo racers of the OSTAR have done their homework for them.

But these wonderful, wild, one-man vessels don't appeal to everybody. There are vociferous critics. It seems that the idea of a sailboat displacing a hundred tons or two crashing across the ocean on self-steering chills the blood of folks who think nothing of a half-million-ton supertanker rumbling over the sea on autopilot. (Sure I know, the singlehander has to sleep some time, while on the tanker there's supposed to be a man always on watch, but how hard is that man really watching and how much can he really see back there several hundred yards from the bow and what can he do about it if he does see something out there ahead?)

The loud-mouthed and influential critics of the OSTAR usually claim to be motivated largely by the competitors. This is, of course, not entirely true. Three other considerations have figured prominently in the arguments: (1) The unfairness of the unlimited rule to the less well-heeled competitors who can't afford to build super-boats; (2) The costs of the rescue operations; and (3) The threat to other vessels along the route.

The first objection is, to date at least, obvious nonsense—just check the records. The super-boats have by no means dominated the race. In the light-air 1972 event, *Vendredi 13* was cleanly beaten by *Pen Duick IV,* only a little more than half her length. In stormy 1976, when two "monsters" were entered, the renamed *Vendredi* damaged her skipper's arm and had to retire, while *Club Mediterranee* snapped halyards like spaghetti and tore up sails like toilet paper, and had to stop for repairs, letting *Pen Duick VI*—one-third the length and slowed by her non-functioning self-steering gear—drive through for the win.

The fact is that the race is working exactly as Colonel Hasler had hoped in the beginning, although on a scale much grander than he'd anticipated (which, unfortunately, makes him very unhappy). The easily handled smaller boats are still pretty well holding their own against the potentially much faster, but also much more demanding, giants. Consider the four top finishers in 1976: First—*Pen Duick VI,* 73' mono-hull; Second—*Club Mediterranee,* 236' monohull; Third—*Third Turtle,* 32' trimaran; Fourth—*Spaniel,* 38' monohull.

Only a little more than a day's time separated these four boats after over three weeks of sailing. Any handicapper who could bring off such a close finish in a 3,000-mile race involving such extremes of boat size and type would be justified in ordering champagne for breakfast. When tiny and inexpensive *Third Turtle* can cross the line within a few hours of enormous, and enormously expensive, *Club Mediterranee,* somebody's clearly doing something right. Objection overruled.

As far as rescue operations are concerned, any time anybody gets into trouble at sea in a slightly unconventional way, and public funds are expended to help him, there's a great outcry about this terrible waste of the taxpayers' money. Well, I'm a taxpayer myself, dammit, and I hope nobody ever has the nerve to tell me to my face—I feel rather strongly on the subject—that my taxes are supposed to pay for the "rescue" of every careless creep who forgot to check his gas tank before he took his girlfriend for a speedboat ride, and not for that of a participant in a great ocean race.

Which brings us to the question of the danger the racers present to other vessels sharing the same ocean. This wasn't really a problem as long as the competing boats were reasonably small: the risks were all on the side of the competitors, who were willing to assume them. But as the boats grew larger, more and more protests were heard about the dreadful menace they presented to uninvolved vessels along the way.

What uninvolved vessels along the way?

I find myself approaching this subject with a sense of total bafflement. I've discussed it with some highly emotional OSTAR critics, and they don't seem to listen to what I say; I get no answers to questions that seem quite sensible to me. But let me try once more—these racers are *sailboats,* aren't they? And the International Rules of the Road have very definite things to say about the rights of sailboats, don't they?

SAILING VESSEL RIGHT OF WAY: ART. 20 (a) When a steam vessel and a sailing vessel are proceeding in such directions as to involve risk of collision . . . the steam vessel shall keep out of the way of the sailing vessel.

I memorized that passage many years ago at the request of the U.S. Navy. Undoubtedly my elderly, dog-eared seamanship textbook is now somewhat out of date, but I haven't heard of that particular article being repealed. The Rules further state that the words "steam vessel" shall include any vessel propelled by machinery. In other words, the rule applies to just about any ship an OSTAR competitor is likely to meet out on the Atlantic. There are no "uninvolved" vessels out there. With very few exceptions, they're all involved to the extent that they're legally obligated to move over when they see a sailboat coming.

As I say, there are a few exceptions; another sailing vessel on a privileged course, an overtaken vessel, a commercial fishing vessel. In the first two categories the only craft a competitor is likely to encounter is a fellow competitor, and we may assume that the contestants accept this slight risk—there aren't many other sailboats cruising around in mid-ocean. And even *Club Mediterranee* isn't likely to be going fast enough to run down a freighter or tanker from behind. Commercial fishing craft actually engaged in fishing do have the right-of-way over practically everything, but the fishing grounds are known, and all accounts I've read of the race indicate that the participants habitually keep sharp lookouts while crossing them.

We sailboat people have got into the habit of dodging about the oceans like scared sardines in our efforts not to hamper the commercial traffic out there. We've done this partly out of a sense of self-preservation, and partly out of consideration for seamen who are earning their livings while we're having fun. But we're not legally required to act this way. In fact, we're breaking the law when we do it. As the privileged vessels, we're *supposed* to maintain course and speed; as the burdened vessels, they're *supposed* to avoid us. So if we're going to get legalistic about single-handed ocean sailing, as some OSTAR critics have done, let's consider what the law really says—everything it says.

Who are these critics? Strangely enough, they're not uninformed landlubbers as you might expect, but yachtsmen and yachting writers who somehow have convinced themselves that these lone-wolf sailors and their offbeat race are tarnishing the bright, safe image of yacht racing they're trying so hard to maintain. And the frightening thing about these public-relations-minded sailing folk isn't so much what they criticize as what they don't.

We've heard from them a great deal about the relatively new mandatory watch-keeping rule necessarily broken by the singlehanders (there's some question about whether or not this rule should actually apply to small yachts), but we've heard absolutely nothing about the ancient, mandatory right-of-way rules broken by the commercial vessels that run them down—and some boats have been thus sunk or damaged in practically every recent race. But there have been no fiery editorials about this callous disregard for the legal rights of sailing men and women; no scathing articles about the watch-keeping standards of the ships involved; no indignant demands for legislative remedies. One gets the impression that these critics want to keep the legal rights of the OSTAR racers from being infringed upon by—I'm not kidding—abolishing the OSTAR. By the same reasoning, we could prevent murder by sending all potential victims to the gas chamber.

They haven't managed to abolish the OSTAR—not yet; there's still one big step to take. They're talking seriously about turning the OSTAR into the ODTAR—the Observer Double-handed Transatlantic Race. That's right, they're really considering making it a two-man event.

It seems fairly incredible to me that there are people around the water so obtuse that they don't understand that sailing alone is one thing and sailing with a crew, any size crew, is an activity performed in a totally different dimension, just about as far away as you can get and still go boating. It takes a special kind of person to sail alone—Chichester, Tabarly, Colas, Claire Francis, to mention only singlehanders who've participated in the OSTAR—and this is a contest for that kind of people. Frankly, I feel that anyone who advocates changing this essential feature of the race must be indulging in deliberate doubletalk. He can't help but know he's really recommending the end of the OSTAR; he just doesn't dare come right out and say it.

Can we afford to give up the OSTAR? The end of the singlehanded race will almost inevitably lead, sooner or later, to the end of singlehanded ocean sailing of any kind. The precedent will have been established that sailing alone is evil and dangerous, the arguments used won't be forgotten. They'll be revived as soon as somebody decides to pass a law. You may have no ambition to sail across an ocean all by yourself, but do you really want to see legislation forbidding you ever to take your boat out alone when you can't recruit a crew?

But there is an even more deadly precedent being set here. Let me restate the question: *Can we afford to give up the ocean?*

To consent to the abolition of the OSTAR is to admit that we have no real right to be out there sailing if our presence inconveniences the big-ship people even slightly. It is to say, humbly, that we don't take seriously the maritime law that gives us the right-of-way at sea.

But there are some rays of sunny hope through the gloom: new singlehanded races have been sailed, and more are being planned. In OSTAR we probed—if only vicariously—the outer limits of what one man can handle in a large sailing craft. It was a fascinating adventure; but now let's see what other fields there are to explore by means of this kind of competition.

A race that was sailed for the first time in 1977, and will be sailed again in 1979, has been designed for exactly this purpose. It's called the

Bermuda One-Two, and it's the brainchild of designer Jerry Cartwright, a top sailor who's logged more singlehanded ocean miles than my boat will probably ever sail with any size crew. The first race circular stated: "Although it is a competitive event, the major long-term emphasis will be towards on-going development of offshore rigs, sailplans, gear, boat design and handling techniques for single and short-handed passagemakers." This sounds like exactly what was ordered, but there's one catch. Jerry Cartwright, an OSTAR competitor himself, has patterned his new event on the older race, taking over not only its undoubted strengths but, I'm afraid, some of its weaknesses as well. Let's see what those weaknesses are.

The One-Two, as the name implies, is a race singlehanded to Bermuda and double-handed back. Actually it's two separate races and you can enter either or both, but combined they should teach us a lot about short-handed sailing. Boat limits were 44' top and 25' bottom—and here the questions begin. We've yielded to the shrill voices demanding an upper limit, but why this lower limit?

Boats considerably smaller than 25 feet have sailed and raced 3,000 miles across the Atlantic for years; surely they can make the 600 miles to Bermuda. True, small boats are slower than large ones, and festivities at both ends would have to be slightly delayed to let the mosquito fleet finish, but is this such a terrible hardship? If development is really the name of the game, why ignore what is probably the fastest-growing class of cruising sailboats: the small, rugged, oceanworthy craft that large numbers of people can afford and maintain even these inflated days? (In fairness, I should mention that the Bermuda One-Two committee can make—and has made—exceptions for boats smaller than 25' that satisfy the inspectors, but this isn't quite the same as giving them equal status under the rules.)

Another limitation I feel should be reviewed is the one dealing with motors and generators. Auxiliary power is a fact of boating life. Ideally, a race designed to improve the breed of modern cruising sailboats should make some concessions to the obvious truth. Unfortunately, a sailboat race that permits any use of motors for propulsion will inevitably turn into a motorboat race, which isn't what we're after—but what about the other uses of power on board, particularly electric power? Under the first One-Two rules, aside from emergencies, the engine could only be used to generate electricity for lighting and the radio. Such electricity, if I read the rules correctly, was not to be used to steer the boat. Juice for this purpose had to come from the wind- or water-driven generators, or from solar cells—anything but the ship's own powerplant.

This regulation probably stemmed from the old purist notion that any kind of machinery, and particularly electrical machinery, is basically unreliable on shipboard and therefore unseamanlike—a *real* sailor relies only on muscle and wind. Yet it's my impression that the last, very stormy, OSTAR produced relatively fewer casualties among the electric autopilots than among the windvane self-steering devices. Isn't it time to break with ancient singlehanded custom, in this respect, and permit this very convenient use of the electric power available on practically all modern offshore boats? It might encourage the design of even more reliable and efficient autopilots, as well as more rugged and dependable smallboat electrical systems. Why not allow the skipper to generate shipboard electricity any way he chooses and employ it any way he pleases, in line with modern cruising practice, as long as he doesn't help his boat through the water in the process? (In the 1979 race this was allowed.)

Let's now proceed into rarefied regions of sailboat racing philosophy and reflect on the responsibilities of the race committee vs. the responsibilities of the competitors. The race circular for the 1977 race stated: "Full responsibility for any accident or mishap will rest with the owner or crew under ordinary process of law and no liability or responsibility is accepted by the organizers or sponsors . . ."

Fair enough. Nobody's forcing us to race. We're simply being offered the opportunity. The decision—to go or not to go—is ours. If we go, the responsibility is ours. If we goof, it's our necks; so it's up to us to equip our boats properly and sail them safely. Or is it?

Well, as a matter of fact, it isn't. After telling us that the responsibility is ours, the race organizers then turn right around and present us with two solid pages of mandatory gear—equipment that we *must* have on board before they'll clear us for takeoff. You can see why they might feel obliged to make sure that all competitors in their race comply with the law, but this equipment list goes far beyond what's legally required. I realize, of course, that modern ocean-racing sailors have become pretty hardened to this basic contradiction: being told that it's strictly their baby, on the one hand, and then being told exactly what diapers it's to wear, on the other. However, as a retread sailor I can't help asking a timid question: who's got the buck? If I do it the race committee's way instead of my own, will the committee then take the rap if my boat sinks or my crew drowns? Or am I stuck with *their* mandatory gear and *my* legal responsibility? (Let's remember that a small boat can only carry so much gear: every mandatory item put aboard means a nonmandatory item left ashore.) This philosophical predicament is very much a part of practically all offshore racing these days, and I think it's time for somebody to resolve it in a courageous and sensible manner.

And finally, I think it's time for a good hard look at one specific regulation that was developed for the OSTAR after an early race in which several competitors got into trouble, it was claimed, through having untested and unprepared boats and not being very experienced themselves. In order to weed out the crocks and incompetents, presumably for considerations of safety, a qualification sail was required as a condition of entry for all subsequent events. In the OSTAR it's 500 miles singlehanded with an additional 1,000 miles recently added, I believe, that can be sailed with a crew. For the Bermuda One-Two, a shorter race, a singlehanded 100-mile qualification crew is required.

Of all the weird regulations ever crammed down a race committee's throat by hostile critics in the name of safety, this is probably the weirdest: sending people to sea in order to keep them from killing themselves at sea! Two well-known and experienced sailors have already died trying to qualify for the OSTAR. That's exactly as many losses as have been incurred during the race itself. I don't think race organizers understand the coldly cynical nature of this qualification requirement, which says essentially: *we don't care where the hell you drown yourself as long as you don't make us look bad by doing it in our race.*

I'm not a hostile critic, and I still hope to sail the Bermuda One-Two. That is, if they'll still have me. (The author and his son did participate in the second leg of the 1979 event, without much success. Oh, well, somebody has to be last.)

Well, that's the word on singlehanding from this instant expert. Take it with a grain of salt.

13

A Ride with the Stream

It was a long way to go for dinner, so I started three days early.

The dinner was the yearly fall bash put on by the Seven Seas Cruising Association, an organization of sea-wandering folks who live on their boats. They publish a monthly bulletin of letters from members describing places visited all over the world, cruising problems encountered and solved, bureaucratic stumbling blocks found in various ports and how to avoid or surmount them, and much more. It is a very useful little publication for anybody about to take off for foreign lands in a boat, or even somebody (like me) who just likes to dream about taking off in his boat, somewhere, sometime.

I don't reside on *Kathleen,* so I don't qualify for membership, but they do allow nonqualifying characters like me to subscribe to their bulletin and attend their dinners. I'd been working on the boat down in Marathon and the dinner was to take place only a hundred and sixty miles to the north (in Lantana, on the near side of West Palm Beach). It seemed like a nice warmup cruise to make now that my little ship was in pretty good shape again after a summer of neglect—a good preparation for more serious voyaging planned for the months to come.

In theory I had a choice of routes. I could run the Intracoastal Waterway inside the Keys, or I could head outside and ride the Gulf

Stream up, at least as far as Miami. In practice it was no choice at all. I'd spent enough time chasing elusive buoys and channels and plowing mud with my keel while bringing *Kathleen* east; if there was an open-water, deep-water route available, that was for me. Weather permitting, of course.

I left on Wednesday. The reports were for southeasterly winds, 10–15 knots, diminishing towards nightfall. Great. You don't tackle the Gulf Stream with the wind in the north; it can kick up dangerous seas blowing against the two-to-three-knot current, but southeast was fine. As it had been a last-minute decision and there were several errands to be run in town, I didn't cast off from Boot Key Marina until 1000 hours. When *Kathleen* emerged from the well-marked channel under power, the wind seemed quite brisk, and I snugged down a reef in the mainsail as I set it. Moments later jib and staysail were also set and drawing, the motor was silent, and we were crashing along at a good pace on a port tack.

My plan was to head straight offshore into the favorable current and then come about to see if I could hold a course up the coast. Unfortunately, a glance astern showed me that we were sliding off to the westward rapidly in some kind of inshore counter-current—at this point the Keys run pretty well east and west—so I tacked immediately and found that the wind allowed me to, just barely, sail right up Hawk Channel inside the reef, where I might have less sea to contend with, although I'd miss the boost of the Stream.

From Miami south, the coastal reefs extend several miles out from the Keys and small craft can sail inside them—actually on top of them—in some twenty-odd feet of water, Hawk Channel, dodging the well-marked shoal patches along the way. In adverse weather when the Gulf Stream is acting up, this is the place to be. I didn't think today was all that adverse, but I was now sailing in the right direction, at least, and making headway towards Miami. I figured I could gradually ease out to where I really wanted to sail as the coast curved away to the north; but when the wind started to increase I had some doubts about whether I really wanted to sail out there after all. It was time for the jib to come in—hey, NOAA, what about those diminishing winds, huh?—and when I tried to roll it up the furling gear jammed and the sail wrapped itself up in the headstay. Later I found that I'd run the halyard wrong; at the moment I could do nothing but kneel in the plunging bow as *Kathleen* smashed along on autopilot, and mutter appropriate incantations as I tugged and hauled, until things sorted themselves out after a fashion and the big sail was wound up out of harm's way.

When I went below to mop myself off, I discovered that the ship was sinking—well, there was water all over the cabin sole. Hastily I picked up the hatch and checked the bilge beneath: dry. It had been a long time since I'd sailed in this much wind and sea, and I'd forgotten that I was supposed to close the seacocks to the head and the galley sink. There was also a new deck leak under one of the lifeline stanchions up forward, strategically placed for soaking my bunk.

I swabbed things up and wrung things out, sticking my head out the hatch every so often to check our progress. Three porpoises scared me seriously as they surfaced simultaneously under the bow; for an instant they looked exactly like a jagged three-pronged reef bared by a passing sea. I grabbed a sandwich and a can of beer and considered my strategy. The afternoon was passing. Hawk Channel was okay in daylight, but by nightfall I wanted to be safely out in deep water, where navigation was less tricky. So, having finished my belated lunch, I clambered out into the cockpit, cranked mainsail and forestaysail in hard, and set a new course on the Tillermaster that would take us on a seaward slant out past the light at Tennessee Reef. Hard on the wind like that, we didn't make much progress in the heavy chop, and I started up the motor to help. At this point, there was 20 feet of water over the reef: the question was how big the waves would be when we came off it, out into the deep Straits of Florida proper.

It was a relief to discover, as the spidery lighthouse finally slid away astern, that the offshore seas were really quite manageable—bigger than the ones inshore, to be sure, but longer and more regular and actually easier for *Kathleen* to negotiate. I held on east until we had more than 200 feet under us according to the depthfinder; then I shut down the motor and eased the sheets and twisted Tilly's knob to change course a bit northwards, still working offshore but no longer driving as hard to windwards. The speed and the boat's motion both improved.

It was time to break out the secret weapon: my fancy but accident-prone handbearing compass. Normally, taking bearings by daylight, I use a little gadget the size of what used to be called a dollar watch, but that dial is not illuminated. For night bearings, I'd bought a big, elaborate sighting compass with a pistol grip that housed a bulb and a couple of penlight batteries. The first time I'd tried to use it we'd run aground even before I got a bearing, and in the resulting hassle the instrument had got stepped on and the plastic handle smashed. The next time, after repairs, that I'd had occasion to try it, I'd laid it down on the cockpit seat for an instant and it had jumped off and damaged its sighting vane. (A deliberate suicide attempt; I saw it.) Back to the shop again. Now I loaded it with batteries, checked that its light was functioning, and found a place for its fancy wooden case under the chart table where it would have to work hard to indulge its self-destructive tendencies. A couple of check sights in the fading daylight indicated that I was doing something right; the calculated position agreed reasonably well with my dead reckoning.

It's a well-lighted coast, navigationally speaking. I had plenty of flashing lights to practice on as darkness fell and *Kathleen* drove along to the east and north, staying reasonably dry in spite of the white-capped seas bearing down on her from starboard. Alligator Reef fell astern, and the Hen and Chickens, and Molasses Reef. That brought us to midnight, and things were getting slightly noisy and rugged, as I buckled on my safety harness and hauled down the second reef in the mainsail. It didn't seem to affect the speed much, but the lee rail came up a bit and the motion was considerably more comfortable. (But *Kathleen* didn't like it a bit. *Chicken,* she said. *What do you want to go spoiling a great sail for, chicken?* They sometimes talk to you like that in the dark, disrespectfully, when there's nobody else on board to hear.)

The next light was the Elbow where, as the name implies, the coast turns still more to the north. It came abeam, like all of them, well ahead of schedule; the knotmeter meant nothing out there. The Gulf Stream had us and we were making six and seven knots over the ground with the gauge indicating only four or five. With a fix on the Elbow and Carysfort Reef, next up the line, I changed course once more, easing sheets accordingly. For the moment there were no ships in sight, although there had been a steady procession of passing lights since nightfall. It seemed a good time for a short rest. Coming down Florida's west coast, where there had been hardly any traffic, I'd allowed myself half-hour breaks at night; here fifteen minutes seemed as much as I could take safely—but an uneasy feeling brought me to the main hatch after ten.

It seemed like an odd place for an apartment house to be, I reflected sleepily, off the stern there right out in the middle of the Florida Straits. Then I came awake and realized it was a big ship overhauling us. Quite safe, of course; there was a good separation between the white range lights. It was a pretty picture. I could put myself in that ''apartment house'' back there. I had been there, not too long before—looking out and down instead of back and up.

The ship was the *Korea Galaxy,* a 20,000-ton Gulf Oil tanker. Her port of departure was Wilmington, North Carolina, and her destination was Aruba, off the coast of Venezuela. Her purpose was to take on oil at Aruba and carry it back to the United States. That was *her* purpose; mine was to get material for a novel and also perhaps, just a little, to see how the other half lives. You get certain notions standing on the deck of your own small cruising boat at sea and watching the big boys go rumbling past. It's not hard, sometimes, to get the idea that they're all out to kill you if they can, or at least that they don't give a damn whether you live or die, and probably won't even notice the tiny *crrrunch* as you go down under the keel.

I hadn't told the Gulf people this when I asked for a ride, of course, but I'm sure they had a few misgivings about letting me aboard one of their ships; the tanker industry has been gun-shy ever since Noel Mostert's best-selling book *Supership.* Nevertheless, they had allowed me aboard the *Korea Galaxy,* and had instructed her captain to give me the freedom of his ship. At 20,000 tons the *Korea Galaxy* isn't a supership. She's a relatively small vessel by modern tanker standards— only about 560 feet long, with a beam of some 74 feet, and a draft of 34 feet loaded. She's driven by one giant, seven-cylinder diesel engine putting out 10,500 h.p. at 135 rpm; at 14 knots, her normal cruising speed, the shaft turns at an even 100 rpm. Those who are mechanically minded may be interested to know that there are no gears or clutches. The propeller, 16 feet in diameter, is driven directly by the engine; to get reverse, the enormous mill is simply stopped and started up again, backwards.

By way of comparison, note that a VLCC, as a supership is called—a Very Large Crude Carrier—might well be over twice as long as the *Korea Galaxy* and have well over ten times the displacement.

The *Korea Galaxy* was interestingly international. Sailing for an American company, she was Korea-built (1974), powered by an Italian (Fiat) engine, and registered in Monrovia, Liberia. Her captain and crew were Italian (fortunately for me the officers all spoke some English), and so was her food, which was excellent. When I first saw her, she was being nudged into an oil dock on the Cape Fear River by two tugs. It was a little after six in the evening. I was supposed to go aboard at seven, but I'd arrived early, hoping to see her come in. Figuring that I might not be fed in the confusion of docking, I'd grabbed a quick hamburger before calling a taxi to take me to the waterfront—a serious error in strategy, as it turned out. As soon as the gangway was down, a polite young cadet officer named Salvatore Pellicia took me aboard to meet tall young Captain Sergio Redivo, who almost immediately led the way to the officers' mess, where we were served a large and delicious dinner. By the time I'd fought my way through soup, fish, and meat, my injudicious hamburger was feeling so crowded that I had to pass up the fruit offered for dessert. Afterward, I was shown my quarters.

I was given the pilot's cabin, no less, three decks up in the air-conditioned superstructure aft. Above me were the offices and quarters of the captain and chief engineer; above them was the navigating bridge. From my windows I could look out forward over the open deck with its long catwalk and its incomprehensible maze of pipes and hatches clear to the bow, more than a football field away. That was my "apartment house" window above the sea. I had my own facilities, including a shower, a desk to write on, and a red leather sofa to read on. You could hardly call it a hardship cruise.

We spent a day at the dock unloading. Before daylight the following morning two pilots, two tugs, and a small motorboat descended on us. The pilots were both husky, weathered gents with soft Southern accents. One wore a golf cap with the insignia of a local club; he was the undocking expert. Using a walkie-talkie he soon had the small boat buzzing around releasing the spiderweb of heavy lines reaching out to various strong points in the water. The dock itself was merely a platform accommodating oil lines, hoses, and manifolds, at the end of a long pier reaching out into the river from the storage tank area on shore. Then the tugs started pushing the ship's bow shoreward, so that she pivoted about a cluster of pilings amidships, her stern swinging out. When there was room back there, the aft tug ducked around to the starboard quarter and started shoving the stern out toward the middle of the river. Gradually, between them, they rotated the long vessel, which reached almost from bank to bank, until she was headed downstream.

I heard the pilot say quietly into his instrument, "You're through, Billy. Thank you very much."

The tug aft backed away and took off down the river. The tug forward came alongside. The pilot with the golf cap left the bridge, appeared on the deck below, went down a ladder that had been lowered for him, and was carried away by the tug. By this time it was full daylight.

The river pilot, or channel pilot, had a drooping, black, Wyatt Earp moustache that gave him an old-fashioned rather piratical look. Like his associate, he attended strictly to business; there was no polite chatter, although I did manage to learn from him that the channel was 38 feet deep, and the tidal currents sometimes ran as high as five knots on the ebb, but that morning we had a flooding tide against us, at the most two knots. He gave his commands in a clear, low voice, every so often stepping over to where he could check the receding buoy aft as well as the approaching buoy forward to make certain no current was setting us into danger.

"Ahead full," he'd say, and presently: "Port fifteen . . . ease to five. Amidships. One seven four."

He had all the courses in his head, and there were plenty of them. As he gave them, one of the officers would repeat the figure in Italian for the helmsman, who'd say it back in Italian to indicate that he understood. I spent my time staying out of everybody's way and admiring the impressive instrumentation of the bridge. To starboard were two black-hooded 48-mile radars (S-band and X-band) and the tall, gray box of the collision-avoidance computer that, the captain had explained earlier, could operate off either one. To port was the engine-control console with a recorder to show every engine order given. Amidships was the steering console with autopilot and gyrocompass—a repeater, actually; the master gyro lived in a room of its own across the hall from my stateroom, two decks down. There was also a magnetic compass mounted above the bridge that could be consulted by means of a periscope device over the helm. The steering wheel itself was ridiculously small for the size of the ship since no leverage was needed to operate the power-driven system. Two speed indicators were visible from the helm (one registered speed over the bottom as long as there was bottom within reach) as well as a depth recorder and a large rudder-angle indicator.

Just aft was a chartroom that would turn any small-boat navigator green with envy. It contained Loran A and C for American waters, Decca for Canadian and European waters, and an elaborate radio direction finder; there were also assorted weather instruments, and an electronic chronometer with two faces, for local and Greenwich time. What really set me drooling, after all the years of navigating small boats off my lap, was the large and well-equipped chart table with endless banks of chart drawers underneath. (My charts aboard *Kathleen* live under the bunk cushions.) To port was a radio room stuffed full of electronics I didn't even pretend to understand.

Gradually, that first morning, we worked our way down the long, winding river. We picked up the Intracoastal Waterway with a nice-looking ketch just emerging from the low islands to the north, under sail. I paid careful attention here since I hoped to come this way in my own boat sometime. We left Fort Fisher with its twin radar domes to port, and saw the ICW branch off to starboard; I made note of the fact that there was a sizable marina right at the junction, in Southport, North Carolina.

We had the ocean ahead, with a small inbound vessel about to meet us in the last stretch of narrow channel. The pilot's walkie-talkie cleared its throat and started to speak.

"Outbound vessel approaching Bald Head, I'll pass you on one whistle."

The pilot murmured his assent into the instrument. It took me a moment to remember that one whistle meant port to port, and that was how it was done; then we were leaving the land behind. Up ahead, a black-and-white boat was waiting just outside the well-buoyed channel leading out to sea. Soon I could read her name: *Cape Fear Pilot III.* The ship slowed to let her come alongside. The moustached pilot said goodbye and left us. We watched from the bridge as he descended to the boat, which roared away. Captain Redivo gave the order for full ahead and, as we passed between the outer channel buoys, showed me how the autopilot was engaged.

"Now we have breakfast," he said. He grinned. "You know how it is, even with two pilots on board, the captain is responsible. But now we can eat."

Later I had a chance to chat with the officers about the small-boat problem and get an idea how we look from the bridge of a 20,000-ton tanker. Unfortunately, while in general amateur sailors are regarded with a kind of affectionate if uncomprehending tolerance by the professionals in charge of the *Korea Galaxy*—they have the idea that we must be very brave but very crazy to take such little boats offshore—there are certain specimens they find annoying, particularly: (1) The False Alarm, (2) The Invisible Boatman, and (3) The Darting Dodger.

Like all conscientious seamen, the officers of the *Galaxy* are quite aware of their responsibility to vessels in distress, large or small. But if amateur boatmen want to keep on being able to rely on help from commercial shipping in real emergencies, they should be careful not to inconvenience large ships by pulling them off course to investigate meaningless displays that can be misinterpreted as distress signals.

The *Galaxy*'s chief mate, Giacomo Ballestrino, was quite sharp about one such incident in which he was involved. He was on watch, he said, in the middle of the Atlantic in fairly heavy weather, when he caught a glimpse between seas of a distant sailing craft flying, he thought, a red distress flag high in the rigging. He immediately changed course to render assistance to this yacht in apparent trouble. What he found was a happy yachtsman lounging casually in his cockpit while his little vessel ran before the blow under a storm jib—a *bright red* storm jib!

"But red, that is a signal for emergencies, is it not?" said the mate with some heat. "To make a sail that color . . . I do not understand!"

Frankly, I don't understand, either. Like Ballestrino, I was brought up to think that red (and nowadays blaze-orange) is a crisis color, to be hoisted only when you're in serious difficulties. Yet some years ago I sent my own fishing boat halfway across Long Island Sound at flank speed to "rescue" a boat that seemed to be drifting helplessly with a bright distress signal flying. It turned out that the folks had stopped for a picnic and a swim, and it had never occurred to them, apparently, that their blaze-orange radar reflector could be misunderstood by anybody.

Still another signal that often draws large ships off course these days, I understand, is the masthead strobe light that's becoming more and more popular. Here, I admit, I have some difficulty in understanding how a *white* light can possibly be taken as a cry for help, and I would like to be able to use my own strobe for the purpose for which I had it installed: to tell big ships I'm there and please stay the hell away from me. Yet the fact seems to be that some people, including some professional seamen, do consider the white flasher to be an emergency signal. Therefore, until the strobe is clearly and officially defined (I hope) as a simple locator beacon—the flareup light specified in the rules of the road for avoiding collision—I intend to be very careful not to turn it on when it may be misinterpreted.

The point is simply that ships like the *Korea Galaxy* are more than willing to help you if you need help, but for Pete's sake be careful about causing them to waste fuel and lose time detouring when you're not in trouble, by doing or displaying anything that can possibly be taken for a signal of distress. The fact that you may think your red jib or blaze-orange radar reflector or masthead strobe is a perfectly acceptable piece of equipment for everyday use is beside the point if the watch officer of a tanker or freighter thinks otherwise. After being stung once rushing to your rescue mistakenly, he'll be just a little slower to react to any signal next time, and if somebody drowns as a result, the fault will be yours.

Now let's tackle the subject that's probably closest to the hearts of all boatmen who venture offshore, whether under sail or power: the danger of being run down by large vessels like the *Korea Galaxy*. There's a popular notion—I'm afraid I used to hold it myself—that all these vessels plow blindly across the oceans with total, callous disregard for any small craft that may get in their way. Some rogue ships undoubtedly do proceed in this manner. However, as I've already indicated, I found no signs of this attitude on the *Galaxy*'s bridge. Every watch-standing officer with whom I talked, from the captain down, was prepared to do everything in his power to avoid us. He just wished we wouldn't make it so hard for him.

A lot has been made of the fact that these ships take practically forever to stop—three miles in the case of the *Korea Galaxy*. Actually, while the engine room telegraph does make special provision for an emergency crash stop, nobody on board considers this a feasible avoidance tactic, when changing course is so simple. It's a two-finger operation: just turn the knob of the autopilot through the desired number of degrees. On the *Galaxy*'s bridge I saw it done all the time, whenever there was any question of passing too close to other ships. After the danger was past, the autopilot was simply returned to its previous setting, and the ship swung back on course automatically.

It's no big deal, the captain doesn't have to be called, no assistance is required and hardly any effort, so there's no reason for the officer on the bridge to hesitate to take avoiding action—no reason at all, *if* he can see that there's something ahead to avoid. Here's the catch, as far as small yachts are concerned: Contrary to popular belief, big ships do not run on radar all the time. Out at sea, when the weather was clear, the *Korea Galaxy*'s sets shut down and lookout was kept visually, not electronically. There were two men on bridge watch always, an officer and a seaman. The latter had only one duty: to look and keep looking, generally from the open wing of the bridge. He only sought protection when the weather was bad, and then the radar was switched on.

So if you're the kind of amateur sailor who bumbles along offshore trusting to your radar reflector alone to keep you safe, you're living in a dream world and may well die in it. In the daytime, sure, you'll be seen— the eagle-eyed lookouts on the *Korea Galaxy* were forever picking up their binoculars to study distant vessels that I, standing right alongside, hadn't spotted—but at night, in good weather, the professionals expect to see your *lights* (as required by law) and to hell with your radar reflector. Captain Redivo, normally a very mild person, was quite bitter about the kind of yachtsman who, totally invisible in the dark, would suddenly light up his boat like a Christmas tree when almost under the *Galaxy*'s bow.

"What can I do then?" he asked. "My ship turns in more than 400 meters. I can do nothing then; I can only hope. Why won't they keep some adequate lights shining so I can avoid them in good time?"

You'll note that the captain's attitude was not the one that's often attributed to big-ship officers, who are supposed to expect you to keep out of their way, and if not, to hell with you. As a matter of fact, all the deck officers on the *Galaxy* took for granted that, in any doubtful situation involving another vessel no matter how small, their ship would simply obey the rules of the road at sea. The other craft was expected to do the same.

The young third mate, Catello di Martino, was in fact highly disturbed by the unpredictable and illegal behavior of many of the yachtsmen he encountered offshore.

"I see this small yacht coming from starboard," he said. "It has the right of way, no? Naturally I change course to pass astern, but suddenly this boat, it turns in a panic and heads back the way it came, right in front of the ship! It is too late to change the course again; I can only pray. Why do they not obey the rules?"

Well, there you have the word from the bridge of the *Korea Galaxy:* Avoid false alarms, show adequate lights at night, and if you have the right of way, keep a steady course (as required by law) so the boys don't get heart failure trying to stay clear of you.

At night, from the wing of the *Galaxy*'s bridge, the dark sea held no menace. And it held no menace from the deck of *Kathleen*—except for that apartment building back there.

It really was a pretty picture. The trouble was, it was a pretty picture that didn't change as it should have if that vessel back there were passing well to seaward. The bearing wasn't changing, either. Then the light of the half-moon showed me the great black shape of the oncoming hull against the gleaming, broken sea. I scrambled into the cockpit, let the main sheet run, flipped Tilly out of the way, and bore off hard at right angles to the course. The tanker passed some fifty yards to windward, all cabin lights shining, leaving a sharp smell of gasoline behind her. Well, maybe she'd have missed us anyway; but as I said, there are rogue ships . . .

It was four in the morning. After getting back on course, and polishing off the last lukewarm coffee in the thermos to settle my nerves, I took a look around for Carysfort Light, which should still have been visible off the port quarter but wasn't. There was nothing in sight but a tiny firefly blinking well aft of the beam. I timed it—four seconds—but couldn't find it on the chart until I checked Pacific Reef, which should have been well ahead. It wasn't; we'd already passed it. With the southeaster behind it, the Stream was rushing us northwards at more than eight knots over the ground.

Unbelievably, it was time to start looking for Fowey Rocks light at the entrance to Biscayne Bay, where there's a wide shallow gap between the north end of Elliot Key and the south end of Key Biscayne. Deep down, I guess I really hadn't believed all those crazy Gulf Stream stories—a rushing river in the sea, for Pete's sake!—and I had expected to reach this point around noon if everything went well; but here it was still dark and Miami was in sight, a halo of light off the port bow.

Actually, I overshot the mark. I suppose I couldn't quite convince myself we were going that fast in spite of the navigational evidence. By the time I got the light of Fowey Rocks sorted out from the lights of a passing tug and its tow, and persuaded myself that it *had* to be the light I wanted and I could safely turn shorewards, I had to jibe around and come back almost closehauled on the port tack to fetch the channel against the inexorable northward push of the Stream. It was like jumping off a fast-moving train.

The Biscayne Channel looks tricky on the chart and, in the first light of day, I took down all sail and approached it cautiously under power as the helpful southeast wind gave me a few screaming puffs by way of saying goodbye. But apart from one sharp turn, well marked, it was straightforward enough, taking us right through the middle of Stiltsville, as it's called—that odd, controversial little community of cottages perched on pilings in the shallows. In the clear morning light, *Kathleen* powered the five miles across Biscayne Bay in a flat calm and found an overnight slip in the large Dinner Key Marina, which is surrounded by masses of boats moored and anchored so close together it would make me very nervous indeed.

A day's rest, an offshore power run to Fort Lauderdale in calm weather, and a final short day of hooting at bridges on the ICW, brought me to anchor off Lantana, where cheerful Bill Osterholt of the Seven Seas Cruising Association greeted me with a stiff drink as I paddled the Avon ashore. Like I said, a long way to go for dinner. But to be with a bunch of friendly smiling people spinning cruising yarns into the night, well worth it.

Note: Those interested can get in touch with the SSCA at P.O. Box 14245, North Palm Beach, Fla. 33408.

14

Thinwater Cruise

It's an easy 100 miles to Miami from Marathon, down in the Keys but it's a hard 100 miles back.

The difference is the northward-flowing Gulf Stream that, a couple of weeks earlier, had given me a fast, exciting ride up the coast. Now, having been joined by Kay up in West Palm Beach, I was back in Miami after taking a postgraduate course in bridge transit—there's practically a span a mile in that stretch of the Intracoastal Waterway—and we were waiting out a spell of windy late-fall weather in the convenient Miamarina right on the city's waterfront.

The question was whether to make the return trip to Marathon by going "outside" the way I'd come but hugging the coast and the reefs to avoid the now unfavorable current, or take the sheltered ICW south "inside" the Keys, skirting wide and shallow Florida Bay. This time the inside route won the toss, mainly on the grounds of novelty. I hadn't been that way in a good many years and never in a sailboat; and Kay had never seen that intriguing maze of sounds and creeks and mangrove islands. The only catch was that below Miami the Waterway is not maintained to any reliable depth. We'd been warned that the water gets pretty thin down there, even in the marked channels.

On the third day of the blow, the winds began to moderate, and we

167

made a short afternoon run down to the well-protected Dinner Key Marina in Coconut Grove in order to have the restricted Rickenbacker Causeway Bridge, Miami's last, behind us. In the morning we motored down wide, calm, shallow Biscayne Bay toward our first hurdle: Featherbed Bank, where a narrow cut leads through the shoals blocking the south end of the bay.

"Watch out for Featherbed Bank!" we'd been warned.

The warnings had been emphasized by stories of violent currents sweeping through this slot to carry the hapless mariner out of the channel and helplessly aground. Even if you fight these wicked maelstroms successfully, we'd been told, and remain between the marks, you aren't really safe; boats have often stranded on unpredictable sandbars suddenly materializing right in the middle of the channel. It was therefore with a grimly set jaw, and a white-knuckled hand clutching the tiller, that I sent us into this hell-passage with Kay as lookout in the bow. Nothing happened. *Kathleen* held her course as if she were running on tracks in the still water. The depthfinder never indicated less than eight feet.

"What was all the fuss about?" Kay asked, returning to the cockpit to watch the markers of terrible Featherbed Bank falling away astern.

"We must have hit the tide just right," I said. "Let's hope we can keep it up."

The shores were closing in now. The bodies of open water between banks and shoals were becoming smaller: Card Sound and Little Card Sound. Then we ran under the high bridge leading from the mainland out to Key Largo, with plenty of mast clearance, and ran by compass across sizable Barnes Sound until we could pick up the inconspicuous marker indicating the entrance to Jewfish Creek, hard to spot against the dark mangroves. The current was against us in the tree-lined creek, which was just as well since the bridge at the far end would have to open for us; besides, our slow progress gave Kay lots of time for studying the plentiful bird life along the shores. The bridge tender turned out to be commendably prompt and actually let us through without delay. We pulled into Gibson's Marina just beyond for ice and advice. The attendant was quite informative.

"Featherbed Bank?" he said. "Hell, that's nothing. But watch out for Cross Bank about fifteen miles ahead; it's shoaling badly. Boat the size of yours or a bit smaller spent six hours stuck there in Cowpens Cut the other day before somebody got them off."

With that cheerful news ringing in my ears, I decided to anchor around the corner in Sexton Cove—we'd agreed that, on principle, we simply had to spend at least one night at anchor like real sailors—so we could tackle fearful Cross Bank in the morning when we were fresh and strong. With *Kathleen* lying to her big CQR in six feet of glassy-calm water, I read up on Cross Bank in the Waterway Guide. The man was perfectly right. Three-point-seven-foot depths had been reported in the channel known as Cowpens Cut (named after the seacow, or manatee). Considering that *Kathleen* draws at least four-point-three feet we had a problem or, let's say, a discrepancy amounting to about zero-point-six feet. I'd got this far with my theoretical calculations when the mosquitoes took advantage of the still evening to attack in force and it became necessary for me to deal with practical matters like screens and sprays.

In the morning, with the weather uncertain and the wind light, we picked up the hook and motored across Blackwater Sound to twisty, picturesque Dusenbury Creek, which led us into Tarpon Basin. Beyond was Grouper Creek and Buttonwood Sound, where the Waterway markers seemed to direct us right out to sea—that is, to open Florida Bay. There was a lot of water here, horizontally speaking, but it was very skimpy in a vertical direction. There were many times when, following the Waterway meticulously, I had less than a foot under *Kathleen*'s keel. Kay and I glanced at each other uneasily. If piloting was so hairy in these wide open spaces, what was it going to be like in the narrow confines of Cowpens Cut . . .

Let me digress slightly at this point to explain about Keys navigation. The essentials are a chart (11451 will take you from Miami to Marathon) and a pair of *good* binoculars, backed up by depthfinder and compass. Truly sharp binoculars are required for reading the numbers on the ICW markers at long range. As you approach one of the many cuts or passes you'll see a small, confusing forest of signposts, sometimes right out in what seems to be open water. Your problem is to sort them out in good time and approach them in such a way that you take them in the proper order. If you jump to conclusions and head for the wrong one, which may be the biggest and therefore look closer than the rest, you can find yourself in serious trouble. So the primary rule is never to commit yourself to a narrow cut until you've actually *read* the numbers on the navigational marks ahead and determined exactly how the channel runs.

The second rule is to stay inside the lines between the marks, particularly on longer runs. Keep checking the post you've just passed as well as the one coming up ahead to make sure no current is carrying you off course; sometimes, in a slow boat like *Kathleen,* you have to proceed in a ridiculously crabwise fashion in order to remain in the channel. Here the depthfinder serves as an early-warning device. If the channel has been giving you consistent eight-foot readings and you suddenly find the instrument indicating five feet or less, you're probably doing something wrong. You may have lost the channel and you'd better, quick, figure out which way to go to find it before things come to a screeching halt.

The compass is needed when crossing some of the larger sounds where there may be five miles or more between marks and you can't pick up the next one until you've run a while—the small-craft chart generally gives you the exact compass course, saving you from the terrible fate of having to figure it out for yourself.

The wandering signposts brought us close to the town of Tavernier, on Key Largo, and then swung away toward what looked like a solid mangrove island to seaward. The readings of the faithful digital EMS depthfinder were still nerve-wrackingly small. As we approached, the single island seemed to split in two, showing a narrow gap into which the Waterway turned. There was an obvious shoal on the channel side of the red marker at the entrance. Still with less than a foot under the keel, I made the sharp turn to port well clear of the visible shallows—and the bottom promptly dropped away to six feet or better. It stayed there as we chugged cautiously between the two mangrove keys and out into the even deeper water (by this time I was considering an eight-foot hole as practically a bottomless chasm) of Cotton Key Basin.

"Phew, this suspense is wearing me out," I said. "Let's pull into the nice marina over there that I stopped at in *Kay IV* the last time I came through."

The Plantation Key Yacht Harbor had a slip for us and, having done it the hard way the night before, at anchor, we pampered ourselves with a motel room complete with that great institution, a bathtub. We had a pleasant lunch in the marina restaurant and Kay, who'd wrenched her back, went back to the room to rest while I spent the afternoon scrubbing up the boat. I consulted the dockmaster about the dangers ahead.

"Featherbed Bank?" he said. "Cross Bank? Easy, no sweat; but you'd better watch out for Steamboat Channel just ahead. It's getting real tricky these days and they've been hanging up in there like driftwood."

In the morning, the sky looked dark and mean as we motored back out into Cotton Key Basin. We'd hardly picked up the Waterway again before a black cloud bore down on us from the northwest and a preliminary spit of rain warned us that there was serious precipitation on the way. We anchored hastily and ducked into the cabin as the heavens opened up with a roar. It was a real cloudburst for half an hour but there was no wind to amount to anything and no lightning at all. We simply drank coffee, munched cookies, and waited for the visibility to improve so we could tackle menacing, terrifying Steamboat Channel . . .

Well, I won't go through that routine again. Steamboat Channel turned out to be no tougher than any of the other cuts through which we'd made our way quite safely. We had a good five feet of water all the way; and except for dodging crab pot buoys—whole minefields of crab pot buoys—the rest of the day's run offered no problems either. We arrived in Marathon's friendly Boot Key Marina in plenty of time to clean up for the Christmas party being held on the dock that evening.

Local knowledge can, of course, be very valuable; but it's always well to remember that folks do like to boast a bit about their local navigational hazards. In California, Cape Mendocino is touted as the deadliest promontory on earth (with Point Concepcion a close second), and I'm sure that people in the Carolinas, on the other side of the continent, will rush to tell you proudly what a grisly deathtrap their Cape Hatteras is. And of course they're perfectly right; and I'm sure that occasionally, under certain conditions, a boat can have a lot of trouble negotiating Featherbed Bank, or Cowpens Cut, or Steamboat Channel. On the other hand, I know of at least two sailboats larger than *Kathleen*, with five-foot drafts, that have recently come down the same way without any difficulties at all. So listen to what the helpful gent on the dock has to say, but don't let him scare you away if you really want to go.

15

First Cruise to Cuba

After all the general briefings and special skippers' meetings it was good to be off at last. *Kathleen* seemed to have the same feeling of release as I shut down the diesel and let her go to work under sail, carrying main, forestaysail, and working jib. The course from Marathon to Varadero, Cuba, was almost due south (actually 187°), but we'd been advised to compensate for a Gulf Stream current running 060° at a speed of 2 knots, which made our required heading, I figured, about 205°. The distance was ninety miles.

"*Kathleen, Kathleen,* this is *Love Is.* Channel 68. What is your position?"

I turned the tiller over to Kay while I performed the appropriate VHF routines. "We've got Sombrero Light off the port beam about two miles," I said.

"Okay, I see you. We're off Sisters Creek heading your way."

"Do you want us to wait for you?"

"No, keep going. We'll try to catch up."

Because of the pioneer nature of the expedition, this first cruise by a large group of U.S. yachts into Cuban waters in decades had been very carefully organized, with the 52-boat fleet divided according to speed into groups that were being sent off at different times in the hope that they'd all wind up at the 12-mile limit off Varadero (60 miles east of Havana) more or less simultaneously. As the two smallest sailboats in the fleet, my 27-foot *Kathleen* and Rick Baker's 28-foot *Love Is* were leaving Marathon ahead of everybody else, with Rick as group leader. However, berthed up the Keys a ways, *Love Is* had had a few miles farther to go to our proposed rendezvous west of Sombrero Light, and now I could barely make her out off the port quarter. Well, I'd offered to wait, but as *Kathleen* roared along on a fine beam reach I was grateful to Rick for not asking me to. I'd have hated to slow down; it was obviously going to be a beautiful sail.

It was. In the two-and-a-half years I'd owned *Kathleen,* I'd never had a better: a full-sail, rail-down charge southward under a clear blue sky. The motion got to Kay after lunch and she retired below. I regretted that she wasn't enjoying the crossing, but I'd had enough singlehanded practice by now that her disability created no other problems. As the afternoon wore on, the bigger sailboats that had started three hours later came up over the horizon astern. Alone out there in front of all those white sails—*Love Is* never did catch up—I felt a little like Captain Horatio Hornblower in his fast frigate racing to warn Admiral Nelson that the French fleet was heading for Trafalgar.

I'd expected them to catch me before nightfall, but *Kathleen* continued to make splendid time for a boat her size, and it was 2300 before the lights of the leading vessel pulled abeam. She identified herself over the VHF as the yawl *Simba.* Three or four more went past, including the big trimaran *Rivka*—those things can scare hell out of you coming up astern in the dark with running lights spread like an aircraft carrier's—and that was all; the rest of the lights remained behind us. The wind freshened and I considered reducing sail but compromised by spilling the top of the main in the stronger puffs to keep her on her feet. Tilly, the autopilot, did most of the steering, maintaining full control despite the steep beam sea while I navigated, stuffed myself with keep-awake snacks, and tended the sheets as required.

The whole thing had started over a year before when Sid Carlson, then Commodore of the Marathon Yacht Club, and George Butler, Fleet Captain, had been discussing possible club cruises over a few stimulating libations. This was at the time when the easing of restrictions on travel to Cuba had first hit the news, so the idea was born: Why not Cuba? A letter was fired off. Nothing happened for months. Then abruptly the telephone rang and an unfamiliar voice sputtered incomprehensible words in a foreign language. After communications had been established, it turned out that the Cuban authorities would be happy to welcome a group of American cruising yachts to their marina at Varadero. The required red tape was formidable, the necessary preparations were staggering—on the Cuban side, Varadero apparently had to be practically rebuilt, with new electricity and water lines installed—but eventually the thing was done. Originally limited to members of the Marathon Yacht Club, the cruise was later thrown open to members of any recognized club. (I gather that the Cubans had the idea, correct or not, that they'd get a higher and more reliable type of visitor by requiring proof of yacht club membership—which seems a rather elitist attitude for a bunch of dedicated revolutionaries.)

To touch on a delicate subject: The cruise plans weren't formed without opposition. There were club members and others who were violently against the project, contending that a visit to Cuba implied endorsement of the Cuban regime. I won't argue the point beyond stating, speaking only for myself, that I've visited a number of foreign countries, and even some U.S. states and cities, whose politics turned my stomach, without ever feeling that I was showing approval of the governments involved. Well, the disapprovers stayed home. The rest of us, Cuban visas in our pockets, were now approaching the Cuban coast.

At dawn the bulk of the fleet was still astern, and no land was in sight ahead. The wind that had carried us through the night gradually faded away, and motors were started to maintain an adequate rate of progress. *Kathleen*'s 12-horse Yanmar couldn't compete with the heavier machinery around; she began to fall back toward the rear of the flotilla. A hazy coastline appeared. At 0915, a gray-green Cuban gunboat some sixty feet in length, with rounded turrets fore and aft that caused her to resemble a speedy toy battleship, popped up from nowhere and approached a large ketch up ahead. There were some moments of suspense; then the VHF cracked:

"To all boats of the Marathon Yacht Club Cruise: we've just been warmly welcomed by the commanding officer of a Cuban patrol craft, speaking good English, who says we should proceed straight into harbor . . ."

That should have been all; but apparently my usually reliable little Japanese diesel entertained some unsuspected anti-Castro sentiments. A half-mile off the Varadero jetties it quit and stubbornly refused to restart. We were rescued by a shabby gray runabout that, despite the civilian costumes of its three-man crew, seemed to have official connections. It towed us part way and then turned us over to a large white fishing-type vessel with the unlikely name *Ferro Cement #3,* which deposited us gently and skillfully in our assigned dock space.

Kathleen's little Japanese diesel refused to have anything to do with the land of Fidel Castro, so some helpful Cubans had to tow us in. (PHOTO BY BUDDY MAYS)

Varadero is a pleasant marina with all customary services, located in a sheltered lagoon at the base of the long, narrow Hicaco Peninsula. Dredged channels connect it with the open Straits of Florida from which we'd come, and also with wide Cardenas Bay inside the peninsula. After docking with much friendly help from earlier arrivals, we were greeted, first, by an official who handed us a Cuban courtesy flag and explained that it should be flown with the point of the white star up. Some military characters asked if we had firearms and were satisfied with our negative answer. There were customs forms to be filled out; and *Migracion* gave us receipts for our passports and took them away. In the meantime, more boats were arriving—the powerboat groups, with better convoy discipline, now started descending on the marina in solid bunches—and the place was a scene of organized confusion. In the midst of it, I noted some divers in wetsuits; and discovered that the Cubans, determined to avoid international incidents (maybe they were remembering the *Maine*), were checking the bottoms of our boats for attached and possibly explosive objects.

At last Kay and I managed to retrieve our passports and find somebody to take our customs declarations. Later we learned that these papers caused a bit of confusion. *Kathleen*'s name is on the side, invisible when lying against a dock, and her hailing port is on the stern. Apparently the customs folks, checking up, were seriously disturbed at not being able to find a vessel called *Kathleen,* and at having an extra boat in the harbor named *Seattle Wash.* Unaware of this misunderstanding, soon cleared up, we'd hauled our luggage to the marina building and taken a taxi to the Kawama Hotel a mile away where, along with several other crews, we'd made reservations, since hot weather could be expected at this time of year and *Kathleen* is not air-conditioned.

We'd made it; we were actually in Cuba, and we would be there for well over a week. We didn't really learn much about the political, social, and economic aspects of the Castro regime, but they've got a lot of enormous new housing projects and schools of which they're very proud. They've also got strict rationing of just about everything; and they have soldiers at just about every crossroad, and you can't step onto a beach without seeing an armed patrol craft on the horizon—stationed there, apparently, not only to keep foreigners from invading the country but to keep its citizens from escaping.

Of more practical importance to the visitor from the U.S.A. is the fact that a hundred bucks will buy you only about seventy-five Cuban pesos, and nothing seems to be particularly cheap. On the bright side, our boats were perfectly safe. I heard of no instance of theft. And we all drank the water and used ice in our drinks and nobody, as far as I'm aware, contracted the usual south-of-the-border gastric ailments. There seems to be no tipping in Cuba; the boys who towed us in even refused the *cervezas* I offered them.

Considering the state of hostility that's prevailed so long between our countries, everybody was surprisingly friendly. Our guides did treat us to a rather unfamiliar version of, for instance, the Bay of Pigs incident; but on the whole there was no real attempt at indoctrination or brainwashing. Some limits were established beyond which we could not sail our boats or drive the bikes and motorcycles carried on the larger yachts; but we were free to take the local bus to neighboring towns and walk around at will and if there was surveillance it was quite inconspicuous.

Not that our movements went entirely unobserved. This was demonstrated on the second day after our arrival when we headed east along the Hicaco Peninsula in our boats for a scheduled day on the water. Rather than trust *Kathleen*'s sulking powerplant (although we'd got it going again), Kay and I hitched a ride on Joe and Bobbi Pluhar's big motor-sailer *Escape*. After stopping in a couple of places for snorkeling, visiting a deserted coast-defense installation, and running lightly aground, we decided to return to the marina by the back door, so to speak, using the channel from Cardenas Bay. As soon as our intentions became obvious, a small, unmarked blue runabout appeared to intercept us. It was crewed by a couple of men in military uniforms. They told us, through the guide we had on board, that we had to turn around and use the other entrance; our fifty-odd-foot main mast would not fit under a certain high tension wire over this end of the channel.

Earlier we'd been officially briefed about the area and informed that this wire was seventy feet in the air; but when our guide made a protest to this effect the instructions were simply reiterated: turn back. And on the other side of *Escape,* we suddenly noticed, was one of the turreted little high-speed Border Guard battleships, materializing out of nowhere to enforce the order. Later we learned that a power boat in the group had been allowed to use this rear entrance to the marina, so apparently the motive for sending us back the way we'd come was genuine concern for our safety (or their high tension wire), but it did show that Big Brother had his eye on us.

Varadero had a beach that must rank with the best in the world, and the water was crystal clear; the swimming could hardly have been improved upon. The fishing, I was told, was great offshore; there's also excellent fresh water fishing for bass within easy driving distance. According to my snorkeling friends, the diving in this particular area is only adequate. Two Cuban organizations are concerned with the tourist trade: INTUR provides the facilities, and CUBATUR arranges to fill them. After letting us have a little time to rest and play, the CUBATUR people got to work to earn their pesos and show us the country.

There was an overnight trip to Havana, and a bus ride down into the area of the Bay of Pigs, although we were not taken as far as the actual landing place on the south coast of the island. In addition to housing projects and schools, we were shown some of the historical and cultural sights (Ernest Hemingway might be surprised to learn that he's a great Cuban culture hero), but the emphasis was on restaurants and nightclubs, the latter featuring regiments of substantial ladies in bright costumes dancing athletically to extremely loud music. The shows had a nostalgic flavor of Flo Ziegfeld and Busby Berkeley, and we half expected Al Jolson or Ruby Keeler to come skipping out of the wings to entertain us—and if any reader is too young to know what I'm talking about, that's exactly the point I'm trying to make. It was very old-fashioned, gaudy, noisy, bourgeois-type entertainment and we couldn't help wondering how they could reconcile it with their stern Marxist principles. Concerts and ballets would have seemed more in keeping with the pure revolutionary spirit.

Nevertheless, it was a well-run and enjoyable program, unfortunately marred, near the end, by a heart attack that took the life of a member of our group (the U.S. doctors in attendance were favorably impressed with the quality of the medical care provided, even though it was ultimately unsuccessful). Then, suddenly, it was time to leave. On the evening before the day of departure we left our passports with the immigration officials. Here the efficient arrangements faltered slightly for the first time; it was close to midnight before all passports were returned. Furthermore, the people whose firearms had been impounded, who'd been promised them back at the same time, were now told that the guns would not be delivered until just before sailing time in the morning, bringing uneasy visions of delay to the people in fast boats planning to make a daylight dash back to Florida. However, at 0515 the military did appear with the guns in plenty of time for the scheduled 0600 departure.

Then motors roared all over the marina, and I found a small hole in the line of traffic in the channel and stuck *Kathleen* into it. Soon the whole fleet was pouring out between the Varadero jetties, heading back north. I'll admit to a certain feeling of relief as, a few hours later, we passed the 12-mile limit and the vigilant gunboats and emerged into international waters. The homeward crossing, although not a wild, glorious sail like the trip south, was pleasant enough except for a navigational misjudgment on my part that brought us to the Florida Keys about 12 miles west of our destination. (Somebody'd forgotten to turn on the Gulf Stream, dammit!) In bright, beautiful moonlight, we finally fumbled our way into Boot Key Marina at 0100 in the morning, the last boat in, and fell into our bunks. In the morning, U.S. Customs appeared to make us legal, and our pioneer voyage was officially at an end.

I'm told that Cubans are not yet prepared to deal with single U.S. yachts roaming casually along their coasts. I don't say it absolutely can't be arranged, but the negotiations might take practically forever. The Cubans are, however, prepared to welcome other *groups* of yachts; and they don't require giant armadas such as ours.

As for me, I must confess that I'm probably not going back unless things change drastically. I'm delighted to have done it once; but those gunboats give me claustrophobia. But it certainly was a beautiful sail, an enjoyable visit, and a fascinating glimpse of what life is like in a regimented, militarized society that yet manages to retain something of the cheerful, easygoing Latin spirit.

16

Bahamas Bound

The current problem was current.

Kathleen and I were back in Miami, waiting for Gordon to join us for a cruise to the glamorous islands we'd dreamed of ever since leaving the cold and rainy Northwest. We were heading for the Bahamas; and while waiting I was trying to determine the right conditions for crossing the Florida Straits to Bimini, 45 miles away across the Gulf Stream. Normally, a 45-mile run would be nothing to worry about. It's the swift current of the Stream, combined with the normally unfavorable winds, that makes it tough.

Of course, in local powerboat circles it seems to be something of a status symbol to have dashed over to Bimini for lunch and come home in time for supper. It can certainly be done in good weather; but in a fast powerboat the Stream is not a serious adversary. A 30-knot flyer would need to allow only about five degrees for drift. The way the helmsman would be bounding around at 30 knots he probably couldn't read his compass that closely; and it wouldn't really matter anyway. Even if he forgot to make any correction whatever, he'd be exposed to the current for less than two hours for an error of less than five miles at the far end, not enough to make him miss his landfall.

A sailboat, however, is a different matter; and a sailing skipper who neglects to allow for the effect of the Gulf Stream for the ten hours or more it may take him to make the crossing may wind up being swept so far to the north that he'll never be able to fight his way back to his destination. This is particularly true if he's slowed down by calms or head winds, and as I've already indicated, head winds are the rule on this run. It's inadvisable to tackle the Stream when it blows from the north; the wind fighting the current may kick up dangerous seas. Westerly winds are rare. That doesn't leave much choice.

So, how do you figure the current allowance?

There's the empirical method. It was explained to me by a local sailor whose name I never caught, who used to ride as mechanic with one of the big names in offshore powerboat racing. Perhaps he got tired of blazing across the water at 80 knots; at any rate he's now got a sailboat. His procedure for getting to Bimini is simple. Figuring that he's going to drift some twenty-odd miles north during the crossing, he compensates in advance by leaving Miami early and running down sheltered Biscayne Bay to Angelfish Creek, twenty-odd miles south. This narrow channel through the Keys puts him out in the Florida Straits. He heads due east and, eventually, sees Bimini appear on the horizon somewhere ahead. He says he's never missed yet.

Well, that's fine, but Angelfish is a moderately tricky little passage for a stranger, and the method does involve a considerable detour. Let us therefore consider various methods for determining how to get directly from Miami to Bimini or one of the associated islands, Gun Cay or Cat Cay. You'd think that, popular as this crossing is, somebody would have come out with a table giving the current allowance required for boats of different speeds. You'd be right; somebody has. The well-known *Yachtsman's Guide to the Bahamas,* edited by Harry Kline and updated yearly, has a rudimentary table showing the chart courses from a number of U.S. ports to several different destinations and vice versa, as well as the courses that would have to be steered by vessels moving at certain velocities in order to make these headings good. A more complete table appeared in the February 1978 issue of *Southern Boating* magazine; this one also gives the actual speed made good towards the destination in each case—not at all the same thing as the speed traveled through the water, when you have to head off by a significant angle to counteract the effect of the current. There are undoubtedly other, similar aids to Gulf Stream navigation; but the two tables mentioned, at least, suffer from a serious deficiency for our purposes. They assume boat speeds from ten to twenty-five knots in one case; ten to thirty in the other. Us poor sailing folks who often crawl along at five knots or less apparently don't count.

So we've got to figure it out for ourselves. Here we've got a number of different ways to go. First is the straight mathematical approach. A very bright boating writer named Jim Martenhoff, who loves to juggle figures, has, if I remember correctly, published two easy solutions, one involving some neat mathematical gimmicks that will let any fool figure it all out if the fool can only remember them, but I never can. The other employs a slide rule in a very straightforward fashion; but although I do use a slipstick occasionally, I never can keep that method in my head, either. (Sorry about that, Jim.)

Next we can buy ourselves a full-dress electronic pocket computer programmed to perform this work for us along with many other useful navigational operations—a very good solution for folks who have a few hundred bucks that don't happen to be working at the moment. Unfortunately, my funds were all employed elsewhere.

Or, we can obtain a simple little plastic gizmo called a current correction calculator, costing less than ten bucks. I've got one; but these folks also have pretty grandiose notions about boat velocities. At least my gadget isn't really designed for speeds under five knots—although some extrapolation is possible—and when *Kathleen* is doing five knots she's moving right along, for her. Four and three knots show up quite frequently on the knotmeter, and the figure two is not altogether unknown in unfavorable conditions. Who's going to guarantee that our conditions are going to be forever favorable? If we hit light winds or, more likely on this run, steep head seas, and slow down significantly, I want to know what additional current allowance I must make to get me where I'm going. Another disadvantage is that I find it hard to work this calculator in reverse. It will tell me readily enough the heading I must hold in order to make good a certain course: but when conditions force me to hold a different heading I find it hard to figure back to find the course I'm actually making good.

A general drawback to all the mathematical and instrumental approaches is that errors are easy to make and hard to spot. For the experienced, current-wise boatman these methods are fine; for the beginner at current sailing they suffer from the inability to show him clearly what's happening to his boat as it proceeds along one course out there at a certain speed, is swept in another direction by a current running crosswise at a certain angle and velocity, and actually makes good over the ground a third course and speed that's a resultant of these two effects. To visualize the problem, at least at first, he really needs a picture, not a lot of abstruse numbers.

So let's draw a picture (yes, yes, Virginia, you may call it a vector diagram if you insist). We'll take as our example the problem that confronted me as I sat there in Miami hoping to get over to Bimini without too much trouble. Use a blank sheet of paper and call the left-hand edge north and south. Near the bottom of this north-south base line make a dot and label it Florida Light, our point of departure. The course from Florida Light (at the south end of Key Biscayne) to Bimini is 085 degrees. With a protractor measure off 85 degrees clockwise from the left edge of the paper—our base line—and draw a line starting at Florida Light. Run it well out and label the other end Bimini. This is the course we'd sail to get there in still water.

But the Gulf Stream is going to grab us and carry us north the minute we leave the land. The consensus is that while both the direction and speed of the current vary as you cross the Stream, good averages to use here are due north and 2½ knots. So now, from the same Florida Light dot, measure off 2½ inches up the left-hand edge of the paper, due north along our base line. This represents the 2½ nautical miles the Stream would carry us off course in one hour, if we let it. (You can use centimeters if you prefer, or any other unit that suits your fancy.) Give the north end of your 2½-inch line a little arrowhead if you like; that makes it a vector in mathematical parlance, very fancy.

Okay. It's clear from the diagram that if we'd steered straight at Bimini, almost due eastwards, for one hour, we'd already be almost two and a half miles off course to the north due to the current. Obviously we're going to have to compensate by heading drastically southwards, but how drastically? Well, let's just see what it takes to bring us back to our 085° Florida-Light-to-Bimini course line.

Say we've got a pretty good wind and our ship is driving right along at five knots. Break out the dividers and set them at five inches (or centimeters, or whatever unit you've decided to use). Put one point of the dividers at the head, or north, end of the 2½-inch current arrow. Swing the other point in an arc until it crosses the 085° course line we need to maintain. Draw another arrowed line, our boat-speed vector, connecting the two points. Apply the protractor to this line and read off the course we must steer: 110°. In other words, at five knots we have to compensate for the Gulf Stream current by heading 25 whole degrees to starboard of our charted course to Bimini.

At this angle, while we're making our five knots through the water, we're obviously not progressing towards Bimini at five knots in this crabwise fashion. To find out how fast we're actually approaching our destination, measure along the Florida-Light-to-Bimini course line to the point where it's intersected by the boat vector or arrow. The distance is 4.8 inches, equivalent to 4.8 nautical miles in one hour, or 4.8 knots.

Suppose we get a better breeze and achieve a sizzling six knots through the water. Strike an arc of six inches instead of five from the north end of the current vector over to the 085° course line; we see that we now have to steer 104 degrees and we'll make good 5.9 knots towards Bimini. On the other hand, if the seas slow us down to three knots, a similar geometrical process shows that we'll have to steer 136° to make Bimini, and our rate of progress will be only 2.1 knots. And if things go really haywire and our speed through the water drops to two knots, we're in trouble. We're simply not going to get to Bimini. The diagram indicates that we can't get far enough east at this reduced speed, no matter what course we steer, before the current rushes us past our objective. We'll have to change our cruising plans drastically and shoot for West End on the island of Grand Bahama sixty miles north; or just turn back and hope to sneak into a U.S. harbor up the coast with our nautical tails between our legs.

But in any case, a complete vector diagram, or series of diagrams, as shown, provides a clear picture of the situation. It shows what directions we must steer to offset the effect of the current at various boat speeds and hold the course we need to make good. It tells us what speeds we can expect to achieve along that course under various circumstances.

It also—very important—tells us at a glance when wind and sea and boat behavior are such that we're better off not trying to make it at all, because we can't. We'll just have to wait for more favorable conditions.

Which is exactly what I was doing when Gordon arrived.

When we left Miami several days later, I broke out my secret instructions to myself as we cleared Biscayne Channel. I now had one set of vector diagrams for the crossing east to Bimini, calculated for speeds of three, four, five, and six knots; and another, similar, set for the crossing to West End farther north—showing the allowance that had to be made at each speed for a Gulf Stream current flowing due north at two and a half knots. *Kathleen* had never made a six-knot passage in her life, but a man can dream, can't he?

It took only a glance at the compass, after the sails were set and trimmed, for me to discard Bimini as a possible destination with this southeast wind. Considering the large current-correction factor needed, we'd be lucky to lay West End. Well, that was why I'd planned an overnight run to the Islands, to give us plenty of time and leave our options open.

The NOAA weather forecast was for 15-knot winds and seas 5–7 feet high in the Stream. It turned out to be accurate, and things were lively on board as *Kathleen* clawed off the Florida coast closehauled. The skylines of Miami and Fort Lauderdale dropped below the horizon but, as darkness fell, the city lights lit up the sky astern. Ahead there was nothing but blackness sprinkled with stars. She's a dry boat and nothing much was coming aboard, but the knotmeter kept warning me that the heavy chop was doing nothing for our speed, and my little vector diagrams kept insisting that at three knots we weren't even going to make West End before the current swept us past—next stop Bermuda. Reluctantly I started the Yanmar. *Kathleen* began to step out, crashing grimly through the head seas instead of stopping every now and then to fraternize with them. With roller-jib furled, forestaysail set, a reef in the main, and the diesel at half throttle, we hammered our way eastward while the Gulf Stream carried us relentlessly northward. By morning we were picking up lights ahead, too many lights. It turned out that we'd overcompensated for the current and made our landfall close to Freeport, some twelve miles east along the island of Grand Bahama, instead of at West End at the tip of it. (Actually, that was exactly where my DR had placed us, but I hadn't trusted it enough to sacrifice our hard-won easting before I could see what I was doing.)

The error was in the safe direction, but we discovered that there's a strong counter-current running eastwards along the Grand Bahama shore; so strong that in spite of the gusty fifteen-knot breeze that was now under our tail as we eased sheets and ran off to the west, it took us until noon to fight our way out to, and around, the end of the island at Settlement Point, and pick our way through the churned-up mess of broken water off Indian Cay into the pretty, sheltered little marina that was our port of entry. The Bahamas customs and immigration officials were prompt and polite; and soon we were hauling down the quarantine flag and running up the Bahamas courtesy flag in its place.

West End, with its big resort hotel, is pretty much tourist-oriented; but the marina is quiet and comfortable and makes a good place to rest up from the rigors of the Gulf Stream crossing. We spent a full day there catching up on our sleep. The following morning *Kathleen,* under power, poked her nose back out into the Gulf Stream for a moment, but only for a moment. On the north side of Indian Cay, we cut back east and motored onto the Little Bahama Bank by way of the marked channel. After clearing the shoals inside the reef, we drew simultaneous sighs of relief and set sail, winging the big genoa out to starboard.

As we glided peacefully northwards, a dramatic contrast to our violent Gulf Stream bash, Gordon said suddenly, "Hey, this is what we came here for, isn't it?"

He was right, of course. This was it: the clear blue water, the soft favorable wind, the ship slipping along at a gentle three and four knots, and not a cloud in the sunny sky. I had to go and spoil it by trying to get some sights with my new sextant for practice, an exercise that always

Easy sailing in the Bahamas with Gordon at the helm relishing the pleasant contrast with the rough Gulf Stream crossing.

frustrates me because I never manage to get as close as I think I ought to. I forced myself to put the devilish instrument away. To hell with navigation. To demonstrate that this was the proper Bahamas attitude, after a beautiful, lazy, all-day compass run, we saw Walker's Cay appear on the horizon dead ahead, sextant or no sextant. Water was a bit thin in the entrance channel, but this was something we knew we had to get used to. With less than a foot under her keel, *Kathleen* entered the well-protected marina and found considerably more depth inside. We filled her up with diesel and were allotted a comfortable berth next to a small bright-red sloop from Michigan. The owners, Eric and Judy Rusak, had trailered their Chrysler 26 to Florida, crossed the Stream under fairly rugged conditions, and were now working their way homewards after a pleasant cruise of the northern islands.

Walker's Cay is actually just about as far north as you can go in the Bahamas. Right on the edge of the deep Atlantic and surrounded by reefs, it's a sportfisherman's and skindiver's paradise; the visiting sailboat skipper feels a little like a golf aficionado wandering into a tennis club by mistake. But even if you don't speak the anglers' language, you'll find the facilities excellent and the people friendly. We spent several enjoyable days there while waiting for a norther to move through the area.

With the weather clear once more, we headed southeast for Great Sale Cay, but came very close to not making it. There's a lot of loose talk about eyeball navigation in the Bahamas; and the guidebooks all babble blithely about how easy it is to learn how to pilot by the color of the water. Well, maybe *Kathleen*'s got some backward people on board. The trouble is that while dark water is supposed to be deep and light water is supposed to be shallow, there are so many exceptions and variations as to make the whole thing pretty confusing, at least for the newcomer. We soon learned that dark water can indicate either deep water, weeds, coral, rocks, or a cloud over the sun. Light water, on the other hand, can signify shallow water, white sand with plenty of depth over it, a spot of sunshine on an otherwise cloudy day, or that very interesting and startling phenomenon, a fish mud—silt stirred up, sometimes for miles, by schools of feeding fish.

As it happened, we'd encountered a number of these fish muds on our sail across the Bank from West End. After passing through them all unscathed, we'd got a bit blasé about them. Therefore when Gordon, on lookout duty forward, announced more pale water ahead as we were leaving Walker's, I simply shrugged and held my course—until the figures displayed by the digital depthsounder started diminishing at a shocking rate. I chinned myself on the tiller and *Kathleen* jibed all standing. After sorting things out, and working our way out of there, we determined what had happened: avoiding an evil-looking reef called Triangle Rocks, the navigator-helmsman had edged a little too far to the east and got us involved with a perfectly good sandbank marked quite plainly on the chart. So much for eyeball navigation: I recommend careful attention to the chart and a good depthsounder.

Which, however, brings us to the problem of Bahamas charts and the fact that there really aren't many, at least not of an official nature. 26320, *Northeast and Northwest Providence Channels,* covers the whole area of the Abacos and the Little Bahama Bank, which makes it fine for overall planning but not much good for detail. The gap is filled by Harry Kline's old reliable *Yachtsman's Guide to the Bahamas,* with sketch charts that give enough details to get by on where the big chart fails. Even more detailed because it concentrates on a more limited area is Julius Wilensky's excellent *Cruising Guide to the Abacos,* with invaluable sketch charts of practically every bay and harbor you're likely to visit in that area. Both these guides should be on board every Abaco-bound yacht. They supplement each other in many ways, particularly in that Wilensky's book was written a few years ago and has not to my knowledge been revised recently, while Kline's guide is systematically brought up to date each year and therefore shows the latest, or almost the latest, changes.

We had a fine genoa reach to Great Sale Cay. This is a long, forked island, and Northwest Harbour, between the tines of the fork, is sheltered from all winds except westerlies. We ran in and experimented with the Bahamian moor, since all the guidebooks recommend it. It consists of dropping one anchor normally, falling back to twice the scope required, dropping a second anchor, and then hauling in the first rode until you lie, by the bow, midway between them. (There's a more dramatic method, but we'll leave that to the show-offs.) The theory is that as the tide, or wind, changes, you'll swing neatly from one hook to the other, staying pretty much in the same place. It's a nice theory, and in a very small, crowded, or current-plagued anchorage the Bahamian moor is certainly a useful, sometimes even essential, anchoring technique. For normal anchoring it's for the birds.

Even with lots of slack, unless you use chain entirely, there seems to be no way of getting the second rode out from under the keel where it tends to chafe badly, and may even foul if your boat has that kind of an underbody. (Okay, you can run a weight down the rode, adding to the fun and games after the boat has swung a couple of times and snarled things up nicely at the bow.) Furthermore, except in a narrow tidal sluiceway, boats seldom swing a full 180°; instead you're apt to find yourself kind of spread-eagled between your two anchors, with unfair strains on both. And then of course there's the Bahamian corollary of Murphy's Law, which states that if, like most people, you carry a heavy anchor and a lighter one, guess which one you'll find yourself riding to when things get really rugged? (Old Bahamas hands seem to carry identical-twin anchors, presumably for this reason.) But the clincher is that, Bahamas guidebooks to the contrary notwithstanding, very few boats in the average harbor seem to employ this system. When everybody in the place is swinging to fifty-plus feet of rode and you're staying tightly moored in one spot, you're likely to find somebody in your lap when wind and current shift. The Bahamian moor is a great idea, and on our way home we found it very useful one night in Angelfish Creek, but in the Abacos after considerable experimentation we finally wound up just dumping the big CQR and backing down hard to set it unless we could see that everybody around had two anchors out.

But at Great Sale we weren't great Bahamas experts yet—it takes about two weeks, I'm told—so we practiced our two-hook routine. *Kathleen* settled down peacefully in the sheltered harbor, and Gordon performed a culinary miracle involving some fresh-caught grouper he'd been given at Walker's Cay. In the evening we watched three other boats arrive and space themselves for privacy well apart along the weather shore. In the morning we found ourselves still riding to the 35-pound CQR with the 12-pound Danforth still performing no useful function astern. We picked up the little hook and, with plenty of room, sailed out the big one in salty fashion; the first time, I believe, that *Kathleen* has left an anchorage under sail alone.

Hard on the wind after rounding the sheltering point, we cruised lazily east along the shore of the island under short sail, watching a heavy 44-footer leave the harbor astern and come powering after us. He set sail and continued to gain until we succumbed to an un-Bahamian attack of competitiveness and broke out the big roller-furling working jib. It took us a little while to get the double-headsail rig properly tuned for speed; then we found ourselves, much to our delight, first holding him and finally pulling away. After a while he started up his powerplant again and went on by, but we felt that the victory, such as it was, was ours. We sailed out past Great Sale and Little Sale Cays and then, with the wind right on the nose, dropped the headsails and started the Yanmar for the slog to Allens-Pensacola Cay.

But it was a beautiful day with a fine sailing breeze, and after a little of that one-lung-diesel thumpity-thumpity-thumpity, we decided that we'd lost nothing at Allens-Pensacola that wouldn't keep until tomorrow. We shut down the mill, set the headsails once more, and spent the morning

Several thousand adventurous miles, by land as well as water, finally brought Kathleen *to the Bahamas. Here she is anchored at Allans-Pensacola Cay.*

happily short-tacking to the nearby Carter Cays, finally dropping everything and picking our way under power between two threatening sandbanks to a wicked-looking little island of sharp coral where, almost on the rocks, the channel made a sharp left-right . . . In other words, it was a typical Bahamas entrance. Inside, we found our morning's competition at anchor. He turned out to be a very nice man who ran me ashore for ice in his Whaler and then took Gordon snorkeling. Unfortunately, I neglected to note down his name, but his boat was *Scimitar,* of Delray Beach, Florida.

The harbor at Carter's Cays is reasonably well protected by shoals and islets, but a fairly strong tidal current runs through it. When the tide changed in the middle of the night, we found ourselves hanging kind of suspended between the two hooks we'd again put out, but both of them held, which was just as well, since *Scimitar* was lying just downstream. In the morning after an early breakfast we put-putted out of there safely, admiring, through the clear water, the keel-tracks on the bottom left by boats not quite so fortunate. Then we headed for yesterday's destination, Allens-Pensacola, which used to be two islands until a hurricane filled in the dividing channel. It was a pleasant upwind sail—beating to windward is no hardship in those sheltered waters—marred only by the fact that the island we were heading for refused to display the radio tower it was supposed to have, much to the navigator's distress. The chart showed such a tower. Wilensky showed such a tower. The crew quickly pointed out that Kline did *not* show such a tower, suggesting that it might have been removed.

The anchorage was easy to enter and comfortably sheltered. We pumped up the Avon for the first time on the cruise and rowed ashore to determine that there had, indeed, been a tower and it had, indeed, been taken down; only a ghost town remained of the tracking station it had served. By evening, *Scimitar* and two other boats had joined us in the harbor; the home ports represented were Seattle (*Kathleen*), Annapolis, Philadelphia, and Delray Beach.

The next day we had a fine reach under genoa to Green Turtle Cay. We were in the groove now, nice and relaxed, having learned that it's not necessary to knock yourself out cruising the Abacos. Good harbors are seldom more than twenty miles apart; and in settled weather real shelter isn't required, anyway. It's only necessary to find an island that'll give a bit of protection from the prevailing wind. Of course it's nice to have some assurance that the weather intends to stay settled and the prevailing wind plans to prevail. The Abacos are generally out of range of the NOAA weather broadcasts on VHF. However, Fort Lauderdale station WAVS (1190 KHZ) repeats these broadcasts occasionally on AM; and at

0725, courtesy of a marine store called Charlie's Locker, this station gives a complete Bahamas forecast much appreciated by boatmen in the area, who tend to display serious withdrawal symptoms all day if they happen to miss Charlie in the morning.

There are two harbors at Green Turtle Cay, White Sound and Black Sound. Both are impossible to enter with any draft at low tide but we didn't know that; we thought only White Sound was impossible. We crawled through the narrow but well-marked Black Sound entrance on the ebb, therefore, and were greeted by depthsounder readings indicating it was high time to get out and walk. *Kathleen* kept right on moving, however, and gradually the bottom dropped away and we anchored between the most widely-spaced of the several boats already inside, getting the heavier CQR set first and then running out the more easily handled Danforth with the dinghy we were now towing astern—in these tight quarters the Bahamian moor was definitely indicated. Then we paddled ashore to visit New Plymouth.

It is the unanimous opinion of the ship's company that Green Turtle Cay is the nicest place in the Abacos. New Plymouth is a lovely little picture-postcard town, but real people live there, and they're all pleasant and friendly. The skipper recommends the New Plymouth Inn for comfortable drinking and dining; the crew, with more adventurous tastes, states firmly that Miss Emily's Blue Bee Bar is the place to go, man. He should know. He went. There are other restaurants serving excellent seafood; there are two groceries; and if you can't find what you want in New Plymouth you can take the regular ferry over to the fancy marina at Treasure Cay (we did). The only catch is that there's no dinghy dock on Black Sound, which is closest to town, and I don't believe there's one in White Sound either, but if you have a motor on your dinghy, it's not much of a jaunt around to the town dock in the outer harbor.

By this time the one serious lack in *Kathleen*'s equipment had disclosed itself; she carried no dinghy motor. The Avon is a great institution, but you can row one only so far—and that's not very far with a strong wind or tide against you. A great deal of Bahamas exploring is by small boat, and unless you have room on board for a true rowing or sailing dinghy, a motor is definitely required. The crew felt that he missed a lot of good snorkeling and spearfishing (only Hawaiian sling allowed) because he couldn't get to it by oarpower alone. However, as far as Green Turtle Cay was concerned, it didn't matter. The first gent we asked in Black Sound kindly let us tie up the Avon at his private dock for the duration, leaving us only a short hike into town. Like I said, a lovely place. We stayed three days and were sorry to leave.

From Green Turtle, boats with any draft usually make a short hitch out into the Atlantic on the way south; there are ways to get through the obstructing shoals inside, but they're tricky and generally require some help from the tide. The Whale Cay Passage, as it's called, had the navigator in his usual state of nervous anticipation; but as it turned out, there was nothing to it. The day was calm, the sea was flat, and we powered out around Whale Cay and back inside the islands without incident; and stopped for the night at Great Guana Harbor—excuse me, Harbour—where we found that, for two bucks apiece, we could use the shower in an empty hotel room of the pleasant Great Guana Club, a tremendous luxury not encountered since Walker's Cay. Mike and Wilma Lotz, of the Dufour 30 *Papillon,* whom we'd met at Green Turtle, came over for dinner. Later, the wind changed and rose, screaming right into the anchorage from the west, a direction no self-respecting wind should blow from in that part of the world. *Kathleen* found herself (remember Murphy's Law) hanging off the beach by her little 12-pounder instead of her big 35, but the Danforth held although it was a rough night not conducive to dreamless sleep. Early in the morning *Papillon* almost found herself on the rocks; a pin had dropped out of a shackle. Mike and Wilma somehow woke up in time to power out of danger; later, they even recovered their lost anchor.

In spite of the friendly club and its shower, we were glad to get out of that bouncy anchorage. A short reach in the morning put us into Marsh Harbour where, attracted by a big New Mexican flag, we met and invited to dinner J.J. Whitted and his crew Guido Casciano of the 30′ trimaran *Chiquili.* Whitted had built his boat in his, and my, home town of Santa Fe and had trailered it to Florida disassembled. After putting it together and checking it out thoroughly, he'd sailed with his crew to the Bahamas; now he was heading north through the Abacos, gradually working his way homewards.

Marsh Harbour, while it's a big protected anchorage, hasn't got much picturesqueness to recommend it, but there's a government dock where you can leave your dinghy, and the town does have just about everything a cruiser needs to resupply his boat if his needs are not too exotic. We spent a rainy day there stocking up and, in the evening, were invited for drinks aboard the beautiful old wooden cutter *Hother,* a 46′ Rhodes-designed ex-racer now serving as home for George and Peg Culler, who suggested that we should meet in a couple of days in what I'll call Secret Lagoon since that's not its name and we don't want too many people to know about it. (You can find it in one of the guidebooks, but only one, if you look hard enough.)

The following day was bright and clear and a couple of long tacks took us to Man-o-War Cay, where the main harbor was incredibly crowded and the subsidiary harbor hardly less so. An uninspired lunch in the town's only eatery (no drinks served) and a hike around town trying fruitlessly to arrange for a minor boat repair with uninterested boatyard personnel, convinced us that, while colorful enough, Man-o-War wasn't likely to ever become our favorite Abaco port.

We weighed anchor, therefore, and headed for Hope Town, where the small harbor, again, was almost wall-to-wall boats. We were advised by a fellow-yachtsman not to anchor but to pick up a mooring; the man would come out later to collect his fee. (He never did.) Hope Town is an attractive and photogenic little seaport; the people are helpful; and an excellent dinner in friendly surroundings at the Harbour Lodge made us overlook the crowding and give it a second-place rating on our Abaco List. However, of the communities we visited, we still like New Plymouth best. (Comfortable Walker's Cay, we feel, is in a separate category because of its highly specialized and U.S.-oriented atmosphere.)

South of Hope Town there are still plenty of opportunities for the dedicated gunkholer; but our time was running out. We made our way to the rendezvous with *Hother,* and spent two days in a beautiful, hidden pond listening to surf thundering on the rocks at the seaward side of the island and preparing *Kathleen* for the open-water jaunt that came next. The first night, *Hother* gave us a fine demonstration of man-and-wife teamwork when the big cutter dragged and the Cullers had to reset their anchors in the wind and darkness. Leaving, a day later, *Kathleen* gave a demonstration of another kind when skipper and crew, each thinking the other was paying attention, managed to put their ship hard aground on a falling tide. Well, you can't visit the Bahamas without hitting bottom at least once, can you? George Culler ran our Danforth out with his dinghy since ours was now stowed; and the husky Powerwinch on *Kathleen*'s foredeck made its usual growling sound of disgust and disapproval (Oh, God, not *again!)* and got down to work, kedging us off in its usual efficient, electric fashion.

Then out through the reefs by way of the North Bar Channel, another mental hazard for the navigator that turned out to be worry wasted. In deep Atlantic waters once more, with a good reaching breeze, *Kathleen* went roaring south along the Abaco coast, giving the skipper his six-knot passage at last. By evening she was down to staysail and double-reefed main, she'd left Great Abaco behind, and she was still going like stink across the Northeast Providence Channel. By midnight the lights of Nassau were in sight ahead although they hadn't been supposed to show up until morning.

Since I didn't know the harbor entrance, and had no idea what to do

Back at Boot Key Marina, in Marathon, Florida, Kathleen *has a touch-up job done on her name.*

once inside, we lay off until morning, when we let draw and made our way into the Hurricane Hole Marina, where they managed to find a spot for us. This sheltered and well-kept little harbor on Paradise Island (formerly Hog Island) is very convenient if you want to lose money at the nearby Casino; not quite so convenient if you have business across the bridge in Nassau proper. However, a friendly taxi driver ferried us around town at a reasonable price, and in the evening, of course, we made the required sacrifice to the gods of chance.

A brisk day's sail put us in Chub Cay, another comfortable but angler-oriented marina. The following day, with the same friendly easterly blowing, we found our way onto the Great Bahama Bank at Northwest Channel Light and ran before the wind all night in 10–20 feet of water, after deciding to ignore the fact that Russell Beacon didn't seem to be quite where it was supposed to be. (A professional skipper had advised us to pay no attention to Russell, and a Polaris sight at sunset confirmed his advice.) In the middle of the night we had a scare when a bunch of flickering lights seemed to charge down on us with hostile intentions. It turned out that we were charging down on them—three sailing yachts sociably anchored together on the open Bank right on the course. We scraped through without harm; and in the dark early-morning hours *Kathleen*'s nervous navigator managed to find the red aerobeacon on Bimini and the blue-white lights of Cat Cay, but Gun Cay Light eluded him. At dawn, the picturesque lighthouse tower became clearly visible dead ahead; on top of it was a tiny little firefly of a beacon that, at least, shouldn't disturb the sleep of the lighthouse keeper's family much with its feeble flashes.

Emerging from the tricky channel in broad daylight, we found ourselves back in the same Gulf Stream we'd left with relief almost a month earlier. It was in a mellower mood now; and the following day, after resting up in Bimini, we made a very calm and easy crossing to the U.S. under power—dull, some might say, but you won't hear that from *Kathleen*'s company. Any time the Stream wants to be dull it's okay with us. Somewhere off Miami we crossed our outbound track, completing our daring circumnavigation of the northern Bahama Islands.

17

Midnight Thoughts on the Great Bahama Bank

I took over the watch at midnight. On overnight runs we'd got into the habit of standing two hours on and two hours off. Nobody really gets much solid sleep that way; but one night at sea isn't long enough to get into the groove of a more elaborate watch system, like the complicated Swedish routine we'd used coming down the Pacific coast a couple of years earlier. Anybody can put up with one sleepless night if he just gets to lie down a bit occasionally.

"It got a bit shallow back there, about ten feet, but it's back to twelve and fifteen," reported Gordon. "You may have to jibe the main over again; the wind keeps flopping across the stern. Be good."

Yawning, he disappeared down the hatch. Shortly the cabin lights went out, and the only remaining illumination came from the red-green-and-white masthead navigation light forty-odd feet above me; the red numbers of the digital depthsounder; and the rosy glow of the twin compasses, one on each side of the companionway. We were on the Great Bahama Bank heading west for Gun Cay and Bimini, on the final leg of the long, lazy cruise around the Abacos just described.

Kathleen was loafing along downwind under mainsail alone, making about four knots, just about right for a landfall at dawn. For some reason I found myself remembering, some two years earlier after our long offshore passage down the west coast and a perfect landfall on California's Cape Arguello, roaring up the Santa Barbara Channel in the dark with pretty much the same rig, except that the sail had sported two reefs on that occasion. . .

Well, it had been interesting, I thought, listening to the murmur of the bow wave and the soft whirr-whirr as Tilly corrected the course at frequent intervals. There had been a lot to do, a lot to buy, and a lot to learn; and most of it had got done and bought and learned. I realized abruptly that my little ship and I had just accomplished something new, and for us very different: we'd actually made a cruise just for fun. After almost thirty months and five thousand miles we were finally ready to go sailing.

It had been the best nautical apprenticeship in the world for me, and the best testing-and-development program for boat and gear. Our deliberate progress from Pacific to Atlantic waters, from British Columbia in the far northwest to Florida in the far southeast (with a small assist from that truck between Los Angeles and Houston), had exposed us to a wide spectrum of cruising conditions. Now in a sense we'd put it all together at last and used what we'd learned the way it was supposed to be used, because pleasure boating is presumably done for pleasure. I had my boat in the right ocean at last, even in pretty much the right part of the right ocean. The pressure was off. I was no longer worrying about picking the best season for the next jump. I had no more big jumps to make unless I wanted to make them. Maine in the spring? The Virgin Islands in the fall? Well, we'd see; but the real ferry job I'd set myself was completed. And so, to a large extent, was the boat-improvement and self-improvement program I'd necessarily got involved with en route.

I was no longer making endless lists of absolutely essential equipment that had to be put aboard soon because, while I'd managed to struggle along without it to date, I wouldn't always be so lucky. I was no longer lining up important projects in nautical self-education, techniques I simply had to master quickly before I needed them badly. This Bahamas trip had demonstrated that, while my navigation was far from perfect and my seamanship would never earn me a position on an America's Cup crew, I'd managed to acquire enough seafaring skills to get by. And while no boat is ever completely finished, *Kathleen* had finally become a smoothly operating seagoing machine with no important gears or bearings missing. . .

I could feel that the wind had swung around to caress my left ear. It was time to jibe the main over and I did, unclipping the port preventer and snapping on the starboard one as the boom came across; then easing the sheet and setting the new preventer up tight.

Gordon called from below: "Need any help?"

"You're supposed to be asleep," I said.

"I was until you started making all that racket."

I went below and took care of the 0100 entry in the log and measured off the last hour's run along our charted track, crawling slowly across the shallow Bank to Gun Cay. Then I poured myself a cup of coffee from the battered old stainless vacuum bottle and returned to the cockpit to drink it after checking that Tilly was still holding the course on this new tack.

Lessons learned. Well, the first one had come early on, as the British say: pick your builder as carefully as your boat. I hadn't. Months of study had gone into selecting the design—and then I'd casually signed a contract, with only a minimum of investigation, with a young man who was planning to put that design into production. At this point the whole operation had come very close to becoming a horrible and very expensive mistake. He was a nice enough young fellow (I can say that now; at the time I wanted to shoot him), but while he'd acquired a reputation for building sound workboats, it turned out that he didn't know much about finishing yachts and couldn't seem to get around to learning. But never mind. Diatribes against boat builders are too numerous and tiresome for me to indulge in another. I did get my boat before the poor guy went bankrupt, and she works. The moral is, of course, that it's nice to encourage ambitious young chaps who want to make their fortunes building yachts, but if you feel that way very strongly I suggest you just hand your particular candidate a check for a grand or two and write it off as charity. Then take your boat plans to a well-established builder who's proved over the years that he knows what he's doing, and pay his price. You'll be ahead of the game.

As for *Kathleen* herself, aside from a few construction oddities caused by the quirks of the builder, now attended to, she's been exactly what I hoped I was getting when I chose the plans. I wanted the smallest boat in which I'd feel safe going offshore, and I think I've got her; at least, I've seen nothing smaller I'd care to trust out there. I wanted good accommodations for two and I got those. I wanted a rig that could easily be handled by one and I got that.

Sir Francis Chichester's last boat, in which he crossed the Atlantic singlehanded at the age of seventy, was close to sixty feet long. He needed the size for speed—he was trying to set records—but I'll bet there were times when even that incredible old gent got weary of manhandling all those acres of canvas by himself, not to mention the maintenance and housekeeping required by a boat that large. That I've picked a boat the right size for me is shown by the fact that I've never wished for her to be any smaller and easier to handle (except perhaps when I was paying the bills). I haven't often wished for her to be larger, either. Certainly I've never felt, even in the worst gale *Kathleen* has experienced, that my life might be a little safer if she were a few feet longer. More comfortable, perhaps; safer, no. There is, I suppose, a point at which any boat will be overwhelmed by raging storm seas, and maybe that point is slightly farther off in a bigger boat; but I don't feel the difference is of much practical significance. If you get caught out when it blows *that* hard, you're in trouble anyway.

What a bigger boat is for is simply to carry more people, gear, and supplies. Personally, I have no desire to maintain a crowd on board; I have trouble enough trying to find one congenial person to sail with me. I admit it would be nice, for instance, to have a shower on board and enough fresh water to support it—but nice enough to make up for wrestling with 500-square-foot sails and 75-pound anchors? Not for this gent and his temperamental sacroiliac; nor do I relish the thought of maintaining the pumps and plumbing involved. The same goes for a lot of other big-boat equipment like refrigerators, freezers, and air conditioners. I decided at the start that, to me, it simply wasn't worth the hassle; and my opinion hasn't changed.

On the other hand, I don't go nearly as far as the true simplicity freaks who dote on motorless sailboats illuminated by kerosene lights and navigated by chip logs and lead lines. I'm very fond of *Kathleen*'s little Yanmar. It has taken boat and crew into places they couldn't possibly have gone without it, and it has kept her batteries reliably charged to power her electric and electronic goodies.

Some people try to peddle the odd notion that you shouldn't enjoy electricity on board because it may fail. This is kind of like saying that you shouldn't enjoy living because you may die—except that for electricity there's almost always a simple shipboard substitute. I was told, for instance, when I installed my electric Powerwinch, that I was being stupid and shortsighted: how would I get my anchors up if the batteries gave out? On a 27-footer? I'm admittedly lazy to a pathological degree, and I much prefer to let machinery do the heavy work for me, but I'm not so damned feeble I can't lift my 35-pound CQR by hand if I absolutely have to; and if things get really tough, well, there are four big geared manual winches around the cockpit, any one of which will break out a hook for me if I want to go to the trouble of running the rode aft. But in the meantime, for over two years, I've had the pleasure of having endless power available on the foredeck at the touch of a switch (just the other day in the Abacos it had hauled us off another shoal) and even if it should fail me now, which it shows no signs of doing, I'd still feel I was way ahead of the game.

The same negative attitude has been applied to my electric Tiller Master autopilot—but oh dearie me what will you do if it quits or runs the batteries down? Why, I'll steer my boat myself like I did at the beginning, until I can cook up a simple sheet-to-tiller rig; that is assuming I can't solve the electrical problem or crank the mill by hand and recharge the batteries. A small price to pay for all those hundreds of miles (many under power when a vane wouldn't have worked anyway) when Tilly maintained the course faithfully, leaving me free to cook and navigate.

Electric lights are brighter, cooler, and more convenient than kerosene lights; and *Kathleen* carries a built-in charger that keeps the batteries up in port whenever shore power is available. The electric knotmeter and distance log are a lot simpler to use than their old-fashioned predecessors; and the speed indicator, in particular, with its instant readout, makes it possible to learn the effects of sail changes in a way that can't be done without it. As long as they work, these gadgets are fun as well as being useful; and when the impeller picks up weeds, or a circuit shorts out, or a terminal corrodes, which really doesn't happen very often, we simply go back to seat-of-the-pants navigation temporarily, no strain. And my digital EMS depthfinder is a perfectly lovely instrument, totally reliable to date, and anybody who recommends going back to the lead line either hasn't ever heaved a lead or is a masochist at heart. Finally, as far as I'm concerned, good big winches have it all over handy-billies, whips, purchases, and other odd string-and-pulley arrangements when it comes to applying power to sheets and halyards. So far, although shamefully abused, none of *Kathleen's* eight oversized Barlows has ever caused a bit of trouble.

It is, of course, quite true that if you're going to spend several years cruising in remote areas you may be better off keeping things very simple instead of trying to maintain complex modern equipment far from parts depots and trained repairmen. However, let's note that the instruments that have caused most difficulty on board *Kathleen,* strangely enough, are those which can hardly be considered particularly complex or particularly modern: the compasses. I've found it necessary to carry three steering compasses in order to keep two more or less operative: one is at the factory as I write. So it's not necessarily the nonessential luxury-gadgets that cause the trouble.

So much for the boat; what about the boatman? Well, I've managed to master in a practical way a number of navigational techniques and instruments I only knew about in a theoretical way before I got my own cruising boat. The handbearing compass and the sextant are becoming old friends. But this is stuff that, while it must be perfected by use, can be largely acquired by reading books and taking courses.

What's harder to master is the true cruising attitude. I mean by this the feeling that your boat is your world and you really don't need the shore at all—the sense that as long as your little ship is watertight and mobile and adequately supplied with food and water, and the weather is not too disastrously lousy, nothing much can happen to you even if you don't make it to a certain harbor or marina on schedule. Everywhere I sail I find yachtsmen with mental blocks that make whole areas of cruising unavailable to them. They weren't as fortunate as I; they didn't have to put themselves through the long-range initiation I've just endured while bringing my boat from one side of the continent to the other.

Judging by my own experience, I will state that there are three types of sailing that are absolutely essential to the development of a real all-around cruising yachtsman. He must have done a reasonable amount of cruising, enough to develop confidence, under each of the following conditions:

1. offshore
2. overnight
3. alone

I don't think a man can call himself a real cruiser until he understands that the sea is not the enemy; it's that damned hard stuff around the edges. Yet I see people who hardly know the first principles of piloting while creeping cautiously—so they think—among rocks and sandbars that would make my blood run cold if I had to negotiate them, but mostly I don't. I simply point *Kathleen*'s bow seaward and draw a big sigh of relief as the last vestige of land drops below the horizon. Then I know that, like an airplane pilot, I have hardly any worries until the time comes to bring her in for a landing—but unlike the airplane jockey, I can practically always choose my time and place; there's nothing forcing me to tangle with that menacing coast until I want to.

Yet that novice gambling his boat and his life among the coastal reefs and shoals considers me a reckless fool for losing contact with the safe (?) and friendly (?) land. I don't know just what terrible dangers he thinks lurk out there to seaward, now that we no longer entertain the ancient fear of falling off the edge of the world; but I do know he'll never be a real cruiser until he gets out there in his boat for several days, preferably at least a week, and learns that the terrors of the open sea are mostly figments of his imagination. (I wish I could get some insurance agents out there, too; they all seem to have the strange notion that a boat is a lot safer and more insurable playing tag with the rocks.)

Offshore sailing necessarily involves night sailing, since lengthy passages are involved. However, the idea of sailing in the dark seems to trigger crippling fears in many people, even if the boat never gets out of sight of the coast and its reassuring lights. Everywhere I see boat people essentially trapped in a certain cruising area because reaching the next desirable cruising ground involves a jaunt longer than they can make in daylight, and they have the notion that proceeding after nightfall is terribly dangerous. Ironically, trying to do it all by daylight, they often wind up exposing themselves to serious risks rushing desperately into any available harbor at dusk or even, if delayed, after dark. A pleasant, relaxed night sail instead of a frantic race against the sun would have put them at their destination in the morning with all day to find a safe marina or anchorage.

Finally, I feel that the able-bodied sailor with a boat of manageable size who hasn't made at least one cruise of reasonable length singlehanded doesn't really know his boat or himself. Sailing alone as a steady diet isn't for everybody, of course; but knowing that you can handle her by yourself if your crew doesn't show up, or gets sick along the way, or is called away by a business emergency, gives you an added dimension of freedom and confidence—and besides, a boat rigged so that one man can manage her is a better cruiser for two, or even four, since the watch on deck can solve most problems by himself without having to bother anybody below.

Fortunately for me I bought a boat in the northwest that I wanted in the southeast; in the course of the cruise, or series of cruises, I found myself exposed to all these experiences. None of them, it turned out, required any exceptional strength or skill. It was simply a matter of getting the hell out there and *doing* it, and of remembering the basic principle that when things get rugged, and you have no idea what move to make next, a good boat will always take care of you if you give her half a chance. . .

"Hey, down there," I called, sticking my head down the hatch. "Are you planning to sleep all night?"

"Coming. Hold your horses."

"There's some coffee left in the thermos."

"Ugh. That lukewarm stuff!"

"According to the chart, you should pick up Gun Cay Light and the aerobeacon on Bimini during the next couple of hours."

"When did we ever see a Bahamas light that was bright enough to show at its charted range? Okay, I'll watch for them. Sleep tight."

But of course I didn't sleep, not with a skimpy ten feet of water under the keel and a tricky landfall coming up at dawn. But the freedom was the thing, I reflected as I lay in my bunk listening to the gurgling, trickling, creaking noises of my little ship rolling steadily westward across the Great Bahama Bank; the knowledge that my boat and I were now ready, capable of cruising anywhere we wanted to.

Of course in a sense I'd left it until too late. There had been a time, many years ago, when I'd seriously considered sailing around the world alone in the wake of my hero, Captain Joshua Slocum. There were a lot of very practical reasons why that ambition was still unattainable; but there was some consolation in knowing that at least I'd managed to acquire the boat and the knowledge with which I could make the voyage, even though I never would.

Appendices

APPENDIX A

A Seaman's Library

First I'd like to call your attention to a massive, and moderately expensive, book that should be in every literate sailor's library: *Great Voyages in Small Boats: Solo Circumnavigators* (John de Graff 1976). This volume contains the around-the-world classics of John Guzzwell (*Trekka Round the World*), Vito Dumas (*Alone Through the Roaring Forties*), and Joshua Slocum (*Sailing Alone Around the World*). It's a tremendously effective selection; and you'll enjoy the contrast between Guzzwell, the quiet, casual, young British-Canadian who makes his singlehanded circumnavigation (in a 20-footer) seem so easy; and Dumas, the flamboyant, emotional Argentinian who suffered gloriously every inch of the way around the world; not to mention, of course, the dry, tongue-in-cheek old New Englander, Slocum, still the first and the best. (*Trekka* has recently been reissued by de Graff in hardcovers and as a McKay SeaBook in paper, but Dumas is almost impossible to find. Slocum, discussed in more detail later, is available as a Dover paperback.)

Now let's buckle down and concentrate on *Cruising in Seraffyn* (Seven Seas Press, and McKay, SeaBook 12, 1979), 1976, by Lin and Larry Pardey, an opinionated young cruising couple whose nautical opinions are often, in my opinion, all wet. That's one of the things—one of the many things—that make this book a valuable and enjoyable reading experience. I mean, it would be a hell of a dull world if everybody agreed with everybody, wouldn't it?

The Pardeys built their little 24-foot cutter, *Seraffyn of Victoria,* with their own hands, moved aboard and, having sold a successful business and cut practically all other ties with the shore, simply took off—slowly. They had no around-the-world ambitions at the time, they only wished to sail and explore. They wandered south into the Gulf of California, spent months there, and then made their way to, and through, the Panama Canal, after which they spent more months in the Caribbean. Eventually sailing north, they wintered in Virginia and then headed off across the Atlantic; the book ends with England in sight and further leisurely explorations planned. This is not a breathtaking saga of raging seas and superhuman endurance—for which see Vito Dumas, above. Except for a brush with a hurricane in a small Chesapeake harbor, the Pardeys managed without any serious crises; they broke no new nautical trails and set no new nautical records. They simply had a lot of fun in a lot of fascinating faraway places and wrote a book about it that's fun to read.

No argument so far. As a straight cruising yarn, this well-written account is right up there with the best. As a bonus, the Pardeys offer us a survey of the cruising boats they met along the way, tabulated by size vs. yearly cruising expenses; invaluable for anyone contemplating taking up the cruising life, and wondering how big a boat to go for. (Small, say the Pardeys, and their figures back them up.)

As I've said, it would be a dull world if nobody disagreed with anybody; and the Pardeys are as entitled to their sea-going opinions as I am—actually more so, since they have a great deal more cruising experience. Nevertheless, since I'm giving this book such high marks, I feel obliged to point out that what works for their cruising style will not necessarily work for yours or mine. This is particularly true of the boat they selected.

First of all, *Seraffyn* is a wooden boat, and her owners are very high on the advantages of wood. Well, they should be; Larry Pardey is a first-class shipwright who can make a piece of teak or oak sit up and talk. With this skill, he'd be stupid to get involved with fiberglass. But if you (like me) are the kind of halfbaked carpenter who puts the bandaid on his thumb before he picks up the hammer, because he knows he's bound to whack himself eventually, all the old-fashioned virtues of wood—and I don't deny them—don't really make up for the fact that fiberglass is a lot easier to maintain and repair, and there are a lot more people in boatyards these days who can do it for you if (like me) you're too dumb or lazy to do it for yourself.

Next: *Seraffyn of Victoria* is a unique Lyle Hess design derived from husky old British working craft. Don't let her 24-foot length fool you; she's a very substantial little ship with nine-foot beam and almost five-foot draft, weighing close to 11,000 pounds. That's nearly a ton more than *Kathleen,* considered fairly hefty by modern standards. Well, the heavy-displacement vs. light-displacement argument is not something I want to get into here. The fact is that, heavy or light, a good boat will get you where you want to go. *Seraffyn* has done very well by the Pardeys; but let's note that John Guzzwell's *Trekka* was a fin-keel skimming dish embodying exactly the opposite design philosophy from *Seraffyn,* yet she took her young skipper clear around the world without fuss or bother.

What I do want to point out is that *Seraffyn* is a heavy boat and it takes a lot of sail to move her. Since she's short, the rig has to stick out at both ends to achieve the required area. Aft, this is no great problem; an inoffensive boomkin holds the backstay clear of the mainsail (and makes a convenient base for the self-steering). Forward, however, there's a long bowsprit; a hell of a long bowsprit. Modern sailors, particularly small-boat sailors, don't have much chance to get acquainted with these picturesque protuberances. In your innocence, you may just think *Seraffyn's* slim bowsprit looks nice and jaunty, giving the boat a classy, classic air. It gives me the everlasting creeps. I've put in my time out on those murderous widowmakers (as the old-timers called them with good reason) and nobody's going to get me out on one again, thanks, not even if it's as handy for managing the anchor as Larry Pardey says.

But it's not really my intention to knock somebody else's boat. *Seraffyn* is a little beauty out of the past, a nostalgic vision from the lost age of sail. She apparently suits the Pardeys perfectly. She may very well suit you—but you'd better be *sure* of this before you quit your job, sell your home, and take off after Lin and Larry in an old-fashioned wooden vessel just like theirs, because they make it sound so tempting.

Finally, apart from construction and design, *Seraffyn* has a distinctive feature of which her owners are very proud: she has no motor. This is part of their keep-it-simple philosophy of cruising; no unnecessary gadgets—diesel or electric—to cause trouble. Just sails, kerosene lights, and a big oar that will move the boat around the harbor slowly in calm weather if somebody leans on it hard enough.

There is of course a great deal to be said (and the Pardeys say it) in favor of this approach, particularly if the budget is tight. A motor and alternator that don't exist never set you back several thousand dollars in the first place, and will never require repairs at the going rate of twenty-five bucks (?) an hour. Personally, I'm a gadget-freak, and I'm willing to pay in time and money for my aberration, but if you're cruising on a shoestring, particularly in distant places where parts and reliable labor are hard to come by, the Pardey philosophy has a lot to recommend it. And I'm not going to argue convenience or safety; if they're willing to wait out calms, and ride out storms offshore whenever the sheltering harbors available can't be reached in time, or entered safely, without a motor, that's their business.

It's when they promote motorless cruising from a money-saving stratagem to a sterling virtue, when they seem to tout it as a symbol of sturdy, seagoing independence, that I part company with them once more.

I had a symbol of sturdy independence once. On my first cruises in *Kathleen* I didn't carry a two-way radio, in line with my firm conviction that nobody should go out on the water with the idea of yelling for help if things go wrong. Very high-principled, to be sure; and Gordon (who felt the same way) and I made it down the Pacific Coast without a bit of trouble. Then I moved *Kathleen* east and hit the Gulf Intracoastal Waterway, which is simply not organized for radioless boats. Time and again I found myself approaching tugboat pilots and fishingboat skippers and asking them please to call locks and bridges on my behalf. Finally it dawned on me that a symbol of sturdy independence that left me totally dependent on other folks' communication gear wasn't much of a symbol after all. *Kathleen* now carries a very fancy 55-channel VHF/FM radio.

It would be interesting to go through *Cruising in Seraffyn* and list all the times, in their engineless independence, the Pardeys casually mention being towed out of harbor, or into harbor, by other folks' engines; and I have a hunch there were a few more such occasions that went unrecorded. They even borrowed somebody else's outboard motor to get them through the Panama Canal . . .

Well, enough. These are nice people and fine sailors, and if they have some oddball nautical notions, who doesn't? I hope I meet them in a pleasant anchorage some day so we can get together on my boat or theirs and really go at it hammer and tongs. In the meantime, I do recommend their book very highly. Just remember when you read their advice: what works for them will not necessarily work for you. That goes for my advice, too.

Reading is an essential part of serious boating. It's the way we learn more about the craft than we can pick up on the water or around the docks, but it's also the way we expand our enjoyment of boats by sharing the adventures of other boatmen.

There are technical volumes describing exactly how to change the prop of a four-horse fishing motor, or survive a gale off Cape Horn. I won't discuss these how-to books here. They're available, and when you need one to help you solve a specific problem, or to learn more about a specific area of boating, you'll have no trouble finding it. I'd rather list a few more stories of small-boat voyaging that should interest every boatman, for the insights they give into the nature of these ocean wanderers, the waters they navigate, and the little ships they sail. The fact that most of these books do deal with sailing vessels shouldn't discourage the power-boatman, nor should we be put off by the fact that the voyages described are generally more ambitious than most of us will ever get to make. It's still the same old sea.

What are the characteristics of a good boat yarn? Well, as far as I'm concerned, there are two simple questions to be asked of any seaman who presents us with a book about his daring, or not-so-daring, nautical expedition:

1. Does he enjoy sailing?
2. Is he fond of his boat?

These may seem like petty criteria to apply to adventure on the high seas; yet I've time and again found that voyages made for fame or money, or even out of sheer necessity, aren't quite as enjoyable to read about as those made simply for the fun of sailing (or racing) somewhere, nor is a boatman who carries on a constant feud with his vessel likely to write as entertaining a book as one who feels a real rapport with his little ship.

Of course we've got to make some distinctions. We can't really expect Captain Bligh to dote on the open ship's boat into which he was forcibly dumped, in which he made his magnificent Pacific voyage. Nor can we expect the Baileys or Robertsons (those offshore yachtsmen whose vessels were sunk by whales) to love the rubber doughnuts in which they survived so remarkably, or enjoy every minute of the long time they were bobbing around out there awaiting rescue.

However, these mutiny and disaster tales fall into a special category. They have a great deal to teach us, but they're not the standard sailing yarn I have in mind, where a man selects his own vessel and embarks on a cruise of his own choosing. Personally, I don't like reading a lot of griping by such a voluntary voyager, either about his endless nautical sufferings or his miserable clunker of a boat. If he felt that way, why didn't he just turn around and sail the lousy bucket back home and burn it?

The great small-boat sailing classic is, of course, as already mentioned, Captain Joshua Slocum's *Sailing Alone Around the World*. Here is a sailor who meets any standard you care to apply. He built (rebuilt, actually) his *Spray* with his own hands and cherished her accordingly. His preparations, while limited by lack of money, were always adequate. He made no lubberly mistakes. He never asks us to sympathize with his dreadful hardships afloat. In fact, he seems to have enjoyed the whole circumnavigation tremendously—and if there were some rough moments when he didn't, and there must have been, he kept his tough old Yankee trap shut about them. He was a great guy, a great navigator, and a great seaman.

Having said this, I must warn you that friend Joshua may not have been quite the simple, bluff, honest old sailor he'd like us to think him. There have been suggestions that some of the more dramatic passages in his book were written with Captain Slocum's tongue planted firmly in his weathered cheek. I won't spoil the story for those who haven't read it by being overly specific, but let's just consider one intriguing item: the *Spray*'s clock.

Slocum couldn't afford a chronometer, so he started out with a secondhand alarm clock that soon took a spill and lost its minute-hand. It's a very famous clock. The old captain claims to have navigated clear around the world with this crippled piece of junk; and of course we all know that an accurate timepiece is absolutely essential for celestial navigation—or is it? Well, now. It seems that there is a little-known method involving something called lunar distances, so complicated and difficult that nowadays the requisite tables aren't even printed as far as I know. This method does not require accurate knowledge of the time. There is reason to think that Slocum, really a superb navigator, was acquainted with this ancient and involved system and used it frequently—but that beatup old one-handed Westclox, or whatever it was, makes a much better story for his book, doesn't it? So read and enjoy *Sailing Alone Around the World,* still the best narrative of its kind, but keep in mind that the fine old gent who wrote it may just possibly be pulling your leg a bit here and there.

Once Slocum had shown the way, many others followed. A comprehensive wrap-up can be found in *The Circumnavigators,* by Donald Holm (Prentice-Hall), which will lead you to a lot of other interesting chronicles of round-the-world sailing. However, the next lone seaman to fire the world's imagination was Francis Chichester, who dashed around the globe with only one stop, in record time, and was knighted for his effort as was the much less flamboyant Sir Alec Rose. *(My Lively Lady,* McKay SeaBook 3.)

Unfortunately, Sir Francis' description of his epic voyage, *Gipsy Moth Circles the World,* (Pocket Books) flunks our double-barreled literary test. On this cruise, Chichester did not really sail for the love of sailing;

he was out to set records, not to enjoy himself. Furthermore, he hated his vessel, *Gipsy Moth IV,* with a bitter passion, and his book is full of complaints about the obstreperous tub and her man-killing ways. Granted that he had justification—apparently she was not the ideal vessel for his purpose, to put it mildly—it does not, in my opinion, make for the best nautical reading.

You should probably read it anyway, since it is another classic of small-boat voyaging; but just so you don't go away with the wrong impression of Francis Chichester, let me steer you to his later book, *The Romantic Challenge* (Ballantine). Here we see Sir Francis doing his thing and doing it well. True, he set himself an impossible goal: to sail single-handed 4,000 miles in twenty days, two hundred miles a day, a figure nobody had yet achieved alone. It has been pointed out that this is a purely arbitrary and artificial speed test. So what? It was what he wanted to do and he went out and tried to do it, and failed—but this time he loved every minute of it. In fact, he was having so much fun he simply couldn't bear to go home so he sailed his new boat, *Gipsy Moth V*—this one he liked—back out into the middle of the ocean and covered several thousand miles just making speed runs for his own pleasure.

However, the incident that shows us the real man occurred on his way home. He was hit by a severe gale in the Bay of Biscay. *Gipsy Moth V* took several savage knockdowns, one a real capsize, that left her half-swamped and leaking badly. Sir Francis himself was thrown across the cabin and hurt. Nevertheless, he found the hole in his boat and patched it. The pumps were clogged with gear that had gone adrift. This rather small, badly bruised, not too healthy seventy-year-old gent (he'd had one kidney removed, and there was some question about his lungs) then proceeded to *bail* out that great 57-foot, 29-ton yacht with a bucket, after which he cleaned her up and sailed her, not to the nearest continental port, but clear home to Plymouth, England. So I say, to hell with his motives and attitudes; ordinary standards simply don't apply here. I take off my hat to an indomitable adventurer and a gallant gentleman.

After Chichester's circumnavigation, there was only one thing left undone in this line: sailing around the world alone *nonstop.* A race was arranged which resulted in several books, all worth reading. But to balance the fairly upbeat chronicles of success discussed so far, let me call your attention to a terrible narrative of failure entitled *The Strange Last Voyage of Donald Crowhurst* (Stein and Day), by Nicholas Tomalin and Ron Hall. I don't mean to imply that Tomalin and Hall are terrible writers; it's their subject that's grim and tragic. Crowhurst, a brilliant but erratic young man, was sailing an ill-prepared boat launched at the last possible moment. For various reasons, mostly financial, the race was extremely important to him. When he realized he was too poorly equipped to even complete the global course, let alone make a good showing, he apparently lost his grip on sanity. He started faking his radio reports to make it look as if he were in a leading position. Finally, it seems, he realized that his fraud was bound to be discovered and . . . Well, his trimaran, the *Teignmouth Electron,* was found sailing in the Atlantic, which she'd never left, with nobody on board.

In 1960, that dedicated single-handed sailor, Colonel H.G. (Blondie) Hasler, initiated the controversial OSTAR series of races across the Atlantic, well described in *Sailing Solo to America* (Quadrangle Books), by Frank Page. This work actually covers the 1972 event in detail, but first the author brings us up to date by summarizing all previous races. In 1972, one of the racers was of particular interest to small boat sailors. His name was David Blagden, and he sailed a stock 19-foot fiberglass boat beefed up for the occasion, the *Willing Griffin.* Blagden's story, *Very Willing Griffin* (Norton), is highly readable. The skipper has nothing but respect and affection for his tiny ship, and if he asks us to share some sufferings, well, who isn't going to suffer a bit bashing at high speed across the stormy Atlantic in a featherlight 19-footer?

So much for the singlehanders. By the way of contrast, read the late William Snaith's book *On the Wind's Way* (Putnam), an excellent account of a fully-crewed racing yacht's competitive dash across the Atlantic to Sweden. It is entertaining and informative in a manner few such yacht-race chronicles achieve. You will get to know the crew of the yawl *Figaro* very well, not to mention her literate and observant author-skipper. It's a fine, fast boat-ride with a bunch of swell people.

By this time you're probably asking yourself if nobody but Slocum ever went ocean sailing without a stopwatch in his hand and a greedy eye on a prize awaiting him beyond a distant finish line. For an account of just plain ocean cruising that meets all our criteria, try Rosie Swale's *Children of Cape Horn.* Swale, with her husband and two kids, sailed from England to Australia by way of the Panama Canal in a small catamaran, and then returned to Europe the hard way, by sailing around Cape Horn. They apparently trusted their little vessel implicitly, and had a fine relaxed time all the way, even through the gales of the infamous Roaring Forties and Fifties. (I've seen criticisms of this book based on the fact that Rosie, a model, has one photograph of herself in her favorite tropical yachting costume of nothing at all, but I'm sure that if you close your eyes tightly and avert your face, you can turn the offending page quickly without suffering irreparable moral damage.)

I said I wasn't going to deal with how-to books here, but there's now so much sailboat stuff on our list that I think we need at least a dash of power-boating. Captain Robert P. Beebe, USN (Ret.), has made a study of long-range cruising powerboats, and his book, *Voyaging Under Power* (Seven Seas), brings a good deal of much-needed light to a murky subject. Before you mortgage the old plantation to purchase a well-advertised "trawler" yacht for a long ocean voyage, check with Captain Beebe. The man has been there and done it, so listen to what he says.

Finally, we come to the Hiscocks, Eric and Susan, good friends of mine. Although I've never met them or even corresponded with them, I know them well through their books. If I really had to show you what the deepwater bit was all about, but was limited to recommending just one author, there's absolutely no question of whom I'd pick. Eric Hiscock has written two fine how-to volumes, *Cruising Under Sail* (inshore), and *Voyaging Under Sail* (offshore) that should be in the library of every owner of a cabin-type sailboat. However, our one-sided friendship is really based on his wonderful cruising narratives, *Around the World in Wanderer III, Beyond the West Horizon, Atlantic Cruise in Wanderer III, Westward Cruise in Wanderer IV* and *Come Aboard* (Oxford). These are nice folks who sail for fun and love their boats—although I have a hunch they were just a bit fonder of their former little sloop than they are of the hulking ketch that is now their permanent home. They have just finished their third voyage around the world. Since there's very little chance of my ever making the same trip in a boat of my own, I'm happy to make it in theirs, by way of the printed page.

This is what it's all about. Very few of us can, or even want to, spend three years sailing around the globe, but that's what books like these are for. My boating library lets me put myself into the Hiscocks' shoes—or Chichester's, or Slocum's—whenever I wish, and roll across the Atlantic with the trade winds, or search for the opening of a coral atoll in the South Pacific, or ride out a hurricane in the Tasman Sea. I can do it without leaving my comfortable chair by the fire or disturbing the old hunting dog asleep at my feet. It's the sissy way of cruising, I know, but it sure beats no cruising at all.

For further happy armchair voyaging, I recommend:

W.I.B. Crealock, *Vagabonding Under Sail,* McKay
Bernard Moitissier, *First Voyage of the Joshua,* Morrow
Hal Roth, *Two on a Big Ocean,* Norton
Miles Smeeton, *The Sea Was Our Village,* Gray
Gordon and Nina Stuermer, *Starbound,* McKay
Stuart Woods, *Blue Water Green Skipper,* Norton
The Venturesome Voyages of Captain Voss, Gray

Also, a couple of general how-to books for reference:

David Parker, *Ocean Voyaging,* DeGraff
Don Street, *The Ocean Sailing Yacht 1 and 2,* Norton

APPENDIX B

Sextant Capers

I finally discovered where I was.

By careful celestial navigation, I determined my position as Latitude North 35° 41', Longitude West 105° 55'. This should come as no great surprise to anybody who knows I live in Santa Fe, New Mexico, and has access to a good atlas; but it's nice to be able to check these things independently, isn't it?

Taking sights at home by means of an artificial horizon was just the beginning. Now I've been through the celestial navigation mill for the second time; but the first time was a rather dull and complicated correspondence course inflicted on me by the U.S. Navy on the theory that even we dumb, shorebound reserve officers ought to know enough so we wouldn't disgrace the Service. It happened so long ago that it's almost forgotten. I am therefore in a pretty good position to describe the technique from the viewpoint of a raw beginner; but don't worry, I'm not going to tell you *how* to do it. There are dozens of good how-to navigation books available for those who want them. I'm simply going to tell you *what* the guy does when he takes that fancy gadget out of its fancy case and aims it at the sun, moon, stars, or planets.

Well, believe it or not, the first thing he does, even before taking a sight, is determine where he is, roughly. This may sound odd. After all, that's what the sextant is for, to tell you where you are, isn't it? Actually, it isn't. The sextant is for telling you how far you are from where you thought you were.

As far as I'm aware, all modern celestial navigation—I don't know about the real old-time techniques—starts with an assumed position somewhere in the general neighborhood of where you think you are. The exact spot chosen doesn't really matter. It all comes out the same in the end. If you happen to pick your spot a little farther east, for reasons of convenience we won't go into here, why, the final figures will just put you a little farther to the west of it, that's all.

Having your general position, you're ready to start making like a navigator. You want to determine just how high a certain celestial body—let's stick with the sun to make it simple—was in the sky at a certain moment.

Actually, the moment is almost as tricky to determine as the angle and just as important. A mistake of four seconds in time will throw your distance off by as much as a mile. The old boys used chronometers, very accurate and carefully calibrated clocks running on Greenwich time. Nowadays, many people (including yours truly) get by with a cheap stopwatch and a shortwave radio receiver that'll bring in time ticks from special stations like WWV in Colorado. You start the watch on the even minute, and write down the Greenwich Time given by the announcer. (In accordance with the firm bureaucratic principle of never using a simple old name when you can foist a fancy new one on the unsuspecting public, this is now known as Coordinated Universal Time.) Then take your sight, and stop the watch. Add the watch reading to what you wrote down, and you've got the time the sight was taken.

Now, the sextant. You can, as I did at the start, get a plastic Davis instrument for sixteen bucks, or you can split for a German Plath, for six hundred. The difference? Well, a friend of mine who has the Plath goes all pale and shaky—he may even break into tears—if he's as much as half a mile off. With the inexpensive plastic job, I cheered heartily if I came within five miles. (Of course, he's a slightly better navigator than I am, having been at it for years, but why bring that up?)

In any case, both instruments work the same way, with fixed and pivoting mirrors. It's a matter of lining up a reflected image of the sun (dimmed by suitable shades or filters to protect the eye!) with a direct view of the horizon—bringing the sun down to the horizon, as we great navigators say. Then you carefully read the measured angle off the various scales, micrometers, and verniers, depending on how elaborate and accurate your sextant is.

Now the real work is done. The rest is just a little adding and subtracting. First we break out the Nautical Almanac for the current year. In it, we find various corrections that must be applied to the raw sextant reading—for the height of your eye above sea level, for instance. We also find, opposite the exact date and time of the sight, two important figures: the sun's hour angle, and its declination.

These are fancy names for very simple measurements. Just as your latitude tells you how far you're from the equator, so the declination of the sun tells you how far it's from the equator. Just as your longitude tells you how far you're around the earth from Greenwich, so the hour angle of the sun tells you how far it's around the earth from Greenwich. Remember, we assumed an exact spot on earth for our own position. The declination and hour angle tell us the exact spot in the sky the sun was when we took our sight. Obviously, if we're smart enough, knowing the two positions, we can figure out the angle we *should* have got on the sextant, *if* we were actually at the position we assumed.

Years ago, however, you had to be fairly smart to figure it out. Solving the celestial, or navigational, triangle, as it's called, was a real exercise in mathematics. Nowadays it's solved for you in books of tables. There are a number of different ones, and any time you want to create a little excitement in the local dockside pub, just suggest to a seafaring man that HO 249 is really just as good as HO 229, or that HO 214 is for the birds, or that good old HO 211 is still the only way to go. Then duck fast and watch the fun.

As far as we're concerned, to hell with it. The fact is, the tables are there, and any one of them will do the job. And the job is very simple. Just climb into one of the more modern systems with the figures you've got and in less than a minute, once you know where to look, you'll come out smelling like a rose, with a sextant angle and a compass bearing.

Compare this tabulated sextant angle with the one you really got shooting the real sun. Generally they'll be close but not identical. The difference, in minutes of angle, is the distance in nautical miles that your real position is from the position you assumed for working purposes. It's measured in the compass direction you just determined, towards or away, depending on whether your actual sextant reading was larger or smaller than the one you got out of the table.

The final step is to break out the chart and draw your position line proudly thereon.

Well, that tells you roughly *what* to do to find your position by celestial navigation. If you're really serious about it, and want to learn *how* to do it, you'll have to consult books written by folks who know more about it than I do. My own favorite, as mentioned earlier, is Robert J. Kittredge's *Selftaught Navigation,* a slim volume that makes the subject quite simple and painless—well, almost. Another good work that has the same virtue of brevity, I understand, is Mary Blewitt's *Celestial Navigation for Yachtsmen* (DeGraff). For more details, and useful tricks not included in the highly condensed texts above, I keep on hand *Practical Navigation for the Yachtsman* (Norton) by Frederick L. Devereaux, and *Practical Navigation* (Doubleday) by W.S. Kals.

APPENDIX C

Have Tools—Will Travel

Some time ago my mechanically-minded friend Ken Wilde, who sold me two fine boats and later bought the second one back from me, called me up to say that Sears was having a sale of tools at a terrific bargain and I really ought to grab a set.

I said, "Ken, you know perfectly well I don't even know how to use a screwdriver properly. What the hell am I going to do with a complete set of fancy wrenches?"

He said cryptically, "Don't worry, on that new seagoing sailboat of yours, you'll learn."

I got the big box of iron, and for a time it was nothing but an infernal nuisance. We made a place for it up forward in *Kathleen,* strapped down so it wouldn't come adrift. Once in a while we'd dump out everything, squirt it all with WD-40 so it wouldn't rust, and stuff it all back in again. Oh, occasionally the magic box did supply a handy screwdriver or pair of pliers; once I even found use for a funny-looking little allen wrench from a cute little set that had come with the package. And it did save mechanics' time at umpteen dollars an hour. When one of these grim geniuses, installing some new gadget I'd discovered I couldn't live without, would start wiping his hands and muttering about having to go back to the shop for a left-handed 55/164 socket—a journey that never seemed to take less than an hour—I'd rummage around in my Sears Roebuck treasure chest and say brightly that I just happened to have one right there.

But as far as really *using* all those mysterious tools was concerned, forget it. Well, until the time came to take *Kathleen* out of her temporary winter quarters in Port Arthur.

I thought of having some work done on the engine in advance, but Port Arthur, while it has a very pleasant and safe marina, is not an easy place to get boat work done. Anyway, the Yanmar had run well for a year and a half and I'd even changed the oil once. What more could a motor expect? We were 60 miles east of Port Arthur when the loyal little power plant finally lost patience with me and decided to inform me, in no uncertain terms, that enough was enough and even an impractical literary type like me ought to know better than to expect a fine piece of machinery to keep running forever without attention.

The first warning came at mid-morning, when Kay popped out of the hatch to report that the motor smelled awfully hot. Hastily I shut things down, ducked below, and opened up the machinery compartment. It was hot, all right. Logic said that if heat was the problem the solution would most likely be found in the cooling system. I closed the seacock, found the right kind of peculiar-looking screwdriver in the magic box (Phillips?), whipped off the water filter, and found it solidly packed with gray, stringy guck. A scrubbing with the brush we use for the dishes revealed a bright and shiny mesh cylinder, which I reinserted and cinched back down. Starting the mill produced a free flow of water and a cool engine (well, after I remembered to reopen the seacock). Triumph.

It didn't last long. Right after lunch, in a spectacularly deserted stretch of swamp, the motor almost died. It picked up again, but quit completely a few hours later while we were maneuvering at a small town called Forked Island to ask for information about a lock ahead, rumored to be shut down for repairs. The man on the bank said that we could get through all right but for a little it looked as if his statement had been wildly optimistic; without power we weren't going to be getting through anything. I opened the propulsion compartment once more and studied it warily. A diesel, thank God, has no essential electrics. We'd already settled the water problem, at least for the time being. The trouble, therefore, just had to be in the fuel system. In the line leading from the tank I saw two filters, one very large with a petcock on the bottom. Opening this, while holding a plastic cup underneath, gave me a horrible-looking mess of sludge and water. I kept on draining it until the fuel ran clear. Back topside, I turned the key. After a moment the engine fired, hesitated, and started running smoothly once more, but by the time we reached Vermilion Lock it was faltering again. Obviously more drastic remedies were needed; but obviously a busy lock wasn't the place to apply them.

We were in luck, however. At this season the lock was not operating as a lock; both gates were open. After waiting for a tow to emerge, we shot right through. (The lock keeper came out to ask for a lock report, but when he realized we were having mechanical problems, he hastily waved us on—I guess the last thing he wanted was to have his big lock plugged up indefinitely by a helpless little sailboat.) By frantic manipulation of the throttle whenever the motor hesitated, I managed to get us to Intracoastal City where we docked in a small marina that seemed to be home to several crew boats—in case the term is strange to you, as it was to us, I'll explain that these are the big fast diesel launches that service the oil rigs out in the Gulf of Mexico. It had been a long, hot, troubled 60-mile day. We went out to have an air-conditioned dinner at a nearby restaurant, letting our mechanical problems wait until morning.

At daylight, I made a real study of the fuel system. I drained some more goop out of the big filter (the one with the petcock) and rummaged around and found a spare element for the little filter (the yellow one). But now the moment of truth was at hand: in order to replace the filter element, I had to open the fuel line, letting in air. A diesel, I knew, will not run on air. In fact, all air has to be purged (bled) from the fuel system before the motor will operate. I'd watched this being done once on *Kathleen,* and it had seemed like a fairly complicated operation, probably beyond my mechanical capabilities. On the other hand, we couldn't proceed as we were. Obviously, the only thing to do was try it. If I loused up completely, and had to find a mechanic to patch things up, we'd be in no worse shape than we were already.

I unscrewed the old filter element, finding it quite full of sludge, and put the new one in its place. Okay. When all else fails, read the instructions. I studied the motor manual carefully, and had Kay, topside, start the motor. It fired readily enough, ran half a minute and then, as the air in the lines reached the fuel pump, quit. I opened things up here and there. No fuel. I loosened some more stuff—and suddenly there was diesel oil all over the place. Hastily I shut the main valve at the tank, and mopped things up and wiped things off and put things back together. Then I re-opened the valve at the tank. Kay turned the key while I held the decompression lever to lessen the strain on the battery. From time to time I'd release the lever to see if the motor would fire. The third or fourth time we went through this routine, there was a heartening cough. The next effort brought a full three seconds of operation. One more try, and the Yanmar was running. Whoopee!

In my euphoria, I managed to run hard aground leaving the marina. A nice stranger in a small outboard came right out and pulled us off. Later, I smelled diesel very strongly, and opened up the engine compartment to find fuel trickling from one of the connections I'd opened to bleed the line. A study of the situation indicated that I must have dropped an essential washer without noticing it. Without much hope, I removed some obstructive woodwork, hauled the heavy battery out from under the motor; and there at the back of the battery platform lay the tiny errant item. Well, I guess you have to have a little luck if you're going to make it as an amateur mechanic—and, of course, a diesel engine. You can't horse around like that with gasoline and hope to survive.

So our water system was all fixed up, and so was our fuel system, at least for the moment. Nothing else could possibly go wrong, I told myself, and in New Orleans I'd certainly get somebody to give my powerplant a thorough checkup before proceeding eastwards. Of course, there *was* that funny little red light flickering on the Yanmar's rudimentary instrument panel. It supposedly indicated low lubricating oil, but one dipstick showed that the crankcase was quite full, and the other showed that the gear box was also well supplied with lubricant, so it was obviously just one of those crazy electrical aberrations that could safely be ignored . . .

Two mornings later we were lying at the bulkhead of a side canal in Larose, Louisiana, a pleasant spot well known to yachtsmen passing that way. We had about 35 miles left to go to the Mississippi River; and we got up early to have plenty of time to negotiate the two locks that would take us out of the ICW onto the Mississippi, and out of the Mississippi into New Orleans. When I turned the key to start the motor, nothing happened.

I've indicated that electricity is not *essential* to the operation of a diesel. It will run perfectly well without any juice whatever. All you have to do is get it started. But cranking a heavy 12-horse diesel by hand is a totally different class of operation from yanking the cord of a light 12-horse outboard, particularly for a middle-aged gent with a temperamental back.

I made a few tentative efforts with the crank and decided I just didn't have what it took to overcome that ferocious diesel compression. I studied the electrical situation carefully. I found that the whole bundle of wires leading from below to the control panel in the cockpit had come adrift somehow and wound up against the hot exhaust pipe, fusing a multiple-wire connector into a shapeless blob of plastic. That flickering red light had been trying to tell me that something was going seriously wrong down there, but I'd chosen to disregard it. I drew a long breath, got a fistful of tools from the treasure chest, and settled down to cut out the burned part and splice all those wires, matching the colors carefully. Then I wiped the sweat from my brow, mounted the ladder into the cockpit, and turned the key hopefully. Nothing. (Later, I discovered a small, inconspicuous fuse behind the control panel, which had blown; at the time I just didn't look hard enough.)

Larose, Louisiana, may have a good diesel mechanic available, but even if it does I had no idea how to find him. There was only one thing left to do. I stationed Kay at the decompression lever, and put the crank back into place, remembering uneasily that a diesel will often run backwards as happily as forwards, and when it does the crank spins viciously to the detriment of all thumbs and arms that happen to be in the way. Well, to hell with that. Using both hands, I cranked mightily and shouted: "Now!"

Kay flipped the lever closed. The Yanmar fired and settled down to a steady purr, which didn't stop for 14 hours, the time it took us to get through the hostile Mississippi locks with their endless delays, through industrial New Orleans with its endless bridges, to the friendly marina on Lake Pontchartrain . . .

Nothing I've written here should be taken as criticism of *Kathleen*'s sturdy little powerplant. Given half a chance, it started; given half a chance, it ran. The fact that a fumble-fingered amateur mechanic like me could keep it functioning for 300 miles in spite of a year and a half of neglect should be taken as a favorable testimonial to the motor's simplicity and reliability, rather than the contrary.

The obvious moral is that even the most rugged machinery needs some tender loving care if it's to keep running smoothly. And that when you see a warning light come on, it's well to keep looking until you find the cause. And that the next time your local Sears Roebuck store, or its equivalent, offers good tools at a bargain, it wouldn't be a bad idea to pick up a fairly complete set.

As Ken Wilde said, don't worry about learning how to use them. It will come to you. Sooner or later.

APPENDIX D

Self-Steering

I came on deck at 0400 to be greeted by the sad news that Tilly had died.

"She just, well, expired," said Buddy Mays, my crew at the time. "She started steering us around in circles, frozen in one position. Rigor mortis, I guess. I couldn't bring her back to life, so I simply took over."

We were out in the Gulf Stream, heading north along the Straits of Florida. It had been a tough thrash to windward ever since we'd left Marathon early the previous morning. Under those circumstances, the simple joy of steering a sailboat palls very quickly; and we'd been running on autopilot practically the whole time, taking over from the Tiller Master only when the coastal reefs got too close and it was time to tack again. Buddy, a professional photographer who'd had some Coast Guard experience but was new to sailing, had been quite intrigued by Tilly. He'd never seen an electric small-boat self-steering device before. However, his attitude now had a tinge of I-told-you-so, since he'd already expressed some doubt about the practicality of having such a complex mechanism on board a 27-foot boat.

While he continued to steer, I made the obvious checks in the dark: switch and course control. There was no friendly whirring response from the workhorse little motor inside the gray metal case. Okay, the fuse. There had been a time in her younger days when Tilly had devoured fuses like candy; I hoped her childish appetite for them hadn't returned.

Starting for the hatch to get a spare from below, I stopped, frowning. Was my eyesight failing or had the red compass lights got awfully dim? I looked aloft and I could hardly see the normally fairly brilliant Marinaspec masthead light. Hastily I stuck my head down the hatch and flicked on the battery condition indicator. Battery #2, on which we happened to be running, showed almost totally discharged.

A moment later I'd thrown the main switch to Battery #1, fully charged.

"Give her a try now."

Buddy leaned over to hit the autopilot switch. I heard Tilly come to life, trying bravely to correct the course even though her steering arm had been disconnected from the tiller.

"We're back in business," Buddy reported. "Sorry, Tilly, I never thought of the damn battery. It wasn't your fault; you can't be expected to do your work without juice . . ."

Which illustrates two things about autopilots: that you tend to start talking to them as if they're members of your crew (which, of course, they are), and that they do require electricity.

All the time my boat was being built, launched, shaken down, and cruised from Canada to California, I kept looking for a suitable wind-vane self-steering gear. I did so much research on the subject, I wound up thoroughly confused. The difficulties were:

1. Vane gears are mostly ferociously expensive.
2. They're generally complicated to install.
3. They're often tricky to use.
4. They tend to be in the way when they're not in use.
5. They don't work worth a damn under power.

The final factor turned out to be the deciding one. At the time, with the Gulf ICW ahead, I expected to use the diesel a lot more than the sails. There was also a good chance I'd wind up making some of my future cruises with *Kathleen* singlehanded. I needed a self-steering device badly; and the more I thought about it, the more obvious it seemed that I really needed one that wasn't particular about whether we were being pushed along by wind or petroleum.

Studying the subject, I discovered that by self-steering standards the electric autopilots weren't too horribly expensive. They were simple to install and easy to use. The ones suitable for tiller-steered boats like *Kathleen* were mostly nice, compact devices that could be stowed below when not in use, leaving hardly anything to clutter up the cockpit. And of course they did work well—maybe even best—under power.

Since they were so unobtrusive when stowed, even if I bought one there was nothing to prevent me from adding a vane later, if I could ever decide which vane. (Nothing but money, that is.)

So my purchase of the Tiller Master was actually kind of a stopgap measure. I still thought that, like most salty yachting characters, I'd wind up with a picturesque, rugged-looking vane on the stern eventually. Now I'm not so sure. It depends on how many oceans I'll be crossing. For the long offshore haul under sail, a windpowered device is still, probably, the first choice. For coastal work under both sail and power, on the other hand, the electric autopilot has a great deal to recommend it.

But let's deal with the drawbacks first. Like all complex electrical devices, autopilots do tend to be somewhat temperamental and vulnerable. My Tiller Master, for instance, arrived in a nonfunctioning condition. Well, that's not quite correct; except for a certain loose screw it was probably okay when I got it. However, that loose screw—perhaps shaken loose in transit—meant that a couple of delicate inner organs that weren't supposed to touch, did. When we plugged in, a lot of electricity went where it shouldn't have, completely cooking the electronic brain (okay, call it a circuit board if you insist). The company was very cooperative about supplying another, but since we were cruising by this time the logistics were formidable. So please remember: when you get your autopilot make absolutely certain it's properly stuck together before you turn on the juice.

As has already been mentioned, in her early days Tilly also demonstrated an unladylike appetite for fuses, particularly when we were running under power. Several factors seemed to be involved, including the fact that the moving parts were stiff and new, throwing heavy loads on the little motor. Salt and dirt were also involved; a cleaning followed by careful application of fresh lubricant (supplied) went a long way towards solving the problem.

But the basic difficulty seemed to be that the voltage provided by the alternator of *Kathleen*'s Yanmar was right at the top of the voltage range (10½ to 14½ volts) that Tilly was designed to handle; there were indications that when the battery in use was fully charged it sometimes went a bit over the top. Even when the fuse remained intact, this caused Tilly's operation to become somewhat erratic. I suppose there are elegant ways of solving this problem involving voltage regulators and such; my solution was simpler. I merely made a point of turning on the VHF radio and a cabin light or two whenever we were to run under power for any length of time with Tilly in charge. The extra load seemed to take care of things in practice—don't ask me to justify it in theory, since I don't know much electrical theory. In any case I suggest you order plenty of extra fuses along with your autopilot if you do buy one. Trying to locate a 1½ amp SloBlo fuse in a small coastal fishing village can be a very frustrating occupation.

The final count against autopilots is, of course, the fact that being electrical they do use electricity. There's no way around this; it's the nature of the beast. So if electricity is in very short supply on your boat, you're not, or you shouldn't be, a potential autopilot customer. However, the incident described earlier is the only time in a year of fairly heavy use, including numerous overnight sails, when Tilly's current drain has caused any difficulties—and note that we'd been running on autopilot from eight o'clock one morning to four o'clock the next, with instruments, cabin lights, and running lights also drawing juice from that one poor, unreplenished battery, and with the VHF employed from time to time as well.

If I wanted to be scientific, I'd give you the manufacturer's figures for current consumption: Tilly is supposed to average a drain of ⅓ ampere per hour, pulling ¾ ampere when actually correcting the course. Then I'd tell you the ampere-hour rating of my battery (if I could remember it) and we could figure out exactly how long it should last on one charge, assuming that we had exact scientific figures for all the other electrical gadgets also operating from the same battery. When we got through we really wouldn't know much more than what we do now: that on a 27-foot boat with a normal two-battery electrical system charged by a 25-amp alternator the Tiller Master is quite satisfactory from the angle of current drain for regular coastwise cruising involving occasional powering, although some vigilance must be exercised when making long overnight runs under sail alone.

Larger boats with greater battery capacity and recharging power should have fewer problems; smaller boats will undoubtedly have more. Nevertheless, even on a fairly small vessel with only a rudimentary electrical system, I should think an autopilot would be quite practical for the kind of marina-to-marina daylight cruising many people prefer, if a charger were carried to top up the battery at night by means of shore power. As far as offshore work in any boat is concerned, you'd have to be prepared to charge the batteries an hour or two a day.

The big advantage, I feel, of the autopilot over the vane systems is simplicity. That is, all the complications are inside the little gray box, and only an electrical genius can understand them, so you might as well forget about them. They either work or they don't, and that's that. As long as they do work, everything is easy. No herculean labors are required; no death-defying trapeze acts on the transom. There are no levers or gears or cables or flapping windvanes or flopping watervanes all inspired by the devil to exert tremendous power at just the time you're least well braced for it. The autopilot is always under control; it will never run amok, threatening to wrench itself out of the boat and break your arm in the process. Singlehanded literature is full of these epic battles of man-vs-vane, generally staged in howling gales; in fact it sometimes seems no singlehanded cruise is complete without one. The autopilot never fights back.

Unlike the vane devices, which are generally engaged only for the long haul, my Tilly is also useful for all kinds of brief, minor maneuvers. When cruising, she rests at the side of the cockpit, plugged in and ready to be swung into action—a two-second job. When the main has to go up, she holds the boat into the wind under power; when the genoa has to come down, she runs the boat off under sail to blanket the big jib so it drops docilely on the foredeck. Anchoring singlehanded, I'll aim the boat at the spot I want with Tilly's help, throw the motor out of gear, and saunter forward, knowing that the pointy end will remain headed in the right direction as long as there's any steerage way left, regardless of wind gusts or current eddies.

I guess this is the real appeal of the electric autopilot: because it's so easy to use it gets *used,* day in and day out, instead of being saved for that transatlantic crossing or voyage around the world. I find myself coming to the conclusion that the two types of self-steerers actually serve different and, to some extent, complementary purposes. Even if I should get a vane gear eventually (those things do look nice and salty sticking up behind, don't they?), I don't feel my fine relationship with Tilly will suffer much as a result. But let's take a quick look at the alternative.

Wind-operated self-steering involves three components: something to sense the direction of the wind, something to steer the boat accordingly, and something to link one to the other.

The sensor is, of course, that very conspicuous windvane. A vane can be a simple weathercock device like the one on your barn, if you have a barn, only larger: just a sheet of plywood, or cloth laced to a frame, with a vertical pivot allowing it to swing freely and point always into the wind no matter which way the boat turns. There's also a horizontally-pivoted variation. Visualize a large paddle sticking up into the air and hinged at the lower end, carefully counterbalanced so that it just stays upright when the edge is aimed towards the wind. If the angle changes, say as the boat veers off course, the wind hits the flat of the blade and exerts enough pressure to flop the paddle over, one way or the other. Get it edgewise to the wind once more—when the boat returns to its proper course—and the counter-weight brings the paddle back up vertical again.

To go with these sensors, there are two general types of steering systems: those utilizing the main rudder of the boat, and those using a smaller auxiliary rudder hung off the stern—in the latter case, the main rudder is generally immobilized when the auxiliary is in use.

There are three ways of transferring the signal from the windvane to the steering system: direct from the vane to the main or auxiliary rudder, indirect from the vane to a trim tab on the main or auxiliary rudder, and indirect from the windvane to a watervane servo system to the main or auxiliary rudder. (If you didn't follow all that, don't despair. Explanations are forthcoming.)

So much for the pieces. Now let's see how various ingenious gents have put them together to get boats to steer themselves.

By far the simplest system is the one using a windvane operating the main rudder of the boat directly. All you do is mount the vane on the stern, run control lines to the tiller, and you're in business—well, maybe. The catch is that a windvane by itself isn't very powerful. The simple, vertically-pivoted, weathercock type has to be very large to apply force enough to the ropes to operate a boat's tiller. I think I read somewhere that when Francis Chichester used this system, he had a vane area of forty or fifty square feet; some of his storm sails probably weren't much bigger.

The horizontally-hinged vane—my son calls it a flipper-flopper—generates considerably more power; but it's still marginal, I gather, for ocean-going boats, particularly in light winds. However, it's by far the cheapest solution. It requires no modifications of the boat's rudder, and nothing dragging in the water. On the other hand, remember that this is the least powerful system and also, I gather, the least sensitive. If it works, you get a hell of a lot for relatively little money, but you can't expect too much of it. And if your boat is at all hard to steer, forget it.

Like most systems linked to the main rudder, this apparatus functions satisfactorily only with a tiller. Trying to adapt it to a steering wheel just increases the odds against you. If you do have a wheel, you're better off, I gather, going to an auxiliary rudder quite independent of the boat's main steering system. There are several devices available that use a flipper-flopper vane linked directly to a small auxiliary rudder mounted on the stern.

The theory is that you balance the boat pretty well with the sails, and secure the big main rudder so it will keep her on course, roughly. Then you engage the vane and the little auxiliary rudder does the fine steering. This system can, of course, be used for tiller-steered boats, too. Since there's less work for the vane to do, I have a hunch this system is a little more likely to be successful. However, the devices involved seem to be several times as expensive as those first described, and they do involve having a gadget on the stern sticking down into the water.

From the least-powerful system that may not work, let's move to the most-powerful system that always works, judging by what I've read about it. This is the watervane servo system invented by "Blondie" Hasler, the high priest of singlehanded sailing—at least, if he didn't invent the basic principle (and I don't know that he didn't) he certainly put it to use. Incidentally, a servosystem is one rigged to multiply the strength of the signal applied to it. (That's right, Virginia, I looked it up.)

Instead of using air to power his steering system, Hasler used water— the water running past the boat as she sails along. Visualize a pivoted paddle sticking into the wake edgewise. As long as the blade is absolutely parallel to the direction of the boat's travel, nothing happens. The instant the blade is turned even slightly, as by the action of a windvane, the pressure of the water makes it slice sharply to port or starboard. Considerable force is generated—try sticking an oar over the side when your boat is moving right along—and this force is applied to the tiller by a system of lines and pulleys and brings the boat back on course.

This type of gear, in its many variations, seems to work well on practically all types of sailboats. It's a favorite among singlehanded ocean racers. I gather from my research that, properly adjusted, it steers the best course under the most varied conditions of any system available. It isn't cheap, but the simpler versions won't make you die of heart-failure when you read the price, assuming you're already hardened to the idea of buying self-steering in the first place.

So? So it's great, but it's a hell of a lot of gear to hang on the stern of a small boat. Since it generates so much power, jams and breakages are not unknown. It's complicated, with a lot of control lines and linkages to give trouble if not carefully inspected, adjusted, and maintained. If you want the closest thing to self-steering perfection that's available, this seems to be it, but my own very private opinion is that for casual use, particularly on a small boat that's never going to cross an ocean, it verges upon overkill.

In between the weak and simple direct-windvane-systems, on the one hand, and the powerful but complex indirect-watervane-systems, on the other, are the trim-tab self-steering devices. The principle is familiar to aviators. If you mount a small hinged tab at the aft edge of a large rudder, and swing that tab over to starboard, it will drive the rudder to port and steer the boat to port. And vice versa. The resulting steering force produced by the rudder is much greater than the power that was required to turn the tab in the first place—in other words, it's another servosystem. A fairly small windvane can operate, through a trim-tab, a rudder that it couldn't begin to budge if hooked up directly.

It's a neat, clean, and simple system and it will steer a lot of boats quite well, although it's not quite as precise, I gather, as the watervane systems. The big drawback, for those who aren't mechanically minded, is that if you go shopping for a trim-tab device you probably won't find one.

All rudders are shaped differently and hitched onto their boats at different angles. They all require different tabs and different linkages. It seems to be impossible to design a standard apparatus of this kind that will bolt onto all boats, or even many boats. If you want one built, it will have to be drawn up especially for your boat and manufactured on special order. But let's look at the bright side: the trim-tab system is ideal for the do-it-yourself boatman. He simply adds a hinged section to the aft end of his rudder, mounts a homemade vane on the stern of his boat, rigs a couple of bell-cranks and a link between them, and he's in the self-steering business . . .

Well, maybe it's not as easy as all that, but a lot of people have done it, so it can be done. I won't try to tell you how. If you're interested, you'll find a complete discussion in John Letcher's *Self-Steering for Sailing Craft* (International Marine) and a valuable analysis in the chapter on self-steering in David Parker's *Ocean Voyaging* (DeGraff). Trim tabs are really only practical—unless you're mechanical genius—on outboard rudders, but the same principle can be used with an auxiliary rudder, and Parker describes such a device in detail.

Okay. Self-steering, you'll gather, costs money. It doesn't really improve the looks of your pretty sailboat. Is it worth it?

That's for you to answer. Do you, in your ordinary sailing, often run a single compass course for hours at a time, or are you forever wriggling around buoys and islands? Do you do a lot of singlehanded and short-handed sailing, or is there always a mob on board, one member of which is always happy to hold the tiller and dream he's Joshua Slocum sailing around the world? Do you, deep down, find steering kind of boring at times, at least on long watches, or do you always enjoy every minute you've got the helm, yield it up only reluctantly, and grab it back as soon as you decently can?

Well, I like to steer as much as the next man, but I must admit that I don't mind a bit being relieved by Tilly from time to time. I may even get a vane self-steering gear eventually, to relieve her and the ship's batteries on very long hauls under sail.

APPENDIX E

And Last But Not Least—There's Seamanship

Old Ben was standing on the dock when I rowed up. He watched as I made fast the painter of the flat-bottomed rowboat, laid the oars neatly inboard parallel to the sides of the boat as I'd been taught, and removed the oarlocks from their sockets.

"You sure you got that sailboat out there secured good and proper?" he asked.

Actually, I don't suppose he was so old. He may have been all of forty; and I can beat that, now. He took care of things on the large place on which we had a small cottage for the summer; but to me he was the biggest man in Maine. He knew all about boats and—this was what made him truly great—he was willing to share this wonderful knowledge with a nine-year-old landlubber kid.

"Yes. I think so," I said.

Then I looked across the harbor at the little white, wooden, clinker-built craft (fiberglass was still in the future) that was mine for the whole summer—mine, at least, if I proved myself worthy of it. I looked, and I wanted to cry. I was tired and hungry after a long day on the water, and I wanted to run home and eat the dinner I knew my mother was keeping warm for me. And the boat didn't look too bad. The single sail was neatly furled and stopped. The center-board was up, as I was supposed to leave it. The loop of the mooring line was solidly in place around the big cleat forward; and the mooring buoy lay on the deck where it belonged—and, dammit, I'd done a really swell job of picking up that mooring today, coming in fast and shooting up into the wind, right to the buoy, gauging it so she just lay there, dead in the water, sail flapping, while I strolled forward with the boathook, nonchalantly, and reached over the side.

There was only one trouble. The mooring pennant, the light line connecting the buoy and the heavy cable, had somehow got knocked overboard and hung in an untidy bight from the port bow.

I said humbly, "I'm sorry, Ben. I didn't see it."

And I got the oars and oarlocks functioning again, and I rowed back out there to coil the pennant properly, because a real sailor leaves his boat shipshape; and I was trying hard to become a real sailor.

I never, that I can remember, heard the word "safety" all the summers I was growing up on the water. (The growing up I did on shore was called school, and took place winters, and didn't count.) In those days, a lifejacket was a monstrous cork affair they made you put on just once when you got on an ocean liner, kind of a stupid ritual, but you had to humor those cranky adults. The idea of lugging the fool things around in our little boats never occurred to us. The notion of actually *wearing* one afloat—well, really! How ridiculous could you get? We could swim, couldn't we?

As far as I know, that sturdy, borrowed, cat-rigged craft that started me on my erratic nautical career—her name was *Deborah,* as I recall— had no flotation; and I seem to remember that she had several hefty pigs of lead in the bilge by way of ballast. If I'd capsized her, she'd probably have sunk right out from under me. I was reasonably careful not to capsize her (although I'll admit I came close a time or two) not so much because it would have been unsafe, not because I was scared of drowning, but simply because it would have been lousy sailing technique and Ben would have disapproved.

Please understand, Ben had no real authority over me. I suppose, if I'd got too bratty, he might have spoken to my folks, but as far as I know he never did. He had other, more potent, disciplinary methods. He had no siren or badge; he couldn't whistle me down and fine me or ground me or jail me if I misbehaved; and yet, on the other hand, he had all the authority in the world because I knew that, if I did a lubberly job afloat, Ben would suddenly get awfully "busy." He'd get so busy he'd be unable to show me fascinating things like how to make an eye-splice, or scull a boat with a single oar, or tie a bowline . . .

Unfortunately, there aren't many Bens left; knowledgeable watermen with time for kids—time to hammer into their pea-sized brains the fact that the purpose of boating is to take a boat out smartly, sail it well, bring it back smartly, and leave it shipshape, having a lot of fun in the process. Instead, we've got 'boating safety' instruction that seems designed specifically to take as much fun as possible out of boating (you can't get it all, but you can try). Worse, it doesn't seem to be really concerned, as Ben was, with teaching a good, clean, seamanlike job of boat-handling and boat-keeping. It spends much of its time and effort, and that of its hapless students, on dull, peripheral matters like life preservers and fire extinguishers, and illegal wakes and speeds, and not sitting on certain parts of a boat you might fall off of. At least that's the impression I get around the small-boat docks these days, where safety is the word, the only word, and (except for some racing sailboat classes) the basic skills of boating seem to be largely ignored.

I don't know how many bowlines I tied before Ben was satisfied I could get this invaluable knot right every time, not only on the quiet dock where instruction usually took place, but in a wildly rolling boat in a screaming gale, if necessary. Square knots, half hitches, clove hitches, they all got a workout. I don't know how much rope I used up learning long splices and short ones, eye splices, crown splices . . .

I only know that no dock line of mine has ever parted at a splice I made; nor has any boat of mine ever gone adrift because I tied a square knot backwards. And remember, Ben didn't *make* me learn these things. He simply let me know they were intriguing boating secrets that, as a special privilege, he'd let me in on if I was willing to work a little. Did he tell me he was teaching me how to keep safe on the water? Hell, no. He just gave me to understand he was initiating me into the select company of good sailors and seamen everywhere; my safety was my own damned business. It was assumed that I had sense enough to want to stay alive, on the water or anywhere else; most people did.

Weather? There were no small craft warnings or advisories in the small bay on which I sailed, open to the larger expanse of Frenchman's Bay. I was out there practically every day regardless of weather. Nobody ever told me not to go sailing because it was blowing too hard. I remember rowing out to the *Deborah* one morning when the breeze out of the northeast did seem to be a little stiffer than usual. I raised the big gaff sail and cast off anyway, figuring I could ease her through the gusts the way I always had before.

Suddenly we were charging wildly through the anchorage, taking water by the bucket-full over the lee rail; and there was no way I could make that overcanvased boat go where I wanted her to without swamping her completely. There was only one thing to do. I shot her up into the wind and hauled the sail down fast. That left me with a helpless, half-filled boat drifting rapidly onto the rocks with which all Maine coastlines are liberally supplied. I grabbed the anchor and, with a prayerful glance at the rode (neatly coiled according to Ben's instructions), lowered it quickly overboard. The line ran out without a snag; I managed to get it cleated forward; and then came the job of bailing her out, putting in a reef to reduce the sail area to manageable proportions, getting the hook up again, and beating off those rocks in that howling wind.

When I came ashore, there was Ben. "Kind of busy there for a while, weren't you, sailor?" he said.

That was all; but from that day I found myself tucking in a reef before leaving the mooring whenever the situation looked the least bit doubtful—I found that it was easy enough to shake out if it wasn't needed. I also found myself paying a little more attention to the various weather signs that gave me clues as to what kind of a situation I might have to cope with during the day's sail. It turned out that Ben had some valuable and interesting pointers on this subject, too.

As I say, we're kind of short of Bens nowadays. That salty production line has closed down, probably for good. It's too bad; but I don't see why it's got to mean that boating has to be taught as a grim, dismal, boring business of merely staying alive on the water.

A boat, power or sail, is one of the loveliest and most exciting of all human creations. Most people, particularly young people, are eager to learn how to master new sports involving new and beautiful equipment. They want to be shown how to be good at it. They want to learn how to do it *right*. Many of them are willing to work hard at it—I was, and I don't think I'm unique in any way. I think there are still kids around the water willing to practice knots and splices by the hour; willing to spend days and weeks learning how to come in to a snappy landing, or pick up a mooring buoy smartly, or even a thrown life-ring representing a man overboard.

What they're mostly not the least bit interested in is being taught how to be safe. They know how to be safe: just leave the boat at the dock, climb into bed at home, and pull the covers over the head. There may be a few middle-aged folks—and they've got to be a damned sight more middle-aged than I am—who feel that it's their duty to their families and insurance companies to learn "boating safety" the way it's customarily taught. The young ones, of all ages, just want to learn boating, period.

They want to know how to tie the right knot, make the right approach to the dock or mooring, steer the right course at the right speed, and anchor in the right place the right seamanlike way, the way generations of sailors have worked out as best for that type of vessel in that type of situation. It may be very irresponsible of them, but they mostly don't give a hoot about abstract principles concerning the protection of life and property afloat. They don't want to be preached at. They simply want to learn to handle their beautiful new boats, power or sail, smoothly and skillfully under all conditions. They want to be taught how to be *good* at this fascinating sport they've found.

This is why courses in "boating safety" often go begging. Hardly any kid wants to hear any more about safety these days (a prejudice shared by some adults—well, I can name at least one). He's had safety for breakfast, lunch, and dinner since he was a captive audience too young to get up and walk away from it. It's the great, hysterical, modern crusade ashore and afloat. He's had it with safety up to here.

What he really wants to learn, once he discovers boating, is something totally different, something he knows instinctively will keep him far safer on the water than all the "safety" rules and lectures, as well as showing him the way to far more boating pleasure: that wonderful, ancient discipline known as *seamanship*.